MW00826281

The Government-Industrial Complex

The Government-Industrial Complex

The True Size of the Federal Government, 1984–2018

PAUL C. LIGHT

Foreword by Paul A. Volcker

OXFORD
UNIVERSITY PRESS

OXFORD
UNIVERSITY PRESS

Oxford University Press is a department of the University of Oxford. It furthers
the University's objective of excellence in research, scholarship, and education
by publishing worldwide. Oxford is a registered trade mark of Oxford University
Press in the UK and certain other countries.

Published in the United States of America by Oxford University Press
198 Madison Avenue, New York, NY 10016, United States of America.

© Oxford University Press 2019

All rights reserved. No part of this publication may be reproduced, stored in
a retrieval system, or transmitted, in any form or by any means, without the
prior permission in writing of Oxford University Press, or as expressly permitted
by law, by license, or under terms agreed with the appropriate reproduction
rights organization. Inquiries concerning reproduction outside the scope of the
above should be sent to the Rights Department, Oxford University Press, at the
address above.

You must not circulate this work in any other form
and you must impose this same condition on any acquirer.

Library of Congress Cataloging-in-Publication Data
Names: Light, Paul Charles. author.
Title: The government-industrial complex : the true size of the federal government,
1984–2018 / Paul C. Light.
Description: New York, NY, United States of America : Oxford University Press, 2019. |
Includes bibliographical references.
Identifiers: LCCN 2018018177 | ISBN 9780190851798 (hard cover) |
ISBN 9780190851811 (epub) | ISBN 9780190851804 (updf)
Subjects: LCSH: Civil service—United States. | United States—Officials and employees. |
Government contractors—United States. | Contracting out—United States. |
Public contracts—United States. | Government accountability—United States. |
United States—Politics and government—1981–1989. |
United States—Politics and government—1989–
Classification: LCC JK692 .L535 2019 | DDC 352.6/30973—dc23
LC record available at https://lccn.loc.gov/2018018177

1 3 5 7 9 8 6 4 2

Printed by Sheridan Books, Inc., United States of America

To Mort Cohen and Rosslyn Kleeman

CONTENTS

The Volcker Alliance

The Volcker Alliance advances effective management of government to achieve results that matter to citizens. The nonpartisan Alliance works toward that objective by partnering with other organizations --academic, business, governmental, and public interest --to strengthen professional education for public service, conduct needed research on government performance, and improve the efficiency and accountability of governmental organization at the federal, state, and local levels.

The Volcker Alliance was launched in 2013 by former Federal Reserve Board Chairman Paul A. Volcker, who served in the federal government for almost 30 years. Mr. Volcker is known for his commitment to effective government for the public good. The Alliance's work is inspired by his legacy of public service and grounded in a set of beliefs about what constitutes effective government. We believe the following:

- Government should be responsive to its citizens, transparent in its operations, accountable for delivering on its promises, and visibly held to the standard of robust and unbiased measures.
- Public service is a high calling, and that it is critical to engage our most thoughtful and accomplished citizens in service to the public good.
- Government functions best when its system of civil service is independent, stable, and staffed by civil servants who are experienced and expert in their domains.
- Our public workforce and government institutions must be dynamic: designed to encourage innovation, leverage technology, and adapt to the needs of a changing nation in an evolving global context.
- The performance of our government institutions depends critically on the training and education of talented public servants, and that this responsibility is shared by our government, our institutions of higher education, and by leading institutions in every sector of society.

Government must be a responsible steward of financial resources, diligent in avoiding waste, assiduous in seeking evidence to assess the effectiveness of its initiatives, and proactive in helping citizens understand the long-term sustainability of its operations.

FOREWORD

PAUL A. VOLCKER

The size of government has been a matter for debate since our nation was founded. The answer depends in part on what we want and expect from government—and that influences a decision on which side of the political aisle we decide to sit. But it's not so simple as that answer suggests.

Paul Light explains the complications in this fascinating new study. He sets out the sheer numbers in painstaking detail. His research emphasizes the difficulty of accurately calculating and agreeing upon a definition of the actual size of the federal government at different points in time.

Beyond the statistical challenge, Light's analysis emphasizes the importance of how people working under the aegis of the federal government are selected, compensated, and managed. No matter one's political leanings, those are essential questions in reaching a conclusion about the size of government.

Nothing is more certain in American political life than complaints about the performance of the federal government. At the same time, there are insistent demands for government to do more to provide more security, whether personal, national, or financial; to improve healthcare; to protect the environment; to build transport systems; and not least to build a strong and independent judiciary.

But somehow, the implications of the two discordant political opinions—for smaller government and for more government—are never really understood or addressed. The challenge for public administration—what it takes to improve performance whatever the size and policies of government—is hardly addressed.

For all of us interested in government, the present is not a pretty picture. It's really not tolerable for a strong democracy that purports to be the benign world leader, with unique responsibilities in maintaining a peaceful and constructive world order, to be caught up in a crisis of confidence of its own. The evident decline in trust in government at virtually every branch, at every level, is silently but pervasively weakening the foundation of our society.

In that sense, the book is a call for action—action beyond campaign rhetoric or popular catch phrases that typically lack substance or fail to sustain effort. Paul Light goes further. Drawing from decades of experience and analysis, he sets out the substance of what is required for real and lasting reform.

His book should be required reading for every member of Congress and president seriously interested in effective government. The breakdowns and disappointments in administrations that seem to be increasing over time, through administrations of differing political colors, demand a response.

What is at issue is confidence in democracy itself. No policies—no politics, red, blue, or purple—can long survive incompetence.

Paul Light has provided us with an accessible, well-researched road map to reform.

It's time to pay attention.

PREFACE

America has relied on federal, contract, and grant employees to execute the laws faithfully since its first breath of independence. This government-industrial complex, as I label it in this book, helped win the Revolutionary War and has been working to create the Constitution's more perfect union for more than two hundred years and will continue to do so far into the future.

Government and industry will continue to fight the nation's wars, for example. The estimated ratio between contract and military forces during the Revolutionary War was one to six, one to three during the Korean War, and slightly above one to one during the Iraq and Afghanistan wars.[1] Contract forces not only fight side by side with military personnel, they also pay the ultimate sacrifice for their service, including 1,500 lives lost in Iraq and Afghanistan between 2009 and 2016 alone.

The deaths of private security contractors and aid workers are rarely acknowledged. To the contrary, the contract military allows the government to hide the true size of war while diminishing the sacrifices of those who serve under the same flag. "The media's failure to bring contractor deaths more clearly into the public consciousness is inexcusable," writes procurement scholar Steven L. Schooner of the Iraq War. "In a representative democracy, public awareness of the human cost of our nation's security and foreign policies is critical. If the United States is going to continue tallying the human cost associated with military operations then the American public deserves a full accounting."[2]

Government and industry will also continue to pursue what Alexander Hamilton called "extensive and arduous enterprises for the public benefit."[3] Name an international or domestic problem that has faced the nation since its founding, and the government-industrial complex worked to convert bold solutions into great achievements.[4] Federal, contract, and grant employees worked side by side in conquering life-threatening diseases, developing new technologies, assessing new policies for improving quality of life, and implementing audacious strategies for achieving social and economic breakthroughs to help every American citizen.

Whatever the mission, the government-industrial complex will also continue to wield enormous economic, political, and social influence. If not a source of undisputed influence, it will remain a formidable force in who gets, what, when, where, and how from government, including who fights the wars, collects the taxes, and even runs the prisons.[5]

The government-industrial complex reflects the ebb and flow of the national priorities. The true size of the federal government's blended workforce grew under Ronald Reagan, held steady under George H. W. Bush, dropped sharply under Bill Clinton, surged again under George W. Bush, held steady before dropping under Barack Obama, and began to rise again as Donald Trump pressed for increased defense spending in first two years.[6]

Despite its great success in converting bold promises into lasting achievements throughout American history, the government-industrial complex cannot play its imperative role in faithfully executing the laws if it becomes a threat to the more perfect union and liberty it must protect. Nor can it protect great achievements such as helping veterans adjust to civilian life, protecting the environment, rebuilding the US infrastructure, guaranteeing access to education and job training, securing civil rights, and assuring safe and healthy retirements for older Americans without a careful sorting of its responsibilities. The government-industrial complex is often all that stands between government's greatest achievements and catastrophic failure.

Purpose of the Book

This book is designed to explore the government-industrial complex using full-time-equivalent head counts of federal, contract, and grant employees from 1984 to November 2017.

This book measures the true size of the government side of the complex by the number of federal full-time employees who work for the federal executive branch. Although this book excludes active-duty military personnel and US Postal Service employees from the head counts in chapter 2, readers are free to adjust the totals as they wish to reflect their own definitions of the federal workforce.[7]

In turn, this book measures true size of the industrial side of the complex by the number of estimated full-time-equivalent employees hired with federal contract or grant dollars. Many of these employees work for private firms that provide products and services such as fighter planes, roads, computer systems, technical assistance, management consulting, and national intelligence. In turn, many grant employees work for state and local governments, nonprofits, and universities that provide products and services such as job training, legal aid, cancer research, disaster relief, hospital construction, veterans counseling, housing placement, environmental assessment, and school planning.

This book uses these head counts to ask whether the right employees are in the right positions at the highest performance and accountability. Having asked a similar conclusion in his 1975 study of what he called "the shadow government," Daniel Guttman offered three options for directing a workforce that is too important to fail, but too big to ignore:

> First, we can bring much more work in-house than now contemplated or, alternatively, apply to contractors the same rules that apply to officials. Assuming this were politically plausible (hardly likely at present), if the premise of contract reform were correct, this would negate the institutional differences for which contractors are valued. Second, we can hope that current attention will permit us to "muddle through." But again, given the reality, this cannot be assumed. Finally, there is the possibility that we can begin to think of approaches—new tools, if not entirely new visions—to employ if the presumption of regularity cannot be assumed.[8]

This book embraces Guttman's third option by providing new estimates of the government-industrial complex in chapter 1; a history of its growth from 1984 to 2017 in chapter 2; analysis of the pressures that create imbalance between federal, contract, and grant employees in chapter 3; a six-step strategy for a proper reblending of federal, contract, and grant employees in chapter 4; and a discussion of a "next gen" public service in chapter 5.[9]

The Core Question

This book does not ask whether the government-industrial complex is the best arrangement for faithfully executing the laws. The question does arise from time to time in debates about the appropriate balance between federal, contract, and grant employees and the need to set a reasonable border between government and institute. However, these debates are often grounded in hunches about the true size of government and limited information on the distribution of responsibilities across the government-industrial divide.

Hence, this book addresses a much simpler question: how many full-time equivalent federal, contract, and grant employees work for the federal government faithfully executing its laws? The answer leads to a history of growth and decline, a discussion of underlying incentives for using contract and grant employees in lieu of federal employees, and options for strengthening the measurement and monitor of the government-industrial workforce.

This call for measuring and monitoring comes directly from President Dwight David Eisenhower's 1961 farewell address, albeit in a discussion of what he described as an unprecedented "conjunction of an immense military establishment and a large arms industry" whose influence was felt "in every city, every Statehouse, every office of the Federal government."[10] Although Eisenhower's address focused specifically on military-industrial complex, his warnings about the "acquisition of unwarranted influence, whether sought or unsought" are just as relevant to the much larger government-industrial complex that emerged from the New Deal and now employs seven million Americans.

Eisenhower believed that the military-industrial complex was essential for winning a war against a "hostile ideology global in scope, atheistic in characters, ruthless in purpose, and insidious in method." At the same time, he also believed the nation was threatened from within by the total influence, "economic, political, even spiritual" of the military-industrial complex itself. Eisenhower told the nation to take nothing for granted as the military-industrial complex sought advantage, and put the burden on an alert and acknowledgeable citizen to "compel the proper meshing" so that "security and liberty may prosper together."

Unfortunately, Eisenhower did not define "proper meshing" beyond his simple call for action, nor did he provide guidance on how to discipline the movement of jobs and functions across the boundaries between military and industry. Much as he believed that the military-industrial complex was a source of great international advantage, he also saw the need for oversight. The penultimate draft of the draft made the point quite clearly:

> We shall need all the organizing genius we possess to mesh the huge machinery of our defenses with our peace-oriented economy so that liberty and security are both well served. It requires constant vigilance, and a jealous precaution against any move which would weaken the control of civil authority over the military establishment. We must be especially careful to avoid measures which would enable any segment of this military-industrial complex to sharpen the focus of its own power at the expense of the sound balance which now prevails. The potential for disastrous abuse of power in this area is great. Let us watch it carefully.[11]

The focus had to be on balance, not the exploitation of advantage, on protecting existing controls at all costs.

In contemporary terms, Eisenhower might now use "a proper blending" to prevent unwarranted influence.[12] Not only would blending be more relevant to contemporary debates about federal strategic workforce management, but it is also a fitting metaphor for the circumstances at hand. After all, meshing evokes an image of government as a layer cake of clear lines of authority between policy and administration, while blending suggests a marble cake of competition and influence driven more by circumstance and political advantage than rationalists might prefer. Whatever the term, Eisenhower's warnings are directly relevant to the core question of this book: does the federal government have the right people in the right jobs to faithfully execute the laws without threat to liberty itself?

I intend to answer this question by reviewing recent trends in the true size of the government-industrial complex, examining the reasons the federal government may have delegated too many functions to industry, and offering a proposal for sorting responsibilities. Using updated head counts of federal, contract, and grant employees, this book presents an apples-to-apples opportunity to ask how to monitor and police the movement of functions across the divide between government and industry.

These estimates help frame the overall discussion about who works for the government-industrial complex, what they do, how much they cost, where they work, whether they deliver fair value, and why their numbers rise and fall over time.[13] Without arguing that this book will resolve the "information asymmetries" that Guttman has identified in the federal government's relationship with its contract and grant employees, my latest estimates can give Congress and the president a reasonable method for mapping the terrain and good reason to do so.[14]

The True Size of Government Revisited

This book extends my past efforts to identify and count the number of employees who help the federal government faithfully execute the laws.[15] Narrowed to federal full-time-equivalent employees, the answer has been about two million, plus or minus a few hundred thousand since 1950. Expanded to include employees who work under federal contracts and grants, the number has varied from six to nine million since 1984, hitting a low of 6.3 million full-time-equivalent employees in 1996 before surging to 9.3 million in 2010 and falling back to 7.3 million in 2015.[16]

This book is based on my belief that the government-industrial complex is imperative to the faithful execution of the laws. Framed as such, the book draws on four themes from my past work on the true size of government.

First, I believe it is time to acknowledge the shared impact of all federal workers in faithfully executing the laws. Although some government-industry employees operate in secret, almost all are identifiable and countable. Moreover, the contract and grant employees covered in this book deserve acknowledgement and accounting for their essential role in faithfully executing the laws and should be identified and counted as part of the federal workforce. Just as contract and grant employees have played important roles in securing many of the federal government's greatest achievements and deserve appropriate credit for their commitment, they have also contributed in their own ways to the recent cascade of government breakdowns and must be held accountable for their role.

Second, I believe that many contract and grant employees have just as much public service motivation as their federal peers. Many come to work for the chance to accomplish something worthwhile for the nation, are deeply committed to the missions they serve, and see their careers as more public than private. At the same time, I believe there are good reasons to worry about breaches in the border between government and industry that create what Eisenhower called "grave implications" for "the very structure of our society."[17]

Third, I believe that Congress and the president have abdicated their responsibilities in overseeing one of the largest workforces in the nation. I am particularly frustrated by the notion that the government-industrial complex workforce is somehow impossible to measure and manage as a whole. If a lone researcher with a few thousand dollars can produce a reasonable trend line from 1984 to the present, surely Congress and the president can produce estimates with pinpoint accuracy. The subject is no doubt complex and the facts are often in dispute, but the potential for what Eisenhower called "unwarranted influence, whether sought or unsought," demands more than occasional congressional handwringing about the lack of data.[18]

Fourth, I believe federal employees continue to make miracles daily as they struggle against the odds created by employment caps, cuts, and freezes; antiquated systems; and withering criticism by their own leaders and public. It is little wonder that many would feel frustrated in their work or that some would abandon federal service for greener fields. It is more surprising that so many would stay. It is not for the money or the accolades. Rather, it is for the persistent commitment to mission.

Plan of the Book

This book gives a broad analysis of the relative size, recent history, and ongoing effort to manage the government-industrial complex. Although this book acknowledges the essential role that the government-industrial complex plays in faithfully executing the laws, it also asks whether the role is too significant and so undisciplined as to make it fraught with threats to the nation's security and liberty.

Readers should note that this book does not favor one source of employees over another, nor does it recommend more rounds of insourcing or outsourcing, downsizing or dismantling. Rather, it presents a set of proposals for reblending the government-industrial complex to ensure the greatest accountability and performance.

Chapter 1 starts this discussion by focusing on Eisenhower's warnings about the conjunction of what he described as an "immense military establishment" with "a permanent armaments industry of vast proportions" and proceeds to a description of the methods used to calculate the true size of the federal, contract, and grant workforce. As chapter 1 argues, Eisenhower presented a framework for tracking the "unwarranted influence, whether sought or unsought," of any government-industrial conjunction, large or small, and even outlined a method for measuring the true size of government through head counts of federal employees and funding for contract firms and grant agencies.[19]

Chapter 2 explores patterns in the number of federal, contract, and grant employees under Presidents Ronald Reagan, George H. W. Bush, Bill Clinton, George W. Bush, and Barack Obama. The chapter starts with an overview of the measurement challenges in estimating the true size of government, a discussion of threats to accuracy, and a description of an estimating approach based on contract transactions and grant awards. The chapter also offers caveats on using the information and examines the data deficits that currently frustrate efforts to monitor the blended workforces that faithfully execute the laws from both sides of the complex.

The chapter then turns to a history of the changing size of government under Reagan, George H. W. Bush, Clinton, George W. Bush, and Obama. Reagan and George W. Bush pushed the total size of government upward during war, while George H. W. Bush, Clinton, and Obama all harvested the peace dividends that followed. The chapter examines each president's view of the federal workforce and explores patterns of growth and decline as the true size of government surged during war and economic crisis and compressed during peace and recovery.

Readers are urged to pay particular attention to Reagan's role in creating a Cold War peace dividend that reduced the number of employees on both sides of the government-industrial complex. Reagan also helped launch two decades of military base closing that gave his successors enough savings to hope for no new taxes and declare an end to the era of big government.[20]

The chapter ends with a quick review of President Donald Trump's early relationship with the government-industrial complex and ends with a discussion of the federal personnel caps, cuts, and freezes that have done so much to alter the government-industrial balance. Although most of these post–World War II employment constraints had negligible effects on federal employment, they fueled public demand for a government that looks smaller but delivers more and the use of contract and grant employees as a work-around.

Chapter 3 examines the time limits, bureaucratic constraints, and political realities that drive federal functions and jobs across the dividing line between government and industry. Whether by accident or intent, the fifteen pressures catalogued in the chapter give Congress, the president, and federal officers ample incentive to use contract and grant employees in lieu of federal employees. The pressures also frustrate effective deployment of federal, contract, and grant employees. The chapter ends with a short discussion of the prospects for reducing the pressure through comprehensive reform.

Chapter 4 starts with a short history of recent efforts to realize Eisenhower's proper meshing of government and industry. As I argue, six of the past seven presidents focused on one-sided reforms designed to cut big government or discipline the contracting process. Obama is the only recent president who focused on both sides through a broad agenda for government improvement and aggressive reforms in the blend of federal and contract employees. Obama eventually retreated from both efforts, but provided an inventory of options for future two-sided action.

Chapter 4 draws on this history for developing a "reset and reinforce" process that might be used for a regular reblending of the federal government's federal, contract, and grant workforces. Based on rigorous annual head counts and workforce planning, this proper blending involves six steps: (1) clarify terms, (2) force both sides of the government-industrial complex to take social responsibility for their work, (3) track movement across the divide between government and industry, (4) sort functions based on careful definitions of which workforce should do what, (5) monitor and reset caps on the true size of the total workforce, and (6) reinforce the dividing lines between government and industry. Anchored by more precise inventories of who delivers what for government, this reblending process could ease long-standing limits on federal employment, while acknowledging the important role that contract and grant employees play in launching bold endeavors and achieving success.

Chapter 5 ends the book with a discussion of the "next gen" public service. Even following a careful reblending using the sorting system presented in chapter 4, Congress and the president must assure that the government-industrial complex embraces a continued commitment to public service, a mission that matters to the nation's future, and a workforce that bring new vitality to aging institutions. Federal employees are going to retire in record numbers over the next decade, but their departures will create a destructive "retirement tsunami" unless Congress and the president act now to recruit and train the next generation of public servants wherever they work in the government-industrial complex.

Congress and the president must make sure that every federal, contract, and grant employee is committed to faithfully executing the laws, including laws they might oppose. Too many decisions about the choice and deployment of the federal government's blended workforce are made without concern for cost, benefit, performance, accountability, and the underlying public-service motivation that should call all government employees to their work.

Just as Eisenhower argued that the military-industrial complex was imperative to the nation's safety, this book argues that the government-industrial complex is critical for supporting bold endeavors and creating lasting achievements. And just as Eisenhower also argued that a proper meshing of the military and armaments industry was the only way to protect liberty, this book asks how to align a much larger government-industrial complex than Eisenhower could ever have imagined. It is impossible to know whether Eisenhower would describe today's government-industrial complex a conjunction of an immense federal workforce and a large contract and grant industry, but it is easy to imagine that he would say its size creates the same "grave threats" may be perfectly appropriate, if not much too weak.[21]

ACKNOWLEDGMENTS

I could not have written this book without the help of dozens of mentors, funders, and colleagues over the past twenty-five years. Indeed, this book is the capstone of a research agenda that has involved a host of colleagues who helped design the research, conduct the analyses, interpret the results, and correct my mistakes. It has also involved the support of my family and friends, all of whom offered their support as I slowly concluded that the federal service was in sharp decline.

I might not be so worried about the decline or believe that it amounts to a crisis if I had not spent much of my career watching the trends worsen. Although I did not start studying the federal establishment in earnest until the 1980s, even my earliest encounters were troubling. I wrote my first *Minneapolis Tribune* story in 1974 on the role of the Bureau of Indian Affairs in sparking the Wounded Knee crisis, and spent the first year of graduate school in 1976 studying trust in government, which had been plummeting for the better part of a decade.

My confrontation with the decline of the federal service began in 1984 when I became director of research at the National Academy of Public Administration, which is a distant relative of the National Academy of Sciences. My projects allowed me to study every aspect of the erosion of the federal service. I was involved in studies of the presidential appointments process, morale at the Environmental Protection Agency, the politics of assumptions in the 1983 Amendments to Social Security, and the Space Shuttle Challenger accident. I also oversaw an agenda covering everything from continued management problems at the US Postal Service, new rules on leaking underground storage tanks, and addressing what my friends Charles H. Levine and Rosalyn Kleeman labeled the "quiet crisis" in the civil service.

I witnessed further erosion after joining the US Senate Committee on Governmental Affairs staff as a special adviser on public management in 1987. My legislative assignments focused on funding and regulating presidential

transitions, lifting the Veterans Administration to cabinet status, requiring financial statements from federal departments and agencies, overseeing the growing
number of chiefs of staff at the top levels of government, monitoring the increase in presidential appointees across government, and reauthorizing the 1978
Paperwork Reduction Act. I also worked on financial reform, results measurement, pay comparability between federal employees and their business peers,
and contract fraud.

The quiet crisis became even clearer to me when I returned to university life in the
1990s and began work on studies of the federal inspectors general; the thickening of
the executive hierarchy; the federal government's hidden and mostly unaccountable
workforce of contractors, grantees, and state and local employees; declining trust in
government; the rising cost of campaigns; and the changing nature of public service
among graduates of the top schools of public affairs. As part of my work for the first
National Commission on the Public Service, which was chaired by former Federal
Reserve Board chairman Paul A. Volcker, I also learned that most young Americans
would not know how to find a federal job even if they wanted one.

This book began to take shape a decade later after the Brookings Institution
created the Center for Public Service in 1999 and published my first book on
the federal government's blended workforce. That book laid the groundwork for
much of the analysis presented here, but did not fully explore the many factors
that led the federal government to substitute contract and grant employees for
civil servants. Nor did it examine the potential sorting systems that might be
used to rebalance the workforce as it expands and contracts over time. These
oversights are remedied in this start-from-scratch book.

As with all books, the conclusions that follow are mine and mine alone.
Much as I appreciate all the help I have received over the years, I own the
mistakes and misinterpretations that readers will no doubt find in this book.
At the same time, I am ever grateful for the encouragement that Robert
A. Katzmann, G. Calvin Mackenzie, David Magleby, Christine Nemacheck,
Russell Wheeler, and Tom Ross lent to this endeavor and acknowledge the
many dedicated scholars who produced so much of the research on which the
book rests, including the Brookings Insitution, Congressional Research Service,
Governance Institute, the Congressional Research Service, George Washington
University Procurement Institute, Nation Analytics, National Academy of
Public Administration, Partnership for Public Service, Project on Government
Oversight, RAND Corporation, and the US Government Accountability Office.
I also owe a special debt of gratitude to my dean, Sherry Glied; associate deans,
Anthony Bertelli and Rajeev Dehejia; my lead research assistants, Rob Mesika
and Tatiana Hryhorowych; lead data analyst, Anubhav Gupta; and the Volcker
Alliance team that has supported so much of my work over the years. I am par-
ticularly grateful to Emily Bolten for her tireless support, Nerissa Clarke, Megan

Smeaton, Anthony Dowd, and the rest of the talented staff, and am grateful for the support of my Oxford University Press team, including David McBride, Emily Mackenzie, and Julia Turner. I am also forever thankful for the unyielding support of family and friends, including my fearless proof reader, Max, and none more important than my wife and friend, Gail Rosen.

I dedicate this book to Mort Cohen and Rosalyn Kleeman, my dear friends and teachers from early in my career. Each taught me important lessons on everything from accounting for federal funds to the wise stewardship of data and ideas. My work has been infinitely enriched by their mentorship—they taught more than they ever imagined, and I am ever grateful for their lessons and confidence.

I have also been blessed to have worked with and for Paul A. Volcker over the past thirty years. I helped Mr. Volcker draft the final report of his first National Commission on the Public Service in 1988, supported the work of his second National Commission on the Public Service in 2003, and remain deeply committed to his campaign to revitalize the federal service through his Volcker Alliance. He has been a tireless champion of causes I support, a guiding light for the public benefit, and a leader for the tough, comprehensive reforms that are essential for faithful execution of the laws. I remain inspired by his strength, endurance, and wisdom.

Paul C. Light
New York City
December 2018

The Government-Industrial Complex

1

A Warning Renewed

This book draws on Dwight Eisenhower's 1961 warnings about a vast military complex to frame a broad discussion about today's government-industrial complex of even greater size and scope. Eisenhower not only added the term "military-industrial complex" to the national vocabulary but also created the specter of a hidden force in American life. Its total influence—economic, political, even spiritual—is felt in every city, statehouse, and office of the federal government, he said, its grave implications threatened the nation's toil, resources, livelihood, and very structure of society.[1]

Just as Richard Nixon leveraged his anticommunist credentials to open the door to China, Eisenhower used his military credentials and unquestioned patriotism to open the conversation about the military-industrial complex.[2] As James Ledbetter writes, the speech was anchored in irony:

> Eisenhower was a pillar of the military-industrial complex he confronted. His assessment of the dark side of America's military machine would have been unusual coming from any American president; for it to come from a five-star general who had amassed and led one of the largest military forces in human history to win World War II was nothing short of astonishing. (And, of course, some might say hypocritical, given the massive buildup of the nuclear arsenal during the Eisenhower presidency, from about 1,000 weapons to about 23,000 by the time he delivered his speech.)[3]

Eisenhower's sixteen-minute speech is still the standard historical reference whenever stories about military bloat and industry lobbying reach the front page. As the following pages suggest, the military-industrial complex is no longer new or exceptional. It is now part of a much larger and well-established conjunction of conjunctions that involves every department and agency of government.

Eisenhower did not question the need for a strong military. He believed the military-industrial complex was imperative for deterring nuclear war and a source of steady resolve in what promised to be a long, cold war. "We recognize the imperative need for this development," he told the public. "Yet, we must not fail to comprehend its grave implications. Our toil, resources, and livelihood are all involved. So is the very structure of our society."[4]

Eisenhower's warning reflected his own tumultuous relationship with the military-industrial complex, including his role in strengthening both sides of the conjunction during his military career. He was a steadfast champion of a strong military but also was an exemplar of what the liberal Center for American Progress calls "fiscally responsible defense budgeting." Convinced that national security was inextricably linked to the nation's military, economic, and spiritual health, Eisenhower cut defense spending by 27 percent during his presidency, much of it harvested from the post–Korean War peace dividend following the July 1952 armistice.[5] Armed with an untarnished reputation, he had the opportunity to create a "new look" military based on quality, not quantity, and stood fast after Democrats recaptured it. Convinced that an arms race could only lead to nuclear war, he warned the nation that increased spending would create "a life of perpetual fear and tension."[6]

Eisenhower paid a high political price for his restraint as Democrats prepared for the 1956 and 1960 presidential campaigns. In 1956, for example, the Senate Armed Services Committee's new Subcommittee on Air Power launched a deep review of the nation's preparedness for nuclear war. With four Democratic hopefuls engaged in the review, the investigation lasted more than a year, produced forty-one public and closed hearings, and concluded with twenty-three recommendations for rebuilding the nation's air power.[7]

According to the subcommittee, the United States trailed the Soviet Union on almost every measure of military power, including the number of fighter planes, light and heavy bombers, tankers, jet engines, scientific personnel, high-energy physics research facilities, housing, air bases, active air force personnel, and ballistic missiles. The administration had not only underestimated Soviet military progress, but had allowed fiscal considerations to weaken US air superiority and create a missile and bomber gap. Absent an immediate increase in spending, the nation's vulnerability to a "sudden attack" would increase for the near future.[8]

Despite this pressure, Eisenhower held steady on his demand for defense cuts. As he told Congress in 1956, "we must not delude ourselves that safety necessarily increases as expenditures for military research or forces in being go up. Indeed, beyond a wise and reasonable level, which is always changing and is under constant study, money spent on arms may be money wasted on sterile metal or inflated costs, thereby weakening the very security and strength we seek."[9]

Eisenhower never forgot the Democratic attacks, either. As historian Dolores Janiewski writes, Eisenhower's 1961 farewell address offered a chance to correct the record:

> Eisenhower spoke in response to what he viewed as cynically generated hysteria about a nonexistent "missile gap" set off by Sputnik in October 1957 and the opportunistic leaking of a report primarily written for a presidential advisory panel. The exaggerated claims about Soviet superiority in missile technology gave the Democrats what Eisenhower considered "a useful piece of demagoguery" to exploit in the 1958 and 1960 elections. Seeking to reassure an agitated public, the president had repeatedly cautioned against overreaction and argued for the need for tight controls of military expenditure but failed to win the rhetorical battle against his critics.[10]

The speech involved more than political payback, of course. Just as he believed the nation's "arms must be mighty, ready for instant action," he also believed there were "grave implications" embedded in a self-perpetuating military-industrial complex. The only path was to ensure a "proper meshing" of government and industry through steady oversight by the citizenry.

As this chapter will argue, this meshing demands careful side-by-side analysis of the true size of the government-industrial workforce. Although the federal government has detailed information on its own workforce, it knows next to nothing about the millions of people who work under federal contracts and grants. Before turning to methods for counting heads, it is first important to ask why the answer matters. As the following pages show, Eisenhower had the answer in 1961.

The Military-Industrial Complex

Eisenhower delivered his farewell address just three days before John F. Kennedy told Americans in his inaugural address to ask not what their country could do for them, but what they could do for their country.[11] Eisenhower could not compete with Kennedy on soaring rhetoric, but his farewell address still resonates in debates about military power, public service, contracting, and corruption. Moreover, his words conveyed a dark warning about the forces that would soon lead the nation into a divisive war. Nevertheless, his speech received little coverage at the time and has received what Janiewski calls "scant attention" since.[12] Although some historians have described the speech as little more than an afterthought, the available evidence suggests that the speech was long in the making

and tightly linked to the president's long-standing concerns about the lines between government and industry.[13]

It is not exactly clear when Eisenhower began thinking about delivering a
farewell address, especially one that would introduce the nation to the military-
industrial complex, though his interest in a grand exit speech may have dated back
to his childhood memories of Washington's farewell address.[14] Whatever the deep
calling, Eisenhower's interest clearly intensified after the 1958 congressional campaign as Democrats increased their attacks on his defense budget.[15] Asked to explain
a Democratic landslide that cost his party fifteen seats in the Senate and forty-nine
in the House, Eisenhower focused on the "spender-wing of the Democratic Party"
and the forces of left-wing government: "We have been too lavish in too many
things starting, indeed, in my opinion, in certain things in Defense because as yet we
have not eliminated the duplications, the unnecessary expenditures that are going
on, and we must start right from the biggest and go right down to the smallest."[16]
Absent hard choices about which weapons to buy and which to retire, he said, "we
better go into a garrison state, because there is no other way to meet the expenses."[17]

At some point that autumn, Eisenhower told his chief "literary ghost" and
speechwriter, Malcolm Moos, that he wanted a farewell message of some kind.
He was in a "philosophical mood" that day, Moos remembered years later, and
said he wanted to have something to say when he left office: "I'm not interested in
capturing headlines, but I want to have a message and I want you to be thinking
about it well in advance."[18] He returned to the topic the following spring after
reviewing a May 24 memo about future speeches, but remained interested in the
option if it avoided party politics:

> I have, yet, no fixed idea that I should deliver in a so-called "fare-
> well" talk to the Congress, even if that body should invite me to do
> so. . . . Needless to say, there would be no profit in expressing, in such
> a setting, anything that was partisan in character. Rather, I think the
> purpose would be to emphasize a few homely truths that apply to the
> responsibilities and duties of a government that must be responsive to
> the will of the majorities, even when the decisions of those majorities
> create apparent paradoxes. A collateral purpose would be, of course,
> merely to say an official "goodbye."[19]

Eisenhower under Fire

Eisenhower was a student of war and profit long before he entered the presidency. Indeed, he had become an expert on military procurement and battle
planning as a senior officer at the Army War College in the late 1920s and early

1930s. As Eisenhower later reported, this work forced him to confront subjects such as mobilization, the composition of armies, the role of air forces and navies in war, and the military's dependence upon the industrial capacity of the nation.[20] He not only gained a deep understanding of the military-industrial relationship but also examined the history of war profiteering during World War I and even may have stumbled upon a 1930 *Nation* magazine of secret contracts for as-yet-to-be-declared wars.[21]

Eisenhower's research laid the historical foundation for his farewell address and ample confidence in an attack on the "apostles of wholesale reckless spending," "phony doctrines," and "demagogic excess" that emerged during the 1958 congressional campaign.[22] Although he had been a steadfast advocate for a well-equipped military, he was equally concerned about the potential threat to liberty created by what he would call the "conjunction between an immense military establishment and a large arms industry."[23]

He gave almost immediate notice of his intent to cut defense spending just two months into office in 1953 when he told the American Society of Newspaper Editors that every gun made, every warship launched, and every rocket fired signified "a theft from those who hunger and are not fed, those who are cold and not clothed."[24] Having started his "Chance for Peace" speech with a dark vision of an empty future, Eisenhower offered his own cost/benefit analysis of perpetual fear and tension. "The world in arms is not spending money alone. It is spending the sweat of its laborers, the genius of its scientists, the hopes of its children." He then provided a striking list of trade-offs:

> The cost of one modern heavy bomber is this: a modern brick school in more than 30 cities.
>
> It is two electric power plants, each serving a town of 60,000 population.
>
> It is two fine, fully equipped hospitals.
>
> It is some 50 miles of concrete highway.
>
> We pay for a single fighter plane with a half million bushels of wheat.
>
> We pay for a single destroyer with new homes that could have housed more than 8,000 people.
>
> This, I repeat, is the best way of life to be found on the road the world has been taking. This is not a way of life at all, any true sense.[25]

Despite holding the defense budget in check for eight years, Eisenhower described the military-industrial conjunction to the nation with adjectives such as "huge," "immense," "large," and "vast." Framed as the inevitable product of a new kind of warfare and described as and a formidable threat Eisenhower also urged the nation to beware the "weight of this combination endanger our liberties or democratic processes."

> Our military organization today bears little relation to that known by any of my predecessors in peacetime, or indeed by the fighting men of World War II or Korea. Until the latest of our world conflicts, the United States had no armaments industry. American makers of plowshares could, with time and as required, make swords as well. But now we can no longer risk emergency improvisation of national defense; we have been compelled to create a permanent armaments industry of vast proportions. Added to this, three and a half million men and women are directly engaged in the defense establishment. We annually spend on military security more than the net income of all United States corporations.[26]

Eisenhower also had personal measures of unwarranted influence in mind as he prepared his speech. He certainly felt the cumulative pressure of the munitions industry and its allies in Congress and the military. As noted later in this chapter, he could feel the pressure in magazine advertisements and trade journals that drove public support for defense spending. "Like Congressional hearings controlled by Democrats," Ledbetter writes, "these publications became a venue for the largely unfiltered views of the military establishment. They were often harshly, even personally critical of Eisenhower and his Defense Department managers."[27]

The House also gave Eisenhower indicators of unwarranted influence in its 1959 investigation of the munitions lobby. The brief investigation did not focus on the familiar relationship between the munitions industry and the procurement corps but on influence peddling by 726 army, navy, and air force commissioned officers who went to work for the nation's hundred largest defense firms after retiring.[28] "It was not our duty to indict," the subcommittee's chairman, F. Edward Hébert (D-LA), later said of the investigation. "It was our duty to find facts and come up with a law to stop this so-called influence peddling. There is no greater opinion than public opinion, and the opinion is that this influence peddling is going on right now in a broad sense."[29]

The investigation may have been designed more to illuminate than indict, but its twenty-four hearings and structured survey of the defense firms produced more than enough evidence to do both.[30] According to the subcommittee's own opinion survey of retired officers, 261 former general and flag officers and another 485 colonels and navy captains were employed by the defense industry as of June 30, 1959, of whom three-quarters worked under "incentive-type" engagements that gave them a cut of the spending they produced.[31] The subcommittee's final report confronted the standard response from the retired officers:

We were impressed with the obvious inconsistencies in testimony. Some might have a more felicitous term. For example, when discussing influence, some retired officers contended that the retired officer is a "has-been"; that he has no influence; and that his personal contact is resented by active duty personnel. These witnesses contended that the fact of being retired was a handicap, if not a deterrent.

It is just a little difficult to reconcile these assurances about "has-beens," when it is agreed that they could stand to be "cooled off" for, say, 2 years. Surely industry is not hiring historians at lush salaries. Industry buys what the employee knows. It buys knowledge, which can be converted into sales for a profit.[32]

Eisenhower followed the investigation through press coverage, congressional liaison briefings, and his personal contacts with the Defense Department, but resisted the opportunity to endorse the review during a June 17, 1959, press conference. Asked whether he thought the lobbying might have created "improper pressures," he dodged the question with a one-sentence answer: "No one has certainly ever tried to do it to me, and anyway, I don't have anything to do with the contracting business."[33] At the same time, he said the investigation was justified: "I think it's all right to look into these things because we must be careful. I think anyone that is acting in good faith would have nothing to fear of such an investigation."[34]

Eisenhower had also discussed the munitions lobby at a press conference two weeks earlier when he confronted rumors that he used the term to take several senators to task in a White House meeting. Asked to comment on the story, he told the press that he could not remember ever using the term "munitions lobby" specifically, but indicted the industry nonetheless: "I do say this: obviously political and financial considerations get into this argument—rather than merely military ones—that is produced when people have to advertise very strongly about a particular thing companies do; obviously, something besides the strict military needs of this country are coming to influence decisions."[35]

The "something" had to be the military-industrial complex. Eisenhower had yet to use the term, but his staff continued to develop proposals for an address on the "permanent war-based industry" through the summer. One October 31 internal memo even referenced the lobbying investigation in promoting a speech on the "merchants of death."[36] Eisenhower eventually chose "military-industrial complex" instead but continued to complain about the network of defense lobbyists through the summer and fall as he impounded more than $600 million in what he deemed to be wasteful defense spending.[37]

Today's Conjunction of Conjunctions

Eisenhower's farewell address is still referenced whenever defense spending surges but also contained what he could have easily called the government-scientific complex. Although Eisenhower understood that this second conjunction was tied to the military, Eisenhower believed the technological revolution had produced the military demand, not vice versa:

> Akin to, and largely responsible for the sweeping changes in our industrial-military posture, has been the technology revolution during recent decades. In this revolution, research has become central, it also becomes more formalized, complex, and costly. A steadily increasing share is conducted for, by, or at the direction of, the federal government.[38]

Eisenhower rehearsed many of these themes before entering the presidency. He began his five-year tenure as Columbia University president in 1948 by warning students of the dangers of "demagogic appeals to class selfishness, greed, and hate," laid into pressure groups and political leaders who appealed to "all that was selfish in humankind" the following spring, and called upon the American Bar Association the next fall to defend the nation from "the unbearable selfishness of vested interest" and from "the blindness of those who, protesting devotion to the public welfare, falsely declare that only government can bring us happiness, security and opportunity."[39]

Given these and other earlier musings, the question is why Eisenhower did not discuss the conjunction of conjunctions described in this book. After all, elements of the nonmilitary-industrial complex existed in the 1950s at the Department of Health, Education, and Welfare; the Federal Highway Administration; National Institutes of Health; Social Security Administration; US Postal Service; and Veterans Administration. Why not expand the warnings to cover government and industry as a whole?

A first answer is that Eisenhower kept the nondefense agenda under control. He was frequently criticized for his stance on civil rights and social justice, but showed steady support for the social safety net and hewed to an early version of what George W. Bush would eventually call "compassionate conservatism."[40] Eisenhower did end his address with a broad warning about government expansion, but did not name nondefense policy as a specific threat:

> As we peer into society's future, we—you and I, and our government—must avoid the impulse to live only for today, plundering for, for our own ease and convenience, the precious resources of tomorrow. We cannot mortgage the material assets of our grandchildren without

asking the loss also of their political and spiritual heritage. We want democracy to survive for all generations to come, not to become the insolvent phantom of tomorrow.[41]

A second answer is that Eisenhower was able to control domestic spending. Although he supported increased social security spending, accepted the new disability insurance program, took the first steps toward today's national health insurance system, and supported new infrastructure of all kinds, he was one of just two post–World War II presidents to secure a balanced budget during his term. As former Congressional Budget Office director Rudolph Penner writes, Eisenhower's 1960 budget is a prime example of the days when budgeting was easier:

> Although the Eisenhower era was a very different time, some lessons from 60 years ago are relevant to today's fiscal challenges. The most important is that it was much easier to control total spending and to set rational priorities when discretionary spending dominated the budget and the Congress did not have to contend with extremely popular, automatically growing, large entitlements for the elderly.[42]

Despite this leeway, budgeting was still difficult as pressure mounted for a stimulus package as the nation emerged from the 1957–1958 recession. "The Cold War was raging," Penner also writes, "Khrushchev was bellicose, there was much talk of a missile gap, and it was feared that the Soviet's socialist economy would out-produce America's capitalist one—a fear that seems quite absurd in hindsight." In the end, Penner writes, Congress gave Eisenhower exactly what he wanted on defense, a 2 percent cut in a year of unrelenting Democratic criticism:

> It was one of the largest fiscal consolidations of the post–World War II period. Eisenhower was successful in limiting the growth of overall nondefense spending. It fell from 8.4 percent of the GDP in fiscal 1959 to 8.1 percent in fiscal 1960. Admittedly, some luck was involved, as well as a budget gimmick. The good fortune: The recovery from the 1957–58 recession turned out to be surprisingly vigorous. GDP grew a robust 7.2 percent in calendar 1959.[43]

Like the military-industrial complex in the late 1950s, the government-industrial complex is no doubt imperative to the nation's survival in an uncertain world. Also like the military-industrial complex in the late 1950s, the government-industrial complex in recent decades has created the potential for the "unwarranted influence" in every corner of society that framed Eisenhower's message.[44] Finally, like the military-industrial complex in the late 1950s, the government-industrial complex presents the same "potential for the disastrous rise of misplaced power" that Eisenhower discussed in his farewell address.[45]

Asked to further explain his concerns about "misplaced power" during his final presidential press conference on January 18, Eisenhower paused for a moment, and then turned to the visibility of the arms industry:

> When you see almost every one of your magazines, no matter what they are advertising, has a picture of the Titan missile or the Atlas or solid fuel or other things, there is becoming a great influence, almost an insidious penetration of our own minds that the only thing this country is engaged in is weaponry and missiles. And, I'll tell you we just can't afford to do that. The reason we have them is to protect the great values in which we believe, and they are far deeper even than our own lives and our own property, as I see it.[46]

Eisenhower might argue that the government-industrial complex was so large by that point that even an exceptionally engaged citizenry could no longer check its potential for unwarranted influence. According to Janine R. Wedel, author of *The Shadow Elite*, citizens themselves may contribute to the threat: "Ironically, the perennial American predilection to rail against 'big government' is partly to blame for the creation of still bigger government— the 'shadow government' of companies, consulting firms, nonprofits, think tanks, and other nongovernmental entities that contract with government to do much of its work."[47]

Writing of *Federalist*, no. 70, Wedel argues that James Madison's warning about the "tyrannical concentration of all the powers of government in the same hands" is applicable to the federal government's reliance on contract and grant employees:

> Such contracting out potentially erodes the government's ability to operate in the public and national interest. It also creates the conditions for the intertwining of state and private power and the concentration of power in just a few hands—about which Madison warned.[48]

Wedel continues with brief examples of just how far contract employees have gone in confronting the rules on the exercise of intimate government functions such as collecting intelligence, managing bank rescues, controlling databases, selecting and overseeing other contractors, providing high-risk protection for diplomats, drafting congressional testimony, and writing field manuals on the use of contractors on the battlefield.

As Wedel argues, these responsibilities drifted over the dividing line between government and industry precisely to disguise the true size of the endeavor: "Because they are not counted as part of the federal workforce, it can appear as if the size of government is being kept in check. Like the Potemkin village of Russia, constructed to make the ruler or the foreigner think that things are rosy, the public is led to believe they have something they do not."[49]

Members who work in this conjunction do their part to maintain the conceit. They may be easy to spot on packed highways during rush hours on their way to well-known office parks, but they rarely speak without permission and prefer the back of the room during public briefings. They can spend decades working in the same office sitting next to the same colleagues pursuing the same federal mission, yet never be identified as part of the government-industry complex that serves the nation or be held to account for work so intimately related to the public interest that it should have been performed by a fully credentialed federal employee.

Counting Heads

Shadows are difficult to measure almost by definition, which is one reason the term provokes mystery and suspicion. The federal government has a deep inventory of data on its civilian employees, but has almost no systematic information on its contract and grant employees.

As a result, the contemporary debate about the government's blended workforce relies on the same broad apples-to-oranges indicators that Eisenhower used to describe the military-industrial complex in 1961: head counts for declaring the defense establishment "immense," products such as weapons for judging the armaments industry "vast," and corporate income for declaring the conjunction "huge." The following pages will explore several recent efforts to count the contract and grant workforce before turning to the methodology used in this book to estimate the true size of government. The chapter will then introduce the data and discuss the problems that continue to create data deficits in the flow of employee information.

Before turning to methodologies and head counts, however, it is important to acknowledge the role of grants in the changing shape of the government-industrial complex. Although it is common to focus on contracts as the principal tool for outsourcing, grants have long been an essential source of support for research and were central to the expansion of third-party government during the 1960s. Not only did grants produce significant increases in state and local government employment, they also generated new opportunities across the nonprofit sector and even created jobs at the "interstices" of the new federalism where contractors helped governments and nonprofits find the grants, manage the awards, and even evaluate the outcomes.[50]

Failed Counts

The ordinarily unflappable Congressional Budget Office (CBO) produced the most recent analysis of the number of federal contract employees. The nonpartisan agency was drawn into the head count debate only weeks after Republicans captured the Senate in the 2014 midterm elections, when Rep. Chris Van Hollen (D-MD) requested side-by-side comparisons of the federal and contract workforce in all future reports on government employment.[51] As the representative of sixty thousand federal employees in Maryland's Sixth Congressional District at the time, Van Hollen had fought the "Reducing the Size of the Federal Government through Attrition Act" in 2011 and 2013, and helped derail an early Obama administration blue-ribbon proposal for a cut of two hundred thousand in the number of federal employees.[52] Van Hollen expected more downsizing pressure as Republicans prepared for the coming presidential campaigns, and hoped the comparisons would widen the debate to include both sides of the government-industrial complex.

Van Hollen's request came at a difficult moment for CBO. Its director was about to be fired, its small staff was drowning in study requests, and Donald J. Trump was only months from announcing a presidential campaign that would occasionally feature attacks on the agency's budget estimates.[53] Moreover, although CBO has some skill in comparing federal and private pay, it has minimal expertise in federal personnel management. The General Accountability Office (GAO), not CBO, is also the acknowledged expert on federal personnel policy and data.

It is not surprising, therefore, that CBO answered Van Hollen's request with a five-page letter acknowledging its limited knowledge base: "Regrettably, CBO is unaware of any comprehensive information about the size of the federal government's contracted workforce."[54] Although CBO acknowledged the Federal Procurement Data System–Next Gen (FPDS) as the "only comprehensive source of information on contract spending," it criticized the data as incomplete, inaccurate, and difficult to use, and made no mention of its potential value for estimating the number of full-time-equivalent contract employees. Despite its own harsh critique, CBO nonetheless used the database in a quick analysis of federal contract dollars at page 4 of the letter, but could not convert the dollars into head counts with the methods at its disposal. Without a head count database at hand, CBO could not meet Van Hollen's demand. "I would have been stunned if the CBO said anything other than what it did," one federal personnel expert wrote at the time. "Does that worry me? Not really, because it does not tell us anything actionable."[55]

The number might not have been actionable in framing federal policy, but might have prevented unwise legislative action. CBO's letter did little to reduce the pressure for head count caps, cuts, or freezes, and exposed the federal government to another round of standard ridicule. *Government Executive* ran its story under "Even CBO Is Stumped on the Size of the Contractor Workforce," *Daily Caller* went with "CBO Report on Contract Workers: 'We Have No Idea How Many Contractors Work for Us,'" *Federal Times* used "CBO: No Clue on the Number of Contractors or Their Pay," and the *Washington Post* filed under "No One Knows the Size of the Government's Contracted Workforce."[56]

CBO might have been more favorable toward the FPDS had its team consulted with other reputable research agencies. CBO was quite right to express FPDS completeness, but might have discussed the 2007 Acquisition Advisory Panel's broad conclusion that the data "at the highest levels provides significant insight."

CBO was also right to reference long-standing concerns about accuracy, but might have been reassured by GAO's 2015 judgment that FPDS was "sufficiently reliable" for tracking defense spending on contracted services.

Finally, CBO was right to acknowledge the FPDS data problems but might have given more attention to recent improvements that led the nonpartisan RAND Corporation to use the FPDS for a 2017 study of defense contract reporting. Like CBO, RAND acknowledged the FPDS data errors but also noted its value as "the authoritative system for federal contract reporting." RAND also noted recent improvements in data quality.[57]

CBO is not the only oversight agency to discover that counting heads is more difficult than it might seem. Federal departments and agencies have also learned that counting heads is more art than science and continue to struggle to deliver the clean inventories of service contract head counts that Congress established for the Defense Department in 2008 and all civilian departments and agencies in 2010.

These inventories are particularly important for tracking the number of contract employees, who provide more almost $300 billion in services each year. These contracts cover a wide range of services "portfolios" such as electronics and communications, facilities, equipment, management, logistics, and medical services, but all are deemed essential to federal performance. The Defense Department spent $130 billion and 53 percent of its contract budget on services in 2015, while civilian departments and agencies spent $122 billion and 78 percent.[58]

In theory, the inventories were designed to provide exactly what Van Hollen wanted. According to the independent watchdogs at the nonpartisan Project on Government Oversight (POGO), the inventories were designed for maximum transparency on the movement of jobs between government and industry, and are especially important for monitoring defense spending:

> These inventories help ensure that contractors are properly overseen and aren't performing work that must be performed by federal

employees (a.k.a. inherently governmental functions). The inventories also assist in identifying contracts that should be considered for conversion to be performed by federal employees. And the inventories help rein in ungoverned contracting that is wasting billions of taxpayer dollars. When such spending isn't reined in, the DoD ends up wastefully subsidizing big service-contracting companies instead of buying much-needed ships, aircraft, and the like.[59]

In practice, the inventories have been uneven at best. GAO has criticized the "limited visibility" of the data, CBO dismissed the inventories as too new to trust in its 2015 letter, and POGO has frequently called the Defense Department to task for delays and what it alleged as concerted efforts to breach the laws governing implementation of the new systems.[60] Although GAO did endorse the inventories in mid-2017 as an important tool for choosing between federal and contract labor, its analysis suggests that many cost comparisons are based more on hunch than on rigorous analysis.[61]

Like the FPDS, the inventories are improving with practice. There are still problems with data reporting, cost estimates, and definitions of what constitutes a full-time service contract employee.

Sources and Methods

This book measures the true size of the federal government with a mix of exact head counts and estimates of full-time-equivalent employees in five different workforces: (1) federal civilian employees, (2) active duty military personnel, (3) US Postal Service workers, (4) contract employees, and (5) grant employees. As the following pages will show, these workforces come together to reveal a blended workforce in which the military-industrial complex is smaller than the nonmilitary-industrial complex. Before introducing these data in more detail, it is first important to understand the sources and methods used for in calculating the true size of government.

Sources

The first three head counts used in this book are publicly available: the Office of Management and Budget (OMB) publishes annual head counts of full-time-equivalent federal employees dating back fifty years, the Defense Department provides active-duty military personnel head counts dating back to 1954, and the US Postal Service historian provides head counts of the number of "regular" or "career" postal employees back to 1926.[62]

The last two head counts used in this book are not publicly available at all. Instead, they must be created with spending data from the FPDS and the Federal Assistance Award Data System (FAADS). Although neither database is easy to use, they are "sufficiently reliable," as GAO describes the FPDS to generate broad insights on what the federal government buys from whom at what price.[63] As CRS argued in late 2016, decision makers should be cautious when using the FPDS but should not dismiss its value:

> All data have imperfections and limitations. FPDS data can be used to identify broad trends and produce rough estimates, or to gather information about specific contracts. Some observers say that despite its shortcomings, FPDS data are substantially more comprehensive than what is available in most other countries in the world. Understanding the limitations of data—knowing when, how, and to what extent to rely on data—helps policymakers incorporate FPDS data more effectively into their decision-making process.[64]

Forty years after it was created, the FPDS remains a work in progress. The data are better, the underlying data architecture is faster, and accuracy is at 95 percent. CBO was right to challenge its completeness and accuracy but overreacted in rejecting the data outright—a point made in its own use of the FPDS to discuss broad trends in its Van Hollen letter.

The FAADS system is also strong enough to support the broad trend analysis used in this book. As with FPDS, the inventory contains missing data and approximations that include problems sorting grants and agreements across more than seven hundred programs.[65] Indeed, the bigger problem with grant monitoring in recent history appears to be the paperwork burdens in reporting to sponsors.[66]

Methods

The federal contract and contract head counts presented in this book were produced through a two-step estimating method designed to (1) review basic records for errors, and (2) estimate the direct and indirect, but not induced, employment generated by the spending. Both steps were completed under a task-order contract with Nation Analytics, a nonpartisan research firm with extensive experience analyzing federal contract and grant data.[67]

Nation Analytics began the estimating analysis by assembling the records of every federal government contract transaction recorded by the FPDS in 2005, 2010, and 2015. Nation Analytics then inspected and repaired the data where possible, and prepared each purchase for further analysis using the Bureau of Economic Analysis (BEA) RIMS II regional input/output model of the economy.

Nation Analytics also reviewed the records of every federal grant award recorded by the FAADS in the same years. National Analytics also inspected and repaired the data where possible, and only included grants for the purchase of products and services, such as highway construction, university research, and wetlands protection. Working together down the list of all grant categories, National Analytics excluded grants that provide products and services to individuals, such as housing assistance, Medicaid, and price supports, and repaired each award for further analysis.

Once checked and rechecked for errors, Nation Analytics used the BEA model to estimate the total number of contract and grant employees in 2005, 2010, and 2015. Nation Analytics completed the analysis by sorting the results by industry (e.g., professional services, manufacturing), government agency (e.g., Defense, Energy, Transportation), business size (small or not small), contracting process (competitive or sole-source), and deliverable (product or service).

The BEA model allows the separation of employment effects into three job categories for further analysis: (1) employees who work directly for the federal government, contract firms, or grant agencies, (2) employees who work indirectly for the federal government under subcontracts and grants, and (3) employees who work in jobs created, or induced, through household spending by federal, contract, and grant employees. The BEA uses highway construction to illustrate the difference between the three kinds of jobs:

> The idea is that an initial change in economic activity results in other rounds of spending—for example, building a new road will lead to increased production of asphalt and concrete. The increased production of asphalt and concrete will lead to more mining. Workers benefiting from these increases will spend more, perhaps by eating out at nicer restaurants or splurging more on entertainment.[68]

In this example, (1) the construction firm hires the direct employees who use the construction materials under prime contracts to build the new road, (2) the concrete, asphalt, and mining firms hire the indirect employees who manufacture the material under subcontracts, and (3) the direct and indirect employees spend the household income that the hiring of gas station attendants, restaurant chefs, bank tellers, movie ticket takers, automobile sales agents, home builders, and other business employees who benefit from direct and indirect government spending. A new computer system would involve a similar, but more variegated chain of impact as contract integrators pour funding into an array of manufacturing, assembly, programming, project integrators, and hardware suppliers.[69]

This book uses the BEA distinctions to create a simple estimate of the direct and indirect employment created by federal contract and grant spending.

Induced employment is a familiar product of direct or indirect federal spending toward economic growth, but the sandwich makers, business executives, bank officers, and ticket takers who depend on the take-home income created by federal, contract, and grant employees cannot be considered federal employees of any kind. Stripped of this induced employment, the estimates presented this book allow a head-to-head, apples-to-apples analysis of the government-industrial workforce.[70]

Readers should note that contract and grant spending does produce significant amounts of induced employment that are not counted as part of the government-industrial complex in this book, but they are real products of contract and grant spending nonetheless. According to the BEA model, for example, the federal government's direct and indirect contract spending induced the creation of 3.2 million jobs in 2017, while its direct and indirect grants induced another 1.2 million jobs. The effects of government spending on the induced workforce is rarely noted as a form of contract and grant spending, but is a benefit nonetheless.[71]

Missing Data

The FPDS and FAADS are more accurate and complete today than when they were created in 1978 and 1981, but they are only as accurate and complete as the data that departments and agencies provide. Although FPDS had a 95 percent accuracy rating in 2017, the 5 percent error rate is still too high. Moreover, the total head count does not include all federal workforces. As noted below, there are at least two workforces missing from the head counts used in this book.

1. The Active-Duty Military

The federal employee figures do not include the 340,000 active-duty military personnel who occupy positions that are civilian in nature. CBO presented the number in 2012 as part of a compendium of options for changing tax and spending policies to reduce the federal deficit. According to CBO's analysis, converting 70,000 active-duty positions could save $19.4 billion between 2014 and 2023, driven largely by the 30 percent lower cost of civilian employees. Although CBO came to the option because of budget savings, it also argued that civilians might be better employees because they require less job-specific training and are not subject to frequent transfers. CBO seemed to suggest that civilians would be more efficient—that is, fewer civilian workers could provide services of the same quantity and quality.[72]

The RAND Corporation confirmed these cost savings in 2016, but also argued that conversions expose military installations to the uncertainties embedded in civilian hiring caps, cuts, and freezes: "Commanders are concerned first and foremost about having sufficient personnel to cover the workload at their installations," RAND wrote. "Some commanders prefer military personnel because they obey commands and can work long hours without overtime pay. In other cases, there is simply a prevailing comfort level that results from seeing certain positions, such as recruiting and entry control point positions, staffed with uniformed service members."[73]

Much as these conversions would save money and enhance productivity, they would make the federal workforce look larger—after all, active-duty military personnel are not listed in the budget tables that inflame outrage every year on Capitol Hill, while full-time-equivalent Defense Department civilian employees are listed in the first column to the right of total executive branch employees. As such, conversion might create a zero-sum game in which increases in the Defense Department's civilian workforce would create pressure to cap, cut, or free the civilian workforce in other departments and agencies. Converting these jobs from active-duty military to civilian status would increase the number of federal employees and associated stories about the growth of big government.

2. Top-Secret America

None of the government-industrial totals discussed in this book include the number of contract employees who work in the national intelligence community. According to a fact sheet released in 2010 by the Office of the Director of National Intelligence (ODNI), the intelligence community spent 70 percent of its 2010 budget on contracts but not necessarily on contractors. ODNI also reported that core contractors comprised 28 percent of its total workforce.

However, ODNI defined its "core contractors" as employees who collect and analyze intelligence and have access to same facilities as federal intelligence officers. Defined as such, ODNI cautioned that core contractors should *not* be confused with ordinary contractors who deliver products such as satellites or services such as administration or information technology services.[74]

ODNI released its fact sheet just after the *Washington Post* published the first of three articles in its investigation of "Top-Secret America." According to Dana Priest and William Arkin, "National Security Inc." employed an estimated 265,000 contract employees in 2010, who worked for 1,100 government agencies and 2,000 private companies located in at least 17,000 locations across the United States.[75] The estimate was based on a reasonable extrapolation of the number of top-security clearances in effect in 2010, but was far from a hard head count and the kind of anchored estimates tied to an input/output model of the economy.

Priest and Arkin's work left little doubt that the number grew by at least half after the 9/11 attacks and 2010. Indeed, ODNI confirmed the trend in its fact sheet, although it also challenged the notion that the increase was haphazard.[76] Priest and Arkin provided ample anecdotal evidence of the waste, all of which was easily captured in one quote by a Senate staff member: "How much money has been involved is just mind-boggling. We've built such a vast instrument. What are you going to do with this thing? It's turned into a jobs program."[77]

The quote missed one simple point: unlike most federal jobs programs, National Security Inc., keeps its job numbers secret. "This is a terrible confession," Secretary of Defense Robert M. Gates said of his own support staff. "I can't get a number on how many contractors work for the Office of the Secretary of Defense."[78]

The intelligence community appears to have the same problem. It either does not know how many full- and part-time contract employees work in its facilities, or cannot fill in the forms.[79] According to GAO's 2014 review, the community has been unable to produce a reliable inventory of its classified employees. GAO reported it could not complete its reliability assessment of the inventory because the seventeen agencies within the community continued to fight about the fuzzy definition of core contractors. Thus, even if Edward Snowden had stumbled across a federal employee head count, it would have been worthless for estimating the size of the top-secret contract and grant workforce.[80]

The lack of a public head count does not alter the intelligence community's increasing dependence on contract and grant employees. According to ODNI's 2006 strategic human capital plan, contract employees were the only answer to the surge in demand: "Confronted by arbitrary staffing ceilings and uncertain funding, components are left with no choice but to use contractors for work that may be borderline 'inherently governmental,' only to find that to do that work, those same contractors recruit our own employees, already cleared and trained at government expense, and then 'lease' them back to us at considerably greater expense."[81]

Readers are free to add the *Post*'s 265,000 estimate to the totals presented in chapter 2. They need only multiply the total number of top-secret clearances reported annually either by the ODNI by its 28 percent estimate by the *Post*'s 31 percent.[82] The method will produce a 10 percent increase in the estimated number of contract employees in either case. However, readers add the numbers at some risk, not the least of which is the secrecy surrounding the distribution and longevity of the clearances themselves.

An Introduction to the Data

Eisenhower believed that the military-industrial combination threatened the nation's liberties and democratic process for at least two reasons. First, it was just plain large—an immense military establishment came together with a vast armaments industry to put the nation's toil, resources, livelihood, and very structure of society at risk. Second, it wanted power—its presence was already felt in every corner of society, while its potential for unwarranted influence endangered liberties and democratic process.

Eisenhower would find plenty of evidence in the FPDS and FAADS to assess today's government-industrial conjunctions. He could track the flow of dollars and jobs toward every corner of society, the government's choice of products and services, the bidding processes used to award contracts and grants, and even the size of the companies and grant agencies that win the awards. He might also use the FPDS and FAADS identification codes to ask questions about unwarranted influence, favoritism, misconduct, lobbying, and discrimination. He could certainly ask whether departments and agencies favored some industries over others, forced contract firms and grant agencies to follow federal health and safety laws, and gave private enterprises a chance to bid for commercially available services under his Budget Circular A-76.[83]

The more Eisenhower learned about the government-industrial complex, the more he might wonder why presidents always promise to cut the number of federal employees without considering the government-industrial complex in the whole. Trump followed the time-honored practice during the 2016 campaign when he promised to freeze federal hiring on his first day in office and attacked Congress for subsidizing the armies of other countries without recognizing the substantial number of contract and grant employees engaged in the nation's war on terrorism.[84] Even as he criticized cost overruns on Lockheed Martin's F-35 Joint Strike Fighter and Boeing's new version of Air Force One, he never mentioned the contract workforce or lobbying reform as targets in his campaign to "drain the swamp" in Washington.

Trump may have relied on legions of contractors and subcontractors to build his real estate empire but focused exclusively on civil servants in his campaign to reduce the federal workforce. Speaking before the nation in his first State of the Union address on January 30, 2018, Trump celebrated the removal of more than 1,500 Department of Veterans Affairs employees "who failed to give the care they deserve" and his commitment to hire "talented people who love our vets as much as we do." He then asked Congress to extend the authority to every department: "All Americans deserve accountability and respect, and that's what we are giving to our wonderful heroes, our veterans. So, tonight, I call on Congress to empower every Cabinet Secretary with the authority to reward good workers and to remove federal employees who undermine the public trust or fail the American people."[85]

Eisenhower might remind Trump that the federal government's civilian employees are only part of the much larger government-industrial workforce that delivered products and services on the public's behalf in 2017. He might also note that 60 percent of this spending went to the purchase of services, not products.[86] Finally, he might give Trump the map of the government-industrial complex presented in Figure 1.1 along with two bullet points:

1. The military-industrial complex occupies the single largest conjunction on the map with 3.3 million employees.
2. The nondefense departments and agencies occupy the largest amount of territory with 3.8 million employees.

The military-industrial complex would look much bigger if Trump added the Department of Veterans Affairs and its 625,000 employees to the Defense Department total, but the nondefense departments and agencies would still contain more 3.2 million employees and cover almost half of the map.

Moreover, as Table 1.1 shows, departments and agencies vary greatly in the use of contract *and* grant employees within their blended workforces. The government-wide ratio of contract-plus-grant employees to federal employees was 2.6 to 1 in November 2017, but Health and Human Services had thirty-six

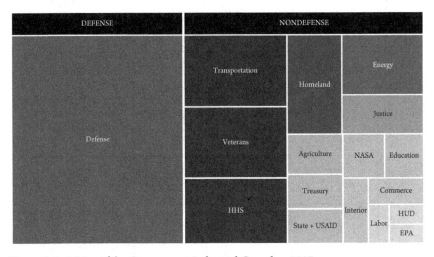

Figure 1.1 A Map of the Government-Industrial Complex, 2017

Table 1.1 The True Size of Government, by Department and Agency, November 2017*

Department or Agency	Grants			Contracts			Totals			Ratios	
	Direct FTE	Indirect FTE	Total Grant FTE	Direct FTE	Indirect FTE	Total Contract FTE	Contract FTE + Grant FTE	Federal FTE	Federal FTE + Grant FTE + Contract FTE	Contract: Grant FTE	Contract + Grant FTE: Federal FTE
Agriculture	4,300	1,300	5,600	35,700	31,000	66,600	72,200	88,400	160,600	11.9	0.8
Commerce	11,500	5,000	16,500	26,400	19,000	45,300	61,800	43,600	105,400	2.7	1.4
Defense	28,800	11,800	40,700	1,326,100	1,164,500	2,490,600	2,531,300	730,600	3,261,900	61.2	3.5
Education	43,000	11,600	54,700	15,700	12,100	27,800	82,500	42,000	124,500	0.5	2.0
Energy	12,000	6,900	18,800	137,500	123,600	261,100	279,900	74,600	354,500	13.9	3.8
HHS	220,200	119,300	339,600	132,400	84,700	217,200	556,800	15,500	572,300	0.6	35.9
Homeland Security	15,500	3,600	19,100	123,400	66,500	189,800	208,900	181,300	390,200	9.9	1.2
HUD	15,900	8,900	24,800	10,400	5,500	15,800	40,700	7,900	48,600	0.6	5.2
Interior	15,700	4,500	20,200	22,000	10,700	32,700	52,900	64,000	116,900	1.6	0.8

Justice	23,200	6,400	29,600	52,300	26,900	79,200	108,700	118,600	227,300	2.7	0.9
Labor	600	300	1,000	33,100	10,000	43,100	44,000	15,900	59,900	45.3	2.8
State + USAID	17,900	3,800	21,700	53,200	25,900	79,100	100,800	36,700	137,500	3.6	2.7
Transportation	336,600	182,500	519,100	36,000	21,800	57,800	577,000	55,400	632,400	0.1	10.4
Treasury	700	100	800	26,200	17,600	43,800	44,600	93,100	137,700	53.5	0.5
Veterans	20,900	5,300	26,200	149,100	92,500	241,600	267,800	356,400	624,200	9.2	0.8
NASA	4,700	2,700	7,400	53,400	55,800	109,200	116,600	17,400	134,000	14.8	6.7
EPA	9,100	5,000	14,100	10,000	6,300	16,300	16,300	15,500	31,800	1.2	1.0
TOTALS	780,600	379,000	1,159,900	2,242,900	1,774,400	4,017,000	5,162,800	1,956,900	7,119,700	3.5	2.6

*All employment figures are expressed in full-time-equivalents (FTE).

contract and grant employees for every one of its federal employees, followed by Transportation with a ratio of 10 to 1, NASA with 7 to 1, Energy with 4 to 1, and Defense with 3.5 to 1.

Departments and agencies also vary greatly in the use of contract *versus* grant employees. The government-wide ratio of contract to grant employees was 3.5 to 1 in 2017, but Defense had sixty-one contract employees for every one grant employee, followed by Treasury with a ratio of 54 to 1, Labor with 45 to 1, NASA with 15, Energy with 14, Agriculture with 12, Homeland Security with 10, and Veterans with 9. In contrast, the government-wide ratio of grant to contract employees was only 0.3 to 1, but Transportation had nine grant employees for every one contract employee, followed by Education with two, and Health and Human Services and Housing and Urban Development both with 1.5 grant employee for each contract employee.

The ratios show significant variations across federal departments and agencies in both the size and funding source for their blended workforce. Some agencies, such as Defense, depend on contract employees; others, such as Transportation, rely on grant employees, and still others have a balance. Whatever the blend, Table 1.1 strongly suggests the need for stronger oversight of the two workforces as part of a much larger whole.

This government-wide variation reflects different tools used to implement the Great Society in the 1960s. Although Eisenhower opposed many of the programs, he also laid the basis for increased nondefense contract and grant spending by supporting new conjunctions of government and industry: transportation through the National Defense and Interstate Highway Act (1956), education through the National Defense Education Act (1958), energy through the Atomic Energy Act (1954), and NASA through the National Aeronautics and Space Act (1958).

Eisenhower also supported the conjunctions that Truman had expanded after World War II, including the Veterans Administration's government-industry complex created under the GI Bill in 1944. He never addressed these nondefense conjunctions or acknowledged their links to the military-industrial complex, but could have added transportation and veterans to his list of expanding ventures that might eventually create the same threats of displaced power that he associated with the military-industrial complex.

Before turning to further analysis of this question, it is important to recognize that Eisenhower was also concerned about research and development, which he believed to be critical to the nation's future. He addressed the technological revolution immediately as another corollary of the war against communism. Not only was research becoming more "formalized, complex, and costly," he explained, but also a growing share of it was being conducted "for, by, and at the direction of the federal government." He even warned the nation about the erosion of academic freedom through what he could have easily described as the government-academic complex:

> Today, the solitary inventor, tinkering in his shop, has been overshadowed by task forces of scientists in laboratories and testing fields. In the same fashion, the free university, historically the fountainhead of free ideas and scientific discovery, has experienced a revolution in the conduct of research. Partly because of the huge costs involved, a government contract becomes virtually a substitute for intellectual curiosity. For every old blackboard, there are now hundreds of new electronic computers. The prospect of domination of the nation's scholars by Federal employment, project allocations, and the power of money is ever present—and is gravely to be regarded.[87]

Eisenhower argued that the solitary inventor had been overshadowed by task forces of scientists working together in laboratories and testing fields, and opined that universities were at risk of losing sight of their primary educational mission. Given the long-term relationships between funders and grantees, Eisenhower might have been quite willing to count these researchers as quasi-government employees, and might have counted other grant-funded employees as quasi-government employees as well.

The Data Deficit

Inaccurate data is only one of several barriers to measuring, managing, and disciplining the government-industrial complex. There is also the doubt created by the data that are never collected at all. Stories abound about highly visible contract failures such as the *Challenger* and *Columbia* tragedies, healthcare.gov collapse, the Abu Ghraib scandal, and continued fraud, waste, and abuse in Iraq and Afghanistan, but the stories do not add up to a systematic analysis of deep patterns in the federal government's blended workforce.[88] The result is a data deficit that prevents the proper meshing of capabilities Eisenhower believed would prevent the disastrous rise of misplaced power.

The data deficit undermines essential questions about the link between broad policies such as hiring caps, cuts, and freezes, and the increased use of contract employees is one example of the data deficit. "If the government is serious about reining in federal spending," POGO noted at the height of the Obama-era budget crisis, "three simple questions about federal and contractor employees must be asked: (1) Who is performing services? (2) What are they doing? and (3) How much do they cost?"[89] Despite all the data coursing through FPDS and FAADS, POGO concluded that much of the data was too weak to use in answering questions about value, performance, and accountability.

The answers will remain elusive until Congress and the president decide how to address at least three sources of deficit deficits.

Confusion

Despite CBO's complaints about the quality of the FPDS data, the greater problem in addressing value, performance, and accountability involves the many pieces of data that now flow through the contract and grant processes. The federal government does not want for information, but clarity and integration.

The confusion is easy to spot in the many stops that acquisition officers make along the path to a final award. Despite decades of streamlining, the process for awarding contracts involves an assembly of reports starting with (1) pulling each bidder's Performance Assessment Report (PAR) either directly from the Contractor Performance Assessment Reporting System (CPARS) or through the Past Performance Information Retrieval System (PPIRS), (2) checking the General Services Administration's Excluded Parties List System (EPLS) to identify and remove any bidder that has been suspended and debarred from competing for contracts, (3) searching the Federal Awardee Performance Integrity Information System (FAPIIS) for any bidder that has failed to maintain a "satisfactory record of integrity and business ethics," and be sure to hit POGO's Federal Contractor Misconduct Database (FCMD) to check any "offense indicating a lack of business integrity or business honesty" such as the seventy-three instances of misconduct and $34 billion in penalties, fines, and settlements British Petroleum (now BP) collected between 1995 and 2017, and (4) eventually certifying that the bidder has the capacity to provide the good or service, including the necessary organization, experience, accounting and operational control, and necessary equipment and facilities.[90]

The award process might look infinitely easier for making grants but puts the burden on the officer once again to make sure every applicant has the right registration and paperwork, a commercial and government entity code, separate cash management and grants management systems, and history of clean audits at the Federal Audit Clearinghouse (FAC). The officer would also be wise to see if the grantee is listed in the FAADS, the Catalogue of Federal Domestic Assistance, and the System for Awards Management (SAM). As for performance, the grant officer might try Google. The contract system may look more complex by comparison, but CRS reports that the system faces significant challenges in providing timely, accurate, and detailed information on awards and sub-awards.[91]

In theory, these checklists would give contract and grant officers more than enough information to make a clear decision. In practice, officers must also have the time, technology, and authority to decide, all of which are too often in short supply in a process that has often been targeted for cuts.

Deception

The Defense Department's acquisition system illustrates how data deficits can create deception. As the largest purchaser of contract and grant labor in the federal government, the department should know a great deal about its blended workforce, but continues to struggle with deep management problems. The department accounted for two of the fourteen items on GAO's first list of high-risk management systems in 1990 (inventory management and weapons systems acquisition) and seven of the thirty-four items in 2017 (supply chain management, weapons system acquisition, financial management, business systems modernization, support infrastructure, and business transformation). Read side by side, GAO's summary of the department's acquisition system has barely changed in the twenty-seven years since it published its first high-risk list in 1990:

> 1990: Following established management controls to deliver capable and supportable weapons to the user when and where needed, and at reasonable cost, has been the exception rather than the rule. As a result, DOD continually buys higher cost systems which substantially exceed original estimates, are delivered much later than originally scheduled, and do not meet the capabilities advertised.

> 2017: Congress and DOD have long sought to improve how major weapon systems are acquired, yet many DOD programs fall short of cost, schedule, and performance expectations, meaning DOD pays more than anticipated, can buy less than expected, and, in some cases, delivers less capability to the warfighter. With the prospect of slowly-growing or flat defense budgets for years to come, DOD must get better returns on its weapon system investments and find ways to deliver capability to the warfighter on time and within budget.[92]

The department's blended workforce has yet to be singled out on GAO's high-risk list, but has been a frequent investigatory target over the decades and is certain to return to the front page as the arms services spend a $160 billion budget windfall in the 2018–2019 federal fiscal year. After laboring under tight budget caps since 2011, Defense was given new funds to increase its weapons procurement and research funding by 15 and 24 percent in 2018 respectively.

Although the 2019 budget contained funding for twenty-four thousand additional active-duty personnel, the focus was on maintenance and modernization, not new boots on the ground. The funding was barely adequate according to the department's chief financial officer: "It is a sign of how deep the hole is that we are in that it takes this big of an increase just to get the department's budget back to where inflation alone would put us."[93]

Comptroller General David M. Walker gave Congress a glimpse of how the increase might be spent when he gave an unusually candid review of the defense acquisitions process on his last day in office in 2008. Testifying before the House Subcommittee on Readiness, Walker gave fourteen reasons why the department could not track its contract employees, including deceit on both sides of the government-industrial complex:

1. Service budgets are allocated largely according to top line historical percentages rather than Defense-wide strategic assessments and current and likely resource limitations.
2. Capabilities and requirements are based primarily on individual service wants versus collective Defense needs (i.e., based on current and expected future threats) that are both affordable and sustainable over time.
3. Defense consistently overpromises and under delivers major weapons, information, and other systems (i.e., capabilities, costs, quantities, and schedule).
4. Defense often employs a "plug and pray approach" when costs escalate (i.e., divide total funding dollars by cost per copy, plug in the number that can be purchased, then pray that Congress will provide more funding to buy more quantities).
5. Congress sometimes forces the department to buy items (e.g., weapon systems) and provide services (e.g., additional health care for non-active beneficiaries, such as active duty members' dependents and military retirees and their dependents) that the department does not want and we cannot afford.
6. DOD tries to develop high-risk technologies after programs start instead of setting up funding, organizations, and processes to conduct high-risk technology development activities in low-cost environments (i.e., technology development is not separated from product development). Program decisions to move into design and production are made without adequate standards or knowledge.
7. Program requirements are often set at unrealistic levels, then changed frequently as recognition sets in that they cannot be achieved. As a result, too much time passes, threats may change, or members of the user and acquisition communities may simply change their mind.

8. Contracts, especially service contracts, often do not have definitive or realistic requirements at the outset to control costs and facilitate accountability.

9. Contracts typically do not accurately reflect the complexity of projects or appropriately allocate risk between the contractors and the taxpayers (e.g., cost plus, cancellation charges).

10. Key program staff rotate too frequently, thus promoting myopia and reducing accountability (i.e., tours based on time versus key milestones). Additionally, the revolving door between industry and the department presents potential conflicts of interest.

11. The acquisition workforce faces serious challenges (e.g., size, skills, knowledge, and succession planning).

12. Incentive and award fees are often paid based on contractor attitudes and efforts versus positive results (i.e., cost, quality, and schedule).

13. Inadequate oversight is being conducted by both the department and Congress, which results in little to no accountability for recurring and systemic problems.

14. Some individual program and funding decisions made within the department and by Congress serve to undercut sound policies.[94]

In short, the Defense Department was unable to distinguish its wants from needs in managing its blended workforce. Equally troubling, it could not tell how many people it had in any place at any given time. Eight years and dozens of congressional hearings, directives, and reports later, GAO made the case in yet another report on weakness in the process. Quickly summarized, the Defense Department still had "limited visibility" on its contract and grant employees, rarely turned in its reports on time, could not link its spending to specific operations, and underreported the number of contract employees engaged in inherently governmental functions that must be performed by federal employees. As usual in most GAO reports, there were occasional notes about progress made, but the analysis showed limited progress at best and a steady drift toward failure at worst.[95] As the report implied, the data deficit comes in many forms—it can involve too little data or too much, misleading data or misleading measurement, and be too complex or too thin.

These complaints were not restricted to the Defense Department. According to GAO's "body of work," all government agencies were having problems dealing with their increased reliance on contract employees, whether in contingency operations such as Iraq, emergency situations such as Hurricane Katrina, or routine purchasing. As a result, the federal government continued to struggle in "determining which functions and activities should be contracted out and which should not to ensure institutional capacity; developing a total workforce strategy to address the extent of contractor use and the appropriate mix of contractor and government personnel;

identifying and distinguishing the roles and responsibilities of contractors and civilian and military personnel; and ensuring appropriate oversight, including addressing risks, ethics concerns, and surveillance needs."[96]

Hidden Data

Data transparency and access is hardly an exciting issue for the President and Congress. In 2009, for example, the Senate's Ad Hoc Subcommittee on Contracting Oversight held a hearing on improving transparency and accessibility to contract information that produced no discernable media coverage and a deprecating opening statement by the chair, Sen. Claire McCaskill (D-MO):

> I think I will start by stating the obvious. This is not a wildly exciting topic. We are not going to have banks of television cameras or eager crowds lined up to see what is happening at this hearing. I saw no linestanders. I saw no rush to grab a seat as the seats became available this morning.[97]

However, McCaskill was quite serious about the need for an integrated system that might help acquisition officers make wise decisions about contract decisions:

> Electronic systems and databases are used in every phase of the contracting process. Government employees use these systems to solicit requirements, review offers, evaluate vendors, and create and administer contracts. Companies use the systems to find and register for opportunities, track when and how and what the government is acquiring, and view their own performance. And, the public should use these systems to understand what the government is doing with their money.... There are now more than a dozen Federal databases and systems with information relevant to Federal contracting. They are managed by at least five different agencies and supported by at least eight different contractors.

Despite McCaskill's well-founded concerns, the federal government continues to design new systems and workarounds for managing the data, including new public sources such as USASpending.gov and next generations of existing systems of the kind used in this book. None of the databases has solved either the transparency or integration problem—to the contrary, the confusion and de facto data denial continues as Congress and the president continue to ignore the need for a reliable one-stop source for essential data. Contracts are still hidden from the public, data on ethics and compliance with existing laws are available only through secondary sources such as

POGO, and contract firms continue to claim proprietary privilege against full disclosure of campaign expenditures, salary information, and the true cost of their products and services.[98]

The topic may not create stampedes to subcommittee hearing rooms, but it is the cornerstone of accountability. Knowledge is just as powerful in contract and grant decisions as it is in politics.

What a Difference a Today Makes

All trends lines, estimates, and head counts have expiration dates for describing current conditions. Some data expire immediately when new data are released, others endure over longer periods of calm, while still others can hold for years until a shock such as a war disrupts the underlying trend. Expired data are generally valid for populating historical trend lines, but are most vulnerable during especially turbulent periods such as the beginning and end of wars or the first hundred days of a new administration.

Expiration dates are particularly important when researchers use the word "today" to frame an urgent problem. The question is whether an issue is so important in real time that expired data must suffice for framing an analysis.

John J. DiIulio answered "yes" in his February 13, 2017, report on what he described as ten "deeply inconvenient truths about the character and quality of present-day American government."[99] His projection of the true size of government was particularly important for refuting the Trump administration's "alternative facts" about its ninety-day hiring freeze and braking its drive to "deconstruct the administrative state."

DiIulio began by reminding readers that "administrative proxies" and "de facto feds" had been essential to federal performance for decades. As he explained, state and local governments, private businesses, and nonprofit agencies were the only option available for answering a simple question: "So, how did the post-1960 United States have a five-fold increase in national spending, establish seven new cabinet agencies, effect a steady expansion in programs and regulations, and yet experience zero growth in the workforce responsible for stewarding trillions of tax dollars and translating 80,000-plus pages of words into action?"[100]

DiIulio answered the question with a deep inventory of data on the total workforce and an accessible calculus supported by his "informed guesstimating and federal workforce arithmetic":

- With one-third of its revenues flowing from government, if only one-fifth of the 11 million nonprofit sector employees owe their jobs to federal or intergovernmental grant, contract, or fee funding, that's 2.2 million workers.

- As noted, the best for-profit contractor estimate is 7.5 million.
- And the conservative sub-national government employee estimate is 3 million.
- That's 12.2 million in all, but let's scale down to call it 12 million.
- 12 million plus our good-old two million actual federal bureaucrats equals 14 million.
- And how many were there back in 1960? The feds had some administrative proxies even then, maybe as many as two million, plus two million actual federal bureaucrats.
- So, let's call it 14 million in all today versus four million back when Ike was saying farewell.[101]

This book confirms Dilulio's conclusion that (1) millions of Americans made their living on February 13, 2017, administering federal programs, and (2) this number was undeniably much larger than it had been in 1961.[102] This book provides a much lower estimate in part because Dilulio's trend lines expired before the Iraq peace divided arrived and the Obama stimulus package obligated its last dollar. As this book shows, these two events produced a multimillion reduction in the number of estimated contract and grant employees.[103] Dilulio was nonetheless right to describe the federal government as a "grotesque Leviathan by proxy," but this book shows that it became a somewhat smaller Leviathan during Obama's second term.

Dilulio wrote his report in part to challenge the Trump's administration's hyperbolic rhetoric about a dramatic expansion of government during the Obama administration. He also wrote the report to support his long-standing call for rebuilding the federal workforce, a concern well illustrated in his *Bring Back the Bureaucrats: Why More Federal Workers Will Lead to Better (and Smaller!) Government.*[104] Finally, he correctly predicted that the hiring freeze would have no significant impact on federal spending while reminding readers that draining the swamp in Washington meant draining state and local governments, private contractors, nonprofit grantees, and middle-class entitlement beneficiaries like most Medicare beneficiaries."[105]

Nevertheless, *Washington Post* columnist George Will used Dilulio's argument to make the case for downsizing in a February 24, 2016, column titled "Big Government Sneakily Gets Bigger." According to Will, government not only was larger than it was in 1961 but also had been "dispersed to disguise its size":

> Many Americans are rhetorically conservative but behaviorally liberal. So, they are given government that is not limited but overleveraged—debt-financed, meaning partially paid for by future generations—and administered by proxies. The government/

for-profit contractor/nonprofit complex consumes about 40 percent of gross domestic product. Just don't upset anyone by calling it "big government."[106]

Contrary to Will, government had actually become sneakily smaller during the second Obama administration. Obama's team would have celebrated the achievement but for the fact that they never measured the true size of government. Nothing measured, nothing claimed.

The next chapter will chart the true size of government looking back from the today at the end of the 2017 fiscal year on October 31, 2017, when the books on federal contract and grant spending were closed. Although it is too early to assess the impact of Trump's budget increases, further hiring reforms, and reorganization plans on total federal, contract, and grant employment, the next chapter will consider his agenda in describing prospects for the future. The defense budget increases are sure to drive contract spending upward, but his cuts in education, health and human services, transportation, environmental protection, climate research, and other domestic programs may more than offset the defense rise.

Only time will tell, as Trump might put it. Future todays will come and go, some driving contract and grant employment upward, others affecting federal head count. The challenge is to use fresh data and trend lines to make judgments about who does what on each side of the government-industrial complex.

2

The True Size of Government

Eisenhower may have been the first president use the term "military-industrial complex" in a presidential address, but he was not the first to recognize the intersection of government and industry in national defense. The federal role in building, protecting, and policing the US defense industry had been on the president's agenda since George Washington urged Congress to promote independent "manufactories" as a source of essential military supplies.[1] Eisenhower knew this history well, if only because of his research on industrial mobilization for war as a staff officer in the War Department in 1930.[2] As noted in chapter 1, he did not know the exact size of the military-industrial complex in 1961 but was nonetheless quite willing to describe its components as "large," "vast," and "immense," and the whole as "huge."[3]

However, Eisenhower did not target the nondefense-industrial complex that had already developed around post–World War II domestic programs in education, interstate highways, housing, hospital construction, scientific research, school construction, and space. Nor did he express concerns about the nondefense-industry complex that would emerge with President Lyndon B. Johnson's Great Society and its wars on poverty, injustice, hunger, and discrimination. Even though he later criticized the Great Society for its "vast and inefficient bureaucracies," Eisenhower did not predict the "government-by-proxy" that employed more than one million nonprofit employees at the height of the great recession in 2010.[4]

It is entirely possible that Eisenhower was less concerned about the domestic-industrial intersections because state and local government was the frequent pass-through. He did worry about defense involvement in academic research, however, and bemoaned the growing dependence on military funding for technological breakthroughs. Having led Columbia University upon retirement, he understood the role of contract and grant employees in science and education policy and spent more time in the speech discussing threats to the "free university" than the military-industrial complex. He may not have expected the growth of nondefense-industrial complex, but he saw grave threats to entrepreneurship in federal engagement nonetheless.

The first section of this chapter will review the history of the government-industrial complex from Ronald Reagan to Donald J. Trump. Contrary to prevailing wisdom, the federal workforce has held steady over the past three decades, while the number of contract and grant employees has flexed with war and economy calamity. After discussing each president's impact on the true size of government, the second section of the chapter will discuss the use of federal employment caps, cuts, and ceilings as discredited tools for managing the movement of jobs and functions across the dividing line between government and industry.

A Presidential History of the Government-Industrial Complex

Eisenhower's farewell address has been used to make the case both for and against defense spending, international engagement, global capitalism, budget caps, and America-first foreign policy. It has also been used to burnish Eisenhower's reputation as a "soldier-prophet" who warned against the war-mongering that would keep the munitions industry rich and powerful, or illustrate his hypocrisy in attacking the machine he had designed.[5]

Interpretations of Eisenhower's speech will no doubt evolve with new readings and further recoveries of old documents, such as the trove of related documents found in the corner of a Minnesota fishing cabin in 2010.[6] For the purposes of this book, however, the address is particularly important for its focus on balance between competing goals. Speaking of the many choices that faced the nation in its pursuit of peace and human betterment just before he introduced the military-industrial complex, Eisenhower urged balance above all: "balance between the private and the public economy, balance between the cost and hoped for advantages—balance between the clearly necessary and the comfortably desirable; balance between our essential requirements as a nation and the duties imposed by the nation upon the individual; balance between the actions of the moment and the national welfare of the future."[7]

Baylor University's Martin J. Medhurst focused on this rhetorical device in a 1994 reconceptualization of Eisenhower's address that still holds to this day. Medhurst finds the search for balance at many points in the speech, but none more significant perhaps than the two stage-setting sentences that juxtaposed the need for the military-industrial complex with the threats to liberty and democratic process it created:

First, he treats the positive aspect of enhanced security, then he turns to the negative potential of "misplaced power" which, it is important to note, Eisenhower locates "in the councils of government." His concern is that the power of decision making, located "in the councils of government"—and especially in the executive and legislative branches—will somehow become "misplaced." That the people who ought to be making the decisions based on the overall good of the nation will, instead, succumb to the power of the military-industrial lobby.[8]

Medhurst understood that his interpretation challenges the more-familiar characterizations of the address as a prophetic warning against the corporatization of war, but marshals compelling rhetorical analysis to suggest a more practical acknowledgment of needs and controls. The military-industrial complex was something to be closely regulated within the councils of government and held to account by an alert and knowledgeable citizenry, but it was essential to the nation's security nonetheless. Eisenhower was not just worried about keeping budget ledgers clean, he also wanted Congress and the president to keep track of who did what for how much and under what oversight.

This chapter uses hard headcounts and estimates to track the size and balance of the government-industrial complex. Table 2.1 includes federal civilian employees, active duty military personnel, US Postal Service (USPS) workers, and contract and grant employees, while Table 2.2 includes only federal civilian, contract, and grant employees. Both tables calculate the government-industrial ratio by defining the industry subtotal as contract and grant employees only. All figures are presented in full-time-equivalents.

The true size of the government-industrial complex in October 2017 varies from 8.6 million in Table 2.1 to 6.8 million in Table 2.2, but both tables tell the same story: contrary to Trump administration claims that there had been a "dramatic expansion in the federal workforce" during the Obama administration, the balance of federal versus contract and grant employees held steady from 1984 to 1994; dropped from 1995 to 1999; increased slightly between 1999 and 2002; and surged to a record high between 2002 and 2010 before falling back to pre-2002 levels in 2015 and holding steady through 2017.[9] The end of the Cold War and subsequent defense downsizing generated the first period of decline, while the wars on terrorism and Obama's economic stimulus plan produced the long period of growth, and the uneasy end of the wars in Iraq and Afghanistan and stimulus spend down spurred the second period of decline.[10] As the following vignettes show, presidents vary greatly in their distribution of employees across the military and civilian conjunction as described in chapter 1, but what went up during war and economic stimulus fell once the wars and economic crises cooled. Figure 2.1 shows the trend.

Table 2.1 **The Government-Industrial Headcount, 1984–2017**

Type of Employee	1984	1990	1993	1996	1999	2002	2005	2010	2015	2017
Federal Employees	2,083,000	2,174,000	2,139,000	1,891,000	1,778,000	1,756,000	1,830,000	2,128,000	2,042,000	2,062,000
Active-Duty Military Personnel	2,138,000	2,044,000	1,705,000	1,472,000	1,386,000	1,412,000	1,518,000	1,384,000	1,315,000	1,282,000
Postal Service Employees	673,000	761,000	692,000	761,000	798,000	753,000	705,000	584,000	492,000	503,000
Contract Employees	3,666,000	3,427,000	3,245,000	3,042,000	2,398,000	2,791,000	3,882,000	4,845,000	3,702,000	4,128,000
Grant Employees	1,234,000	1,352,000	1,344,000	1,351,000	1,415,000	1,236,000	1,578,000	2,344,000	1,583,000	1,189,000
TOTAL	9,794,000	9,758,000	9,125,000	8,517,000	7,775,000	7,948,000	9,513,000	11,285,000	9,134,000	9,164,000
Ratio of Contract + Grant to Federal + Military + Postal	1:1	1:1	1:1	1:1	1:1	1:1	3:2	3:1	3:2	3:2

Table 2.2 **Government-Industrial Ratios, 1984–2017**

Type of Employee	1984	1990	1993	1996	1999	2002	2005	2010	2015	2017
Federal Employees	2,083,000	2,174,000	2,139,000	1,891,000	1,778,000	1,756,000	1,830,000	2,128,000	2,042,000	2,062,000
Contract + Grant Employees	4,900,000	4,779,000	4,589,000	4,393,000	3,813,000	4,027,000	5,460,000	7,189,000	5,285,000	5,317,000
TOTAL	6,983,000	6,953,000	6,728,000	6,284,000	5,591,000	5,783,000	7,290,000	9,317,000	7,327,000	7,379,000
Ratio of Contract + Grant to Federal	2:4	2:2	2:2	2:3	2:1	2:3	3:0	3:4	2:6	2:6

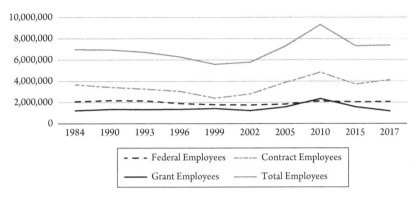

Figure 2.1 The Government-Industrial Headcount, 1984–2017

Ronald Reagan

The third year of Ronald Reagan's administration is the arbitrary starting point for the trend lines discussed in this book. Looking back to Table 2.1, the total number of federal, contract, grant, active-duty military, and USPS employees reached almost ten million as Reagan approached the midpoint of his administration in 1984; this figure had barely changed by 1990. The number of federal, USPS, and grant employees increased, however, while the number of active-duty military personnel and contract employees decreased sharply as the Cold War faded.[11]

The large number of defense contract employees under Reagan is not surprising given his anti-communist agenda. Yet, even given his focus on the Soviet Union, Reagan began his 1981 inaugural address with a surprisingly short discussion of the economic woes that plagued the nation, and then turned to a long discussion of his proposed cuts in domestic spending by starting with his memorable campaign slogan:

> In this crisis, government is not the solution to our problem; government is the problem. From time to time we've been tempted to believe that society has become too complex to be managed by self-rule, that government by an elite group is superior to government for, by, and of the people. . . . We are a nation that has a government—not the other way around. And this makes us special among the nations of the Earth. Our government has no power except that granted it by the people. It is time to check and reverse the growth of government, which shows signs of having grown beyond the consent of the governed.[12]

Reagan started cutting only steps from the inaugural podium where he signed a "strict freeze" on all executive-branch hiring. "I pledged last July that this would

be a first step toward controlling the growth and the size of Government and reducing the drain on the economy for the public sector," he said in the President's
Room of the Capitol Building. "And beyond the symbolic value of this, which is
my first official act, the freeze will eventually lead to a significant reduction in the
size of the Federal work force."[13]

Despite his commitment, the number of federal employees declined by less
than 100,000 during his presidency, hardly the radical downsizing promised.[14]
As GAO would later report, the freeze had a greater effect on government efficiency and effectiveness than it did on the number of federal employees. It also
led some departments and agencies to increase their use of contract employees
while encouraging the use of overtime to cover lost capacity.[15]

The freeze may have had little effect, but the Reagan defense budget produced
a radical change in the distribution of contract employees as the number of defense contract employees fell by a third, from 2.8 million in 1984 to 1.8 million
in 1990, while the number of nondefense contract employees almost doubled,
from 835,000 to 1.6 million during the same span.[16] Setting aside the number
of defense and nondefense grant employees, which did not change significantly,
the question is why contract employment would swing so dramatically in such
a short period.[17]

A first answer is that the number of active-duty military personnel fell 5 percent between 1984 and 1990. Viewed as a leading indicator of contract cuts,
base realignments and closures, and even further military demobilization, the
Reagan administration started to cut the defense budget long before the Berlin
Wall fell in 1989. As the number of military personnel fell, so did the need for
many of the ordinary services that contract employees provided, such as food
and clothing.

A second answer is that procurement scandals cut into defense contract
spending as stories about $37 machine screws, $400 hammers, $640 toilet
seats, and $7,000 coffee makers slowed the buying process.[18] The Defense
Department's chief investigator summed up the scandals in a single sentence
when he testified before the House Armed Services Committee in March
1985: "My job is to say I think these people cheated, and their attitude is 'we
stole it fair and square, you know, and we are not going to give it back.'"[19] Even
though some of the waste was an artifact of arcane accounting rules, the Reagan
administration had little choice but to reduce contract spending even before the
Cold War came to an end.[20]

A third answer is that the Reagan administration cut the defense budget as
the Soviet Union accelerated toward collapse. Although Reagan had increased
defense spending during his first term, his 1981 tax cuts eventually created a
deficit crisis, which in turn drove the administration toward a confrontation
with ethereal weapons systems and obsolete military bases. Much as Reagan

deserves the blame for exploding the budget, he also earns the credit for giving his successors fifteen headcount harvests.

Reagan still found enough room in the defense accounts to keep his "Star Wars" missile defense system on the planning agenda, but abandoned his plans for a six-hundred-ship navy, cut the shopping list for other long-treasured weapon such as the M-1 tank, and stretched out the production schedules for new weapons such as the Blackhawk helicopter. According to defense experts, Lawrence J. Korb, Laura Conley, and Alex Rothman, Reagan's cuts gave his successors ample room and the political cover to harvest even further reductions over the next decade:

> Between 1985 and 1998 the defense budget fell for 13 straight years as Presidents—Reagan, Bush, and Clinton—two Republicans and a Democrat—brought spending down to more sustainable levels as the Cold War wound down. . . . The spending cuts usually attributed to President Clinton and, on occasion, President George H. W. Bush began during the Reagan administration's second term when the United States was still engaged in the Cold War.[21]

A fourth answer is that Reagan allowed domestic spending to rise. Having told the public in July 1981 that "this was not a time for fun and games," Reagan cut real spending in eight of fifteen selected departments and agencies during his first term, including a 33 percent cut at Labor, 29 percent each at Commerce and the Environmental Protection Agency (EPA), 24 percent at Energy, and 19 percent at Education. Although Reagan continued to reduce domestic budgets in his second term, the cuts were much lower.[22] Moreover, Reagan increased spending at grant-heavy departments such as Education, Health and Human Services, and Justice, while even Energy and EPA held steady.[23]

Together, these four explanations help explain the declining number of contract employees at defense, but not the rapid increase at nondefense agencies such as Health and Human Services. However, at least some of the variation in the nondefense agencies could have been caused by uneven implementation of the new reporting Federal Procurement Data System. As GAO reported in 1982, Defense and NASA were the only large spending agencies able to meet the federal government's new reporting rules, while the rest were unreliable at best.[24] GAO's analysis strongly suggests that the sharp drop in contract employees at defense was accurate, while the increases at many nondefense departments and agencies during the early 1980s should be viewed with caution.

Even without a final judgment on what caused the dramatic swing in contract employees, Reagan's cuts generated the savings needed for a large Cold

War peace dividend. Reagan chartered the first base realignment and closure commission in 1988 and supported the Base Closure and Realignment Act that soon followed. He also approved a small reduction in the number of active-duty military personnel and began the downsizing that reduced defense civilian employment by a third.[25] He never changed his standard joke about big government: "The nine most terrifying words in the English language are, 'I'm from the government and I'm here to help.' "[26]

George H. W. Bush

President George H. W. Bush separated himself from Reagan's rhetoric during the 1988 Republican campaign by promising a "kinder, gentler nation," "a thousand points of light," and a positive role for government. "Does government have a place?" he asked. "Yes. Government is part of the nation of communities—not the whole, just a part. I do not hate government. A government that remembers that the people are its master is a good and needed thing."[27]

Bush also issued the audacious pledge that would eventually doom his reelection. "The Congress will push me to raise taxes, and I'll say no," Bush promised the party faithful at the 1988 Republican nominating convention, "and they'll push, and I'll say no, and they'll push again, and I'll say to them, 'Read my lips: no new taxes.' "[28]

Bush knew he could not honor his "no-new-taxes" pledge unless he balanced the federal budget. He also knew that spending cuts and government downsizing offered the only path to success. Yet, having described government service as "a noble calling and public trust" in his first speech after becoming president, Bush understood the need for a respectful relationship with federal employees, as well as the need for steadiness as the nation transitioned from the Cold War to a decade of peace. "There is nothing more fulfilling than to serve your country and your fellow citizens," he told the assembled members of the Senior Executive Service (SES). "And that's what our system of self-government depends on."[29] Although he asked the executives to work with his administration to improve government performance, his tone was overwhelmingly positive:

> I've not known a finer group of people than those that I have worked
> with in government. You're men and women of knowledge, ability, and
> integrity. And I saw that in the CIA. I saw that when I was in China.
> I saw it at the United Nations. And for the last 8 years, I saw that in every
> department and agency of the United States Government. And I saw
> that commitment to excellence in the Federal workers I came to know
> and respect in Washington, all across America, and, indeed, around
> the world. You work hard; you sacrifice. You deserve to be recognized,

rewarded, and certainly appreciated. I pledge to try to make Federal jobs more challenging, more satisfying, and more fulfilling. I'm dedicated to making the system work and making it work better.[30]

With cuts in federal employment off limits, Bush's only hope for substantial cuts in the government-industrial complex came from Reagan's Cold War peace dividend and defense base closings. He placed a one-year freeze on military spending in 1989 to start the harvesting, began withdrawing forces from Europe to what he described as "more appropriate levels" in 1990, negotiated a nuclear arms accord with Russia in 1991, and put more cuts "in train," as his chairman of the Joint Chiefs of Staff, Colin Powell, described them, in 1992.[31] "These cuts are deep, and you must know my resolve: This deep and no deeper," Bush told Congress in what would be his last State of the Union address. "To do less would be insensible to progress, but to do more would be ignorant of history. We must not go back to the days of 'the hollow army.'"[32]

Despite a 175,000 deep cut in active-duty military personnel, Bush still fell short of his initial downsizing target—the number of federal employees had fallen by just 35,000 in total, while the number of contract employees had dropped by 180,000. According to Table 2.3, the cuts came from defense. As a result, the government-industrial ratio remained unchanged between 1990 and 1993 at 2.2 contract and grant employees for every 1 federal employee, suggesting to the public that the federal government had not changed shape much at all.

It is not clear that Bush could have honored his no-new-taxes pledge even if the peace dividend had paid off sooner. But the sagging economy and rising deficits forced him to break his promise at the end of June 1990. The dividend had yielded substantial budget savings, but not enough to balance the budget. And that made all the difference in his battle for a second term. Although his public approval soared to 89 percent just six months later as the military proved its muscle in the brief Gulf War, it dropped to 29 percent by August 1992, and Bush lost his bid for re-election in a three-way race.

Bill Clinton

The Cold War peace dividend was ready for further harvesting when Bill Clinton took office on January 20, 1993, and began the downsizing with a White House hiring freeze and a 100,000 cut in the number of federal employees.[33] "I have to say that we all know our government has been just great at building programs," he told Congress when he presented the caps, cuts, and freezes in his first speech on Capitol Hill. "The time has come to show the American people that we can limit them too; that we can not only start things, that we can stop things."[34]

Table 2.3 **The Defense and Non-Defense Workforce, 1984–2017**

Type of Employee	Location	1984	1990	1993	1996	1999	2002	2005	2010	2015	2017
Federal	Defense	1,000,000	1,023,000	932,000	779,000	681,000	650,000	653,000	741,000	725,000	731,000
	Non-Defense	1,083,000	1,151,000	1,207,000	1,112,000	1,097,000	1,106,000	1,177,000	1,387,000	1,317,000	1,336,000
Contract	Defense	2,831,000	1,816,000	2,083,000	1,926,000	1,466,000	1,780,000	2,532,000	3,087,000	2,204,000	2,410,000
	Non-Defense	835,000	1,611,000	1,162,000	1,116,000	932,000	1,011,000	1,350,000	1,758,000	1,498,000	1,586,000
Grant*	Defense	N/A	N/A	N/A	N/A	N/A	N/A	52,000	74,000	72,000	41,000
	Non-Defense	N/A	N/A	N/A	N/A	N/A	N/A	1,526,000	2,270,000	1,511,000	1,144,000
Active-Duty Military	Defense	2,138,000	2,044,000	1,705,000	1,472,000	1,386,000	1,412,000	1,518,000	1,384,000	1,315,000	1,334,000
	Non-Defense	0	0	0	0	0	0	0	0	0	0
Postal Service	Defense	0	0	0	0	0	0	0	0	0	0
	Non-Defense	673,000	761,000	692,000	761,000	798,000	753,000	705,000	584,000	492,000	509,000
TOTAL	Defense	5,969,000	4,883,000	4,720,000	4,177,000	3,533,000	3,842,000	4,755,000	5,286,000	4,316,000	4,390,000
	Non-Defense	2,591,000	3,523,000	3,061,000	2,989,000	2,827,000	2,870,000	4,758,000	5,999,000	4,818,000	4,575,000

*Grants were not available on a department-by-department basis for this analysis

Clinton expanded the effort the next year by raising his downsizing target to 273,000 under the Federal Workforce Restructuring Act of 1994. Clinton signed the bill only one year into his presidency, but claimed victory in his battle against big government: "After all the rhetoric about cutting the size and cost of Government, our Administration has done the hard work and made the tough choices. I believe the economy will be stronger, and the lives of middle class people will be better, as we drive down the deficit with legislation like this. We can maintain and expand our recovery so long as we keep faith with deficit reduction and sensible, fair policies like this."[35]

Clinton was able to honor the pledge with eight years of economic growth, a dot.com tech surge, the first balanced federal budget since 1969, and a 400,000 reduction in the number of federal employees. Along the way, he reduced federal employment to its lowest level since 1950 and drove the government-industrial ratio to a contemporary low of just 2.1 contract and grant employees for every 1 federal employee.

However, Clinton could not have said "the era of big government is over" in 1996 without Reagan's help and George H. W. Bush's patience. Clinton did not acknowledge his predecessors for bringing the Cold War to a close or putting the defense budget cuts in train, but the Reagan-Bush success eventually produced three-quarters of the personnel cuts that gave Clinton the data to announce the end of an era.[36] Clinton and his secretary of defense, Les Aspin, did add further cuts to the total, but even these reductions can be counted as part of the Cold War peace dividend. As Table 2.3 shows, defense eventually accounted for about 250,000 of the 360,000 jobs that dropped off the payroll between 1993 and 1999, and all 30,000 jobs that dropped off between 1999 and 2002.[37]

Clinton did not acknowledge Al Gore for his effort to create a government that works better and costs less either. Yet, just as Reagan started the downsizing, Gore led the administration's reinventing-government campaign, also known as the National Performance Review (NPR), set and enforced the president's employment ceilings, accelerated the procurement process, produced performance plans from every department and agency, and eliminated 640,000 pages of agency rules.[38]

Gore's reinventors also moved faster than expected to cut the federal headcount and reduced the number of managers and supervisors across government through targeted cuts.[39] Although there are hints that some agencies reduced their layers by merely changing titles from manager and supervisor to "team leader" and "management support specialist," the reductions were so quick that the federal government issued a "wake-up call" to human capital officers about the need to develop the next generation of supervisors.[40]

According to Gore's top aide, Elaine Kamarck, the campaign produced a long list of impacts:

- We reduced the federal workforce by 426,200 between January 1993 and September 2000. Cuts occurred in 13 out of 14 departments making the federal government in 2000 the smallest government since Dwight D. Eisenhower was president.
- We acted on more than 2/3 of NPR regulations, yielding $136 billion in savings to the taxpayer.
- We cut government the right way by eliminating what wasn't needed— bloated headquarters, layers of managers, outdated field offices, obsolete red tape and rules. For example, we had cut 78,000 managers government-wide and some layers by late 1999.
- We closed nearly 2,000 obsolete field offices and eliminated 250 programs and agencies, like the Tea-Tasters Board, the Bureau of Mines, and wool and mohair subsidies. (Some of which have crept back into the government.)[41]

Kamarck was right to claim success, although the peace dividend was ready for harvesting well before Clinton took the Oath of Office. In addition, several of the most significant claims have been stubbornly difficult to prove. GAO could not find solid evidence to support the administration's $136 billion claim and criticized the campaign's strategic workforce planning and follow-through. GAO also criticized the lack of attention to its high-risk list and its inventory of deep-tissue concerns.[42]

Nevertheless, many of the successes were very real, indeed. The number of management jobs did decline, as did the number of federal employees. As the Senate Governmental Affairs Committee chairman Sen. Fred Thompson (R-TN) argued in the first of what would be many congressional reviews, the reinventing campaign produced many of successes, but left many problems unsolved:

> I was generally pleased to see this effort start because you don't have to have necessarily revolutionary results in order to get something positive done. And any positive thing that could be done ought to be welcomed by all of us. . . . We still have tremendous problems. And yet we still seem to have the same core performance problems facing the government that we have always had. Every time GAO updates its high-risk list of Federal activities most vulnerable to waste, fraud, and mismanagement, the numbers of problems increase.[43]

George W. Bush

George W. Bush entered the White House a most fortunate president. He not only inherited a $128 billion surplus, but also a government-industrial headcount that was 600,000 smaller at the beginning of his term than his father's had been at the end. He had room to maneuver as he entered office during Clinton's economic boom.

Bush showed little interest in further downsizing as he prepared for his inauguration in 2001, however. Clinton had already harvested most of the Cold War peace dividend and the total number of federal, contract, and grant employees hovered near a twenty-year low through the spring and summer of 2001, and the government-industrial complex seemed to be moving toward the careful separation Eisenhower envisioned.[44]

Bush faced little pressure to downsize government but had his own targets for winnowing. He began his first congressional address on February 1 by rejecting the "old, tired argument" between "more government, regardless of the cost," and "less government, regardless of the need." Rather, he promised to create a compassionate, conservative government that would "be active, but limited, engaged but not overbearing." He also told Congress that he intended to reshape the budget "as any prudent family would, with a contingency fund for emergencies or additional spending needs."[45]

At the same time, Bush showed little interest in defense policy. After spending forty minutes of his speech discussing America's purpose in a time of blessing, he spent just three minutes on defense transformation based on strategy, not spending, and on vision, not budget. However, three minutes was long enough to warn the nation about a more dangerous future, and prepare them for a different kind of defense:

> Our Nation also needs a clear strategy to confront the threats of the 21st century, threats that are more widespread and less certain. They range from terrorists with bombs to tyrants in rogue nations intent upon developing weapons of mass destruction. To protect our own people, our allies, and friends, we must develop and we must deploy effective missile defenses. And as we transform our military, we can discard cold war relics and reduce our own nuclear forces to reflect today's needs.[46]

Bush did not promise any caps, cuts, and freezes during the speech. Rather, he told Congress that his defense vision would drive the budget, not the other way around.[47] As his new budget showed, Bush had already made the decision to push the defense budget up ever so slightly by $14 billion by 2003, including a bit for military compensation, and a bit more for research and development.

Nor did Bush enter office expecting to become a war president. Contrary to internet conspiracy theorists, he was just as shocked by the terrorist attacks as the rest of the nation, and could not have known he would send American troops to war in Iraq, or that defense spending would rise 30 percent over his first three budgets. Having started with Clinton's $408 billion budget marks, Bush bumped defense spending to $450 billion in 2002, $492 billion in 2003, and $531 billion in 2004, almost all in response to 9/11. Nondefense spending would also rise almost 18 percent during the same period as he pursued several relatively expensive domestic priorities such as the new Transportation Security Administration, a new farm bill, education reforms, and Medicare prescription drug coverage.[48]

As went the defense budget, so went the true size of government. Whereas Clinton's nondefense budget barely moved over his two terms in office, Bush's defense budget moved toward record levels as the wars in Iraq and Afghanistan continued. With mandatory spending for programs such as Social Security and Medicare removed from the totals, the two budgets had almost the same bottom lines, just not the same priorities.

The spending is easy to track in the government-industrial headcount. Between 2002 and 2005, the Bush administration added 1.1 million contract employees, 350,000 grant employees, 100,000 activity-duty military personnel, and 70,000 federal employees to the government-industrial complex. "When the work of national defense dramatically increased after 9/11," Martha Minow explains, "Pentagon reliance on private military companies escalated. Private contractors played key roles in the war in Afghanistan. They served in paramilitary units with the Central Intelligence Agency (the 'CIA') that hit the ground before other combat troops; they maintained combat equipment, provided logistical support, and worked with surveillance and targeting plans."[49]

The increases in contract and grant employees continued from 2005 to 2010, guaranteeing a record redistribution of federal, contract, and grant employees across the government-industrial divide. Whereas there were 2.3 contract and grant employees for every 1 federal employee in 2002, there were 3 for 1 in 2005 and 3.4 for 1 by 2010. Both ratios easily eclipsed the previous high from 1984.

The Transportation Security Administration (TSA) accounted for a large share of the increase in the number of federal employees between 2002 and the end of the Bush administration. Created on November 19, 2001, TSA was required to staff its baggage and passenger checkpoints with federal law enforcement officers, not contract employees. "This is a function of government," Sen. Ernest F. Hollings (D-SC) argued. "No one is putting in measures to privatize the Capitol police or the Secret Service. We are going to give some protection to the traveling public."[50] The rest of the chamber agreed with a 100–0 vote, and nearly 60,000 federal screeners were on the job in time to make the 2002 civil service headcount.[51]

Barack Obama

If Bush entered office a most-fortunate president, Obama entered under intense economic and international pressure. The economy was still reeling from the subprime mortgage crisis that began in 2007, the federal deficit was headed toward $1.5 trillion, the national debt was rising, credit markets were frozen, the United States was fighting two wars, the unemployment rate was skyrocketing toward 10 percent, and the president's promised healthcare package was about to enter a ten-year debate about its cost and consequence.

However, Obama showed no worries when he appeared before Congress to present his economic plan on February 24. Before turning to the specifics, however, he spoke directly to the American people about their anxious nights:

> We will rebuild, we will recover, and the United States of America will emerge stronger than before. The weight of this crisis will not determine the destiny of this Nation. The answers to our problems don't lie beyond our reach. They exist in our laboratories and our universities, in our fields and our factories, in the imaginations of our entrepreneurs and the pride of the hardest working people on Earth.[52]

Obama also told Americans that he rejected the notion that government had no role in creating the foundation for common prosperity, and applauded its work as a catalyst for private enterprise and entrepreneurship. But with his stimulus package already adding billions to the deficit, Obama promised to end programs, not create them:

> In this budget, we will end education programs that don't work and end direct payments to large agribusinesses that don't need them. We'll eliminate the no-bid contracts that have wasted billions in Iraq and reform our defense budget so that we're not paying for cold war–era weapons systems we don't use. We will root out the waste and fraud and abuse in our Medicare program that doesn't make our seniors any healthier. We will restore a sense of fairness and balance to our Tax Code by finally ending the tax breaks for corporations that ship our jobs overseas. In order to save our children from a future of debt, we will also end the tax breaks for the wealthiest 2 percent of Americans.[53]

Obama also could have promised another round of workforce restructuring. After all, he must have known that a peace dividend would emerge from the end of Bush's 2008 troop surge in Iraq. Just as Reagan had given George H. W. Bush and Clinton the Cold War peace dividend after the Soviet Union collapsed, George W. Bush was about to give Obama an Iraq/Afghanistan dividend as his troop surge ended well before the 2008 election. However, Obama outlined the coming cuts as an opportunity to reshape government. Speaking before the University of Michigan's class of 2010, he rejected the traditional debates about big and small government:

> The truth is, the debate we've had for decades now between more gov-ernment and less government, it doesn't really fit the times in which we live. We know that too much government can stifle competition and deprive us of choice and burden us with debt. But we've also clearly seen the dangers of too little government—like when a lack of account-ability on Wall Street nearly leads to the collapse of our entire economy. So, class of 2010, what we should be asking is not whether we need "big government" or a "small government," but how we can create a smarter and better government.[54]

Obama ended his address only six months away from ordering a federal pay freeze that would make his "smarter and better" program arguably more difficult to achieve. "The hard truth is that getting this deficit under control is going to require some broad sacrifice. And that sacrifice must be shared by the employees of the Federal Government," he said when he announced what would eventually morph into a three-year freeze. "I did not reach this decision easily. This is not just a line item on a Federal ledger, these are people lives."[55]

Obama understood that the freeze might affect federal employee recruit-ment, if not potential outsourcing: "In these challenging times, we want the best and brightest to join and make a difference. But these are also times where all of us are called on to make some sacrifices. And I'm asking civil servants to do what they've always done: play their part."[56]

Just fifteen months later still with a new Republican majority in the House, Obama signed the Budget Control Act of 2011. Designed to prevent a govern-ment tumble over the "fiscal cliff" created by the need to raise the federal debt ceiling, the act required Congress and the president to cut $1.2 trillion from the federal budget over the next decade. If they could not do so, Congress and the president would impose a "sequester" composed of what Obama called "dumb, arbitrary cuts" of roughly $100 billion every year until 2021.[57]

The sequester may have been dumb and arbitrary, but the continued budget battles eventually forced the federal government to close during the first two weeks of October 2011 nonetheless. About 850,000 federal nonessential federal employees were sent home for two weeks. Experts do not know exactly how much the shutdown cost, but generally agree with Sen. Rand Paul (R-KY) that "it cost the nation more to shut the government down than to keep it open."[58]

Even as Obama economic stimulus, he began harvesting the post-Iraq and Afghanistan peace dividend.[59] The number of federal employees fell 66,000 between 2010 and 2017, while the number of contract employees dropped 1.2 million, grant employees 1.1 million, active-duty military personnel 70,000, and Postal Service employees 90,000. Although the Bush administration's final budget gave Obama a first Iraq/Afghanistan drawdown with which to work, Obama's greater gains came with the end of the Iraq War in December 2011 and continued with the eventual spend out of the economic stimulus package. As war and economic calamity eased, so did the government-industrial head count. In doing so, Obama reduced the ratio of contract and grant employees from 3.4 to 1 in 2010 down to 2.3 to 1 shortly after leaving office.

Obama's harvesting ended by 2015 as the Islamic State in Iraq and Syria (ISIS) gained new territory, Russia waged a proxy war in Ukraine, the Taliban returned to battle, and the Syria refugee crisis exploded. These events were not entirely unexpected, though the Obama administration can be fairly criticized for sugarcoating ISIS, but the Congressional Research Service (CRS) described them as "uniquely problematic, perhaps even unprecedented" in "the speed with which each of them has developed, the scale of their impact on US interests and those of our allies, and the fact that many of these challenges have occurred— and have demanded responses—nearly simultaneously."[60]

It is impossible to know precisely precisely where the cuts fell, however, if only because the Defense Department financial management system has been on GAO's high-risk list every year since 1995. Revisiting another year of disappointing performance in 2017, GAO criticized the department as one of the few federal entities that could not account for its spending or assets. GAO also criticized the department for inconsistent and unreliable reports to Congress and an impaired ability to make cost-effective choices on pressing issues such as whether to out-source activities to private firms.[61] At the same time, GAO continued to press for improvements in the department's $1.4 trillion acquisition programs and its tendency to pay more than anticipated and buy less than expected.[62]

In addition, it is also difficult to know how much further the true size of government could have fallen by 2015 if Congress had embraced the "21st Century government that's open and competent" Obama promised in his 2011 State of the Union Address. Obama hardly hit the rhetorical peaks with his call to action, but he did make one of the best bipartisan jokes in State of the Union history:

> We live and do business in the Information Age, but the last major reorganization of the Government happened in the age of black-and-white

TV. There are 12 different agencies that deal with exports. There are at least five different agencies that deal with housing policy. Then there's my favorite example: The Interior Department is in charge of salmon while they're in fresh water, but the Commerce Department handles them when they're in saltwater. I hear it gets even more complicated once they're smoked.[63]

Obama never delivered the reform package, however, although he did lobby for restoring the reorganization authority that many past presidents had used to reshape the federal hierarchy. Congress never even discussed the request, and Obama gave up on the comprehensive reform after the House rejected his demand without discussion.[64]

Obama did not need reorganization authority to make at least some changes in the government-industrial complex, however. He also had executive actions and orders. As he said at the start of his second term, "I've got a pen and I've got a phone. And I can use that pen to sign executive orders and take executive and legislative action."[65]

Obama did just that by issuing ten major executive orders between 2009 and 2015 to protect contract employees from discrimination, sanction their employers for violating federal labor laws, and encourage purchases based on administration priorities such as the minimum wage, environment, and human trafficking:

1. Executive Order 13496, January 30, 2009, requiring contract firms to post notices of employee rights under federal labor laws
2. Executive Order 13495, January 30, 2009, protecting contract employees from displacement when their contract switched firms
3. Executive Order 13513, October 1, 2009, prohibiting texting while driving by contract employees conducting while conducting business on behalf of the federal government
4. Executive Order 13627, Sept. 25, 2012, strengthening protections against human trafficking by contract firms
5. Executive Order 13627, January 20, 2014, requiring contract firms to comply with all federal safe workplace and fair labor standards and requiring federal acquisition officers to consider any violations in making contract decisions
6. Executive Order 13658, February 12, 2014, guaranteeing contracting employees a $10.10 minimum hourly wage
7. Executive Order 13672, July 21, 2014, protecting contract employees from discrimination based on sexual orientation and gender identity
8. Executive Order 13673, July 31, 2014, ordering contract firms and bidders to disclose all labor law violations, while requiring agencies to consider such violations when awarding new contracts

9. Executive Order 13693, March 19, 2015, requiring agencies to maintain federal leadership in sustainability and greenhouse gas emissions by establishing purchase preferences for products made from recycled materials, energy efficient products and services, "biopreferred" and "biobased" products, and other sustainable products and services

10. Executive Order 13706, September 7, 2015, requiring paid sick leave for all contact employees[66]

Acting as the nation's "purchaser-in-chief," Obama used the federal government's substantial buying power and his authority as administrator-in-chief to approve policies such as the new minimum wage that Congress ignored. He also believed that the orders sent a signal to the rest of the nation and states. Speaking of his minimum wage increase for contract employees just two days before Valentine's Day 2014, Obama touched on the symbolic nature of his orders:

> Now, this will make a difference for folks. Right now, there's a dishwasher at Randolph Air Force Base in Texas making $7.76 an hour— $7.76 an hour. There's a fast food worker at Andrews, right down the street, making $8.91 an hour. There's a laundry worker at Camp Dodge in Iowa making $9.03 an hour. Once I sign this order, starting next year, as their contracts come up, each of them and many of their colleagues are going to get a raise. And by the way, that includes folks who get paid in tips. They'll get a raise too. . . . And let's not forget—not only is it good for the economy, it's the right thing to do.[67]

It is too early to tell how many of these orders will be rolled back by the end of the Trump administration, but as noted below, the so-called blacklisting rule requiring disclosure of labor law violations was revoked on March 2017. Even if the rest of the rules were to survive, enforcement may be near impossible if the federal government's underfunded acquisitions and oversight offices remained understaffed and under-resourced.

Donald Trump

Donald Trump did not mention the government-industrial complex in any form during the 2016 campaign or his transition into office, but he did discuss each side of the complex separately.

On the industry side, he criticized Boeing for over-pricing the new Air Force One in a December tweet: "Boeing is building a brand new 747 Air Force One for future presidents, but costs are out of control, more than $4 billion. Cancel Order!" he tweeted in December 2016.[68] He also criticized Lockheed-Martin for over-pricing the F-35 Joint Strike Fighter several days later with another tweet: "The F-35 program and cost is out of control. Billions of dollars can and will be saved on military (and other) purchases after January 20th."[69] Lockheed stock fell 2 percent later in the day and fell by 1 percent after Trump repeated his commitment to cost saving in early January.

On the government side, his "Contract with the American Voter" listed a federal hiring freeze as a solution to "corruption and special interest collusion." As former Republican Speaker of the House Newt Gingrich explained, the contract would reassure traditional Republicans that Trump was Republican enough to deserve their support:

> Trump's Contract with the American Voter should also alleviate any concern among traditional Republicans that their party's candidate is somehow not Republican enough. The provisions in the Trump Contract would reduce the size and scope of government as much as any president in our lifetimes, including Ronald Reagan. Its ethics reforms and bureaucracy-cutting measures would significantly reduce the power of the executive branch Trump seeks to lead. And they would help restore accountability and honesty to government once again.[70]

Although Trump criticized contract firms for price gouging, he blamed the federal government for the waste, fraud, and abuse. Asked how he would balance the federal budget in a February 2016 debate, Trump blamed agencies. "Waste, fraud, and abuse all over the place," he answered, "Waste, fraud, and abuse. You look at what's happening with every agency—waste, fraud, and abuse. We will cut so much, your head will spin."[71]

Asked two weeks later how he would pay for his tax cuts, he put the burden on government again. "We're going to buy things for less money," he answered. "We will save $300 billion a year if we properly negotiate. We don't do that. We don't negotiate. We don't negotiate anything."[72]

The First 100 Days

Trump followed through on his complaint when he imposed a ninety-day "across-the-board" federal hiring freeze on January 23.[73] Trump signed the order without remarks, but the administration framed the memorandum as a broad attack on big government. "Look, I think you saw this with the hiring freeze," the president's press secretary, Sean Spicer, explained later in the day. "There's been frankly, to some degree, a lack of respect for tax payer dollars in this town for a long time and I think what the president is showing through the hiring freeze, first and foremost today, is that we've got to respect the American tax payer. They're sending us a ton of money, they're working real hard."[74]

Like the presidential hiring caps, cuts, and freezes that preceded it over the decades Trump order exempted thousands of national security and public safety positions and was too short and poorly timed to have significant effects. Relatively few federal employees exit during winter and many of the vacancies could have been easily filled by contract employees.

Winter turned into spring, however, and the freeze continued in force at the State Department and a hiring slowdown at many other many departments and agencies in advance of personnel cuts in 2019. The effect was far from extreme, but the end-of-year head counts did show a sixteen-thousand-person drop in total federal employment, including noticeable declines at the Bureau of Prisons, Defense, EPA, the Internal Revenue Service, and State Department. There were also reports of accelerated turnover in the senior executive corps and Foreign Service, and a twenty-thousand-person increase in voluntary quits from 5.8 percent in 2016 to 6.7 percent in 2017. "This is going very well," anti-tax lobbyist Grover Norquist said at the time. "Slow and steady— for all the bluster, this is how you downsize government without engendering blowback."[75]

These numbers, while no doubt significant to a nervous workforce, were too small to alter the true size of government trend in Table 2.1. Trump ended his first year in office with a slightly larger government-industrial workforce than he inherited. The freeze may have created a sense of dread that one federal employee described as like the movie soundtrack in *Jaws*, but the administration was slow to follow up with the kind of targeting that made the Clinton downsizing so effective.[76]

The uncertainty increased when Trump signed Executive Order 13781 on March 13. Designed to "improve the efficiency, effectiveness, and accountability of the executive branch," the order gave OMB authority to develop plans after considering three broad questions about government performance:

1. Whether some or all of the functions of an agency, a component, or a program are redundant, including with those of another agency, component, or program;
2. Whether certain administrative capabilities necessary for operating an agency, a component, or a program are redundant with those of another agency, component, or program; and
3. Whether the costs of continuing to operate an agency, a component, or a program are justified by the public benefits it provides.[77]

The answers were not due for 180 days, but the future became clear when Trump released his "skinny budget" for fiscal year 2018 less than a month after his inauguration. Although best described as a "wish list" of future priorities, the budget outline contained a $54 billion increase in defense spending increase to honor the president's promise to make the military "so strong, nobody's gonna mess with us," and a parallel cut in nondefense programs and agencies that included the State Department.

Congress would have to approve the proposals, but all things being equal, the defense increase would almost certainly raise the number of contract and grant employees on the industry side of the federal workforce, while the domestic cuts would almost certainly reduce the number of federal employees on the government side.[78] *Fortune* estimated that the cuts could eliminate 100,000 to 200,000 jobs, which former Clinton administration budget director Alice Rivlin described as "drastic layoffs that would be very hard to do very quickly."[79] Stories about nervous, even terrified, federal employees hit the front pages again, but the effects on the total number of federal employees were ambiguous at best.

However, the administration made no secret about the depth of the cuts in what the OMB director, Mike Mulvaney, called the "America First Budget":

> The President's commitment to fiscal responsibility is historic. Not since early in President Reagan's first term have more tax dollars been saved and more Government inefficiency and waste been targeted. Every corner of the Federal budget is scrutinized, every program tested, every penny of taxpayer money watched over.[80]

Mulvaney stretched the history-making hyperbole all the way back to George Washington when he later said the "skinny budget" would stop 240 years of organic growth in government: "The president of the United States has asked all of us in the executive branch to start from scratch, a literal blank piece of paper and say, 'if you're going to rebuild the executive branch, what would it look like?' "[81]

Finally, Mulvaney explained the president's decision to end his ninety-day hiring freeze as a natural product of organizational learning:

> So we're going from this sort of across-the-board hiring freeze. That's not unusual for any new management team to come in—to put into place when they come into an organization, whether it's the private sector or a government. Not unusual for a new management team to come in and say, look, stop hiring, let us figure out what's going on, we'll get acclimated and then we'll put into place something that's more practicable and smarter. And that's what this is. So you'll see this across-the-board ban tomorrow, and replaced with a smarter approach.[82]

Reinventing Government Redux?

If there was any comfort in the end of Mulvaney's "sort-of" hiring freeze, it came in Trump's early March statements supporting a government that works better and costs less. "We are going to do more with less, and make the government lean and accountable to the people," he wrote in his March budget message to Congress. "Many other government agencies and departments will also experience cuts. These cuts are sensible and rational. Every agency and department will be driven to achieve greater efficiency and to eliminate wasteful spending in carrying out their honorable service to the American people."[83]

Trump had not become a reinventor per se, but he did promise to do something "very, very special" to make government more efficient and "very, very productive."[84] In doing so, he even prompted some of Gore's staff to endorse the effort. "To give them credit, it's time to do it again," Kamarck told *Politico* in March 2017. "It is to time to review the government again and ask the hard questions about what it's doing and what it should be doing. And it is time to focus on obsolete functions and getting rid of them." Trump's remarks may have used reinventing's works-better-and-costs-less cadence, but Kamarck worried that it would be yet another "budget drill" that would generate "fake cuts" with little gains in performance.[85]

On the government side of the complex, for example, Trump's 2019 budget targeted nondefense federal employees for deep reductions in force. The administration did not set a specific downsizing target, but did order all departments to identify opportunities for attrition-based workforce cuts. The budget also scheduled wholesale cuts in nondefense programs such as environmental protection and Medicaid.

On the industry side, the budget gave contract and grant employees cause for celebration. Trump's budget offered 40 percent more for Defense-side operations and maintenance, 20 percent for research and research and development, and 6 percent for procurement. Meanwhile, the budget promised the army, navy, and air force 55 percent, 49 percent, and 46 percent respectively for operations and maintenance, somewhat smaller increases for air force and navy research and development, and 16 percent for navy shipbuilding and conversion. These increases all promised large increases for the contracting and grant workforce.[86]

Deconstructing the Administrative State

The number of nondefense federal employees could fall much farther in subsequent years if Trump pursues his early plan to "deconstruct the administrative state." Conservatives commonly use the term to describe the wholesale dismantling of the "deep state" that perpetuates government growth and interference.

Trump endorsed dismantling when he appointed Stephen Bannon to the White House staff. Bannon used his close ties to Trump's right-wing base to press for administrative and regulatory reform. Speaking before the Conservative Political Action Conference in late February 2017, he used the term "deconstruction" to describe as the third "bucket" of the president's America-first agenda:

> The third, broadly, line of work is deconstruction of the adminis-trative state. . . . If you look at these cabinet appointees, they were selected for a reason and that is the deconstruction. The way the progressive left runs, is if they can't get it passed, they're just going to put in some sort of regulation in an agency. That's all going to be deconstructed and I think that that's why this regulatory thing is so important.[87]

Bannon was forced out of the administration in six months later, but his agenda was already widely shared by key allies such as Mulvaney and his team of budget cutters. Mulvaney did not use the term specifically, but he acknowledged Bannon's thesis in April when he described executive orders as a poor substitute for legislative success: "To the extent that we only do stuff within the execu-tive branch—as with any executive orders—they can be overturned by the next administration if they see things differently. That's the way the executive order system works. And that if we wanted real permanent change, the best way to go about that would be to do legislative change."[88]

Trump never adopted Bannon's terminology specifically but did embrace de-construction when he launched a new regulatory review process on January 30 to reverse Obama's environmental and contracting orders, created a yearlong government-wide reorganization planning process on March 13 to eliminate any and all federal programs and units that Mulvaney would later describe as "un-necessary, outdated, or not working," and established a new White House Office of Government Innovation on March 27 under the leadership of his son-in-law, Jared Kushner, who would soon be denied access to top-secret information.[89]

These administrative actions were hardly revolutionary, however. As noted later in this chapter, Trump was not the first president to impose a hiring freeze nor will he be the last to reorganize government, attack the regulatory process, criticize cost overruns, freeze federal pay, or question employee commitment. So noted, he is undeniably the first to characterize the federal government and its employees as agents of a "deep state" intent on removing him from office. Other presidents may have said as much in private, but none matched Trump's delight in going public.

Reversing Orders

Trump was particularly active in reversing Obama's executive orders on a host of issues from the clean coal plan to a planned phaseout of private prisons, and seemed to take special pleasure in reversing course on the contract workforce.[90] Trump's first target was Obama's Executive Order 13673, which required contract bidders to disclose any labor law violations in the three-year period prior to the solicitation.[91] Federal contract officers were ordered to use the information to assess the bidder's record of integrity and business ethics; determine whether the violations were serious, willful, repeated, and/or pervasive; and list the findings on the federal government Awardee Performance and Integrity Information System for other departments and agencies to use. Firms with violations could still bid for contracts, but the rule sent a clear warning that violations could matter in the final decision.

Trump had promised to revoke the rule during the campaign and welcomed business leaders to the Oval Office when he sat down to sign the rollback on Monday March 27:

> When I met with manufacturers earlier this year—and they were having a hard time, believe me—they said this blacklisting rule was one of the greatest threats to growing American business and hiring more American workers. It was a disaster they said. This rule made it too easy for trial lawyers to get rich by going after American companies and American workers who contract with the federal government—making it very difficult.[92]

Democrats and labor unions did not agree. With the rollback already on the president's desk awaiting signature, Sen. Elizabeth Warren (D-Mass) released a caustic report titled *Breach of Contract: How Federal Contractors Fail American Workers on the Taxpayer's Dime*. Drawing upon federal databases, congressional investigations, and POGO's misconduct data, Warren concluded that "the violation of labor laws and abuse of workers by federal contractors is common, repetitive, and dangerous." Warren acknowledged that contract firms supported critical federal missions, but often did so by underpaying workers and putting health and safety at risk. Warren warned her colleagues that the risks would rise if contract firms took the rollback as permission to reduce employee protections even further.[93]

Warren's report had no impact on Trump's agenda. As the president said when he revoked the rule in a White House ceremony, Obama's workplace rule was only the first of many rollbacks ahead: "I will keep working with Congress, with every agency, and most importantly, the American people, until we eliminate every unnecessary, harmful and job-killing regulation that we can find. We have a lot more coming."[94] Trump had inherited Obama's pen, but intended to use it to reverse direction.

Reskilling the Federal Workforce

Trump's government reform agenda was still under development when the president celebrated his first anniversary on January 20, 2018, in the midst of a three-day government shutdown. Most departments and agencies had submitted reorganization plans in time to meet the president's 2017 order, but the details were scarce, while the White House fact sheet offered little more than talking points about the need to do better.[95]

The administration's budget request for fiscal year 2019 was equally opaque in its broad commitment to strengthen the federal workforce, streamline the federal bureaucracy, and "reskill" federal employees. Although the budget contained deep personnel cuts in most departments and agencies, it never explained how it would eliminate what it called "transactional work" and "legacy positions," and avoided specifics on how it would improve government performance and reorganize the federal organization chart. As the *Washington Post*'s Joe Davidson argues, the generalities disguised a much deeper attack on federal pay and protections:

> President Trump and his budget director, Mick Mulvaney, must have been in a jocular mood Monday when they issued their fiscal 2019 budget appendix titled "Strengthening the Federal Workforce." It could have just as easily been called "Picking the Pockets of Federal Employees."[96]

The administration did make one major concession on the true size of government. After acknowledging the federal government as the single largest direct US employer, the administration also described the "even larger 'indirect' workforce" that delivers much of the work paid for by federal funds: "These are the Federal contractor personnel, as well as the State, local, and nonprofit employees—many of whose jobs are entirely funded through Federal grants and transfer payments—located all across the Nation, in every state and territory."[97] Although the administration concluded that the size of the workforce was "unknown and a subject of dispute," this passage almost dares Congress, federal employee unions, think tanks, GAO, and even CBO to produce the side-by-side comparisons that could be used to reskill the contract and grant workforce.

The President's Personnel Agenda

The Trump administration's plans for the federal workforce has become much clearer by spring 2018 when the Senate finally confirmed the president's Office of Personnel Management administrator, Jeffrey Pon. Pon was broadly welcomed as a nonpartisan human-resource specialist and advocate of comprehensive civil service reform. He won support from federal senior executives and the Partnership for Public Service, and did not provoke federal union opposition.

Pon was not the only actor in the civil service field, however, and began his term under immediate fire when the administration released a laundry list of personnel proposals that included curbs on federal union activity, "quick hire" authority for hard-to-recruit skills, deep retirement cuts, a one-year pay freeze, and an accelerated disciplinary process. As the next chapter suggests, there are good reasons to support the general call for reform—the disciplinary process is too slow, the retirement system needs repair, and quick hiring authority is long overdue.

However, the fusillade of proposals felt more like a random assortment that a cohesive agenda, a point made by Pon himself in declaring that he intended to mount a full court press for reform all the way through the midterm elections. "Do I anticipate everything to work and go through? No," he said in late April. "I've already heard from some of my colleagues, 'Maybe Pon is taking on too much, maybe he's biting off too much.' But I actually look at it a different way. I'm going to ask, and the worst they can say is, 'No.' "[98]

Pon also struggled to defend an unexpected flood of White House reforms that included three presidential orders on hiring, firing, and unions. He also stumbled early in explaining his general reform philosophy. It may have been rooted in the best traditions of human resource management, but needed careful explanation and a degree of cauti9on. Although his role in the more draconian cuts remains unclear, he was quickly forced to play defense, arguing at one point explaining pay reform that he did not support a "peanut butter" pay system that gives every employee an even spread. Nor did he burnish his reputation for good timing when he announced his proposal for a $144 billion federal pension roll-back at the start of Public Service Recognition Week. "President Trump really knows how to say thank you," Davidson wrote of the proposal.[99]

Looking for Variation

As noted in chapter 1, Eisenhower described the military-industrial complex as an integrated force with total, not divided economic, political, and even spiritual influence. However, he also acknowledged the multiple workforces that worked for the "defense establishment" and the "armaments industry" on different sides of the military-industry complex.

Table 2.4 suggests that today's government-industrial complex contains more variety than Eisenhower's military-industry complex implied. Whereas Eisenhower described a whole composed of two integrated parts, Table 2.4

Table 2.4 **Inside the Government-Industrial Complex, 2017**

Measure	Contracts		Grants*	
Deliverable	Products	1,286,000	N/A	N/A
	Services	2,842,000	N/A	N/A
Source	Small Business	1,103,000	N/A	N/A
	Large Business	3,025,000	N/A	N/A
Bidding Process	Sole Source	1,051,000	N/A	N/A
	Competed	2,670,000	N/A	N/A
Industries	Professional and Business Services	1,907,000	Construction	523,000
	Manufacturing	1,193,000	Professional and Business Services	384,000
	Construction	290,000	Administrative & Support Services	98,000
	Educational	231,000	Hospitals	77,000
	Transportation & Warehouse	134,000	Educational	47,000
Largest Buyers	Defense	2,491,000	Transportation	519,000
	Veterans Affairs	242,000	Health and Human Services	340,000
	Energy	261,000	Education	54,000
	Health and Human Services	217,000	National Science Foundation	59,000
	Homeland Security	190,000	Defense	41,000
	National Aeronautics and Space Administration	109,000	Veterans Affairs	26,000
	Justice	79,000	Housing and Urban Development	25,000

*The grant data did not allow estimates of deliverables, sources, and bidding process.

reveals suggests a whole composed of highly varied missions and methods in which in which professional and business services accounted for more than half of all contract and grant employees.[100]

Deeper analysis of this variation is almost impossible without using expensive search regimes designed to combine spending targets, products, and amounts simultaneously.[101] It is relatively easy to analyze the spending data by deliverable OR source OR bidding process OR industry, but much more difficult to analyze the data by deliverable AND source AND bidding process AND industry. Ask a simple question and these databases will answer; ask a complex question and the databases may refuse. Hence, the rise of an entire industry of data divers who earn their profits by mapping the messy world of federal contract and grant data.

Complex questions will be easier to answer in the not-too-distant future using the new spending database created by the Digital Accountability and Transparency Act of 2014, otherwise known as the DATA Act.[102] The new database passed its first milestone in April 2017, when the Treasury Department released its inventory of codes and formats to be used in publicly available reports, and its second milestone a year later in May, when all departments and agencies began submitting their spending reports to DATA Act's "data broker" for validation and eventual publication as the sole source of spending information on USASpending.gov.

The database cannot honor its promised revolution in government transparency unless departments and agencies faithfully implement the fifty-seven codes. Once assigned and verified, the codes will provide common links between all federal spending decisions based on award history (e.g., appropriation account, budget authority, total obligation), type (e.g., contract, grant, or loan), characteristics (e.g., purpose, start and end dates, primary place of performance, industry code), and recipient (e.g., legal name and address, Dun & Bradstreet number, congressional district, and the names and total compensation of the recipient's five most highly compensated "executives").[103]

According to the nonprofit DATA Foundation, these codes will make all spending information "interoperable," thereby creating a more transparent contract and grant world in which government-wide analyses that take years today will become trivial exercises, auditors receive and retrieve spending reports automatically, presidents can see the consequences of their decisions in a nanosecond, Congress can write appropriations bills electronically, and trust in government will increase.[104]

However, this transparency will only be as accurate as the individual coding decisions made deep inside each department and agency. Some agencies may resist the codes as an exercise in compliance, while antiquated information technology may require hand coding, vague definitions may create inconsistent reporting, public interest groups may lack the skills to query the system, and persistent funding shortages and job cuts may weaken employee productivity.[105]

As of late spring 2017, GAO was still urging caution regarding the government's readiness to report. "We don't expect agencies' spending data to be uniformly complete of accurate," GAO told its *WatchBlog* readers on May 6. "Previously identified weaknesses in agencies' accounting and financial management processes, as well as financial systems and IT security, increase the risk that inaccurate, incomplete spending data will be reported." Nevertheless, GAO still supported forward movement: "Why? Because reporting this amount of spending data is not easy, and it will be a process of continuous improvement, where agencies report, are transparent about their weaknesses, and work to improve subsequent rounds of reporting."[106] Although December 2017 analysis of the first round of reports showed problems with timeliness, accuracy, and completeness, many of the errors came from simple reporting glitches that can be easily fixed.[107]

Even with perfect coding, the database is unlikely to address Eisenhower's concerns about unwarranted influence unless good-government groups are able to download the USASpending.gov data for further analysis using nongovernmental data. For example, the nonpartisan Center for Responsive Politics could use the data to search for deeper patterns in the relationships between campaign spending, lobbying activity, and federal awards, while POGO could add federal grantees and loan recipients to their Federal Contract Misconduct Database.

The DATA Act has already broadened the discussion of federal spending beyond the traditional focus on entitlements and national debt. It is also well positioned to strengthen oversight of the government-industrial complex and its conjunctions of conjunctions. At the same time, the DATA Act is unlikely to affect trust in government unless its new database is fully open, accurate, searchable, machine-readable, and downloadable.

Eisenhower would likely have agreed. He was the definitive "hidden-hand" president who cultivated an image of political innocence to secure significant impact, yet also believed that transparency was essential for countering the disastrous rise of misplaced power.[108] He was also gifted at keeping secrets and hiding covert action, yet also worried that government contracts could become both a substitute for intellectual curiosity and a threat to scientific progress. Full disclosure of spending data just might appeal to a president who had spent most of 1930 searching for insights on the military-industrial complex in World War I. It might also appeal to a president who saw "a great influence, almost an insidious penetration of our own minds" in magazine advertisements that featured photos of missiles and bombers."[109]

Caps, Cuts, and Freezes

As the next chapter will argue, all federal departments and agencies work under broad personnel and management policies set by Congress and the president. Although many of these policies were created to improve federal performance, they often create unintended incentives for using contract and grant employees in lieu of federal employees as government missions change, skill gaps emerge, and polarization rises.

As the next chapter also shows, some of these incentives also reflect the caps, cuts, and freezes that Congress and the president frequently impose on federal hiring and employment to prove their allegiance to smaller government. These limits are easy to promise, quick to implement, and advertise. However, past research strongly suggests that caps, cuts, and freezes rarely produce significant impacts on the number of federal employees. Rather, they either produce federal shrugs or drive jobs across the government-industrial divide as departments and agencies backfill empty posts with service contract employees. Moreover, caps, cuts, and freezes appear to have disproportionate effects on the bottom levels of government where quit rates are high and the calls to service contract employees are inevitably louder.

As Table 2.5 shows, Congress and presidents placed twenty-four caps, cuts, and freezes on the number of federal employees between 1940 and March 2018. Some of these orders established "not-to-exceed" limits on total headcount, others set a specific downsizing targets, still others froze federal hiring for a fixed period of time, and one created multiple rounds of quasi-independent commissions that closed or realigned 350 military bases between 1988 and 2015, thereby trimming thousands of government-industry jobs.

All but five of these efforts were poorly designed and of such limited duration that they produced more anxiety and evasion than any positive consequences.[110] They may have provided momentary surges in public support, but they did not change the trajectory of federal employment. "That's good politics," Schooner writes of caps, cuts, and freezes, "because the bipartisan tale of a shrinking Federal Government, despite its dubious veracity, offers broad-ranging appeal."[111] It also produces what Guttman calls the "hydraulic force" that underpins the use of grant employees to create and expand domestic programs such as Medicare and Medicaid.[112]

Most of the caps, cuts, and freezes were little more than political gestures, but there is one cap that has affected federal employment levels for almost three-quarters of a century. Authored by Rep. Jamie L. Whitten (D-MS) in 1950, the Whitten Amendment prevented the federal government from filling vacant federal positions with permanent replacements during the Korean War emergency, thereby setting a two million cap on total federal employment.[113] Called before

Table 2.5 **Caps, Cuts, and Freezes, 1940–2017**

Measure	Goal	Tool	Origin	Time Horizon	Impact on Federal Employment
1. Byrd-Langer Joint Resolution of 1942	Urged executive attention to the size of federal employment	Disclosure	Congress	Until war's end	None
2. War Overtime Pay Act of 1943	Required periodic counts of total federal employment	Disclosure	Congress	Until war's end	None
3. Federal Employees Pay Act of 1945	Funded federal pay increases through equivalent reductions in total personnel	Cut	Congress	Five years	Minimal
4. Supplemental Appropriation Act of 1950 implemented under Executive Order 10180 Establishing Special Personnel Procedures	Prohibited hiring and promotions	Freeze	Executive	Indefinite	Major
5. Supplemental Appropriation Act of 1952 adding further controls to the Whitten Amendment	Limited promotions to higher grades	Freeze	Congress	Indefinite	Minimal
6. Revenue and Expenditure Control Act of 1968	Set fixed numerical targets	Ceiling	Congress	Indefinite	Minimal
7. Reductions in Civilian Employment of 1971	Reduced budget for civilian personnel	Cut	Executive	One year	Minimal
8. Department of Defense Authorization Act of 1974	Set fixed numerical targets	Ceilings & reductions in force	Congress	One year	Minimal

9. Department of Defense Authorization Act of 1975	Set fixed numerical targets	Ceilings & reductions in force	Congress	One year	Minimal
10. Fiscal Year Adjustment Act of 1976	Strengthened implementation of fixed numerical targets	Ceilings	Congress	Indefinite	Minimal
11. Department of Defense Authorization Act of 1976	Lowered but retained fixed numerical targets	Ceilings & reductions in force	Congress	One year	Minimal
12. Presidential Memorandum Creating a Limitation on Hiring in the Federal Government of 1977	Prohibited hiring	Freeze	Executive	Three months	Minimal
13. Civil Service Reform Act of 1978	Set fixed numerical targets	Ceiling	Congress	Three years	Major
14. Presidential Memorandum Creating a Limitation on Hiring in the Federal Government of 1978	Prohibited hiring	Freeze	Executive	Three months	Minimal
15. Presidential Memorandum Creating a Limitation on Hiring in the Federal Government of 1980	Prohibited hiring	Freeze	Executive	Nine months	Minimal
16. Presidential Memorandum Directing a Federal Employee Hiring Freeze, January 20, 1981	Prohibited hiring retroactive to November 5, 1980	Freeze	Executive	Two months	Minimal
17. Budget Targets for Fiscal Years 1982 and 1983	Set fixed numerical targets	Reductions in force	Executive	Two years	Minimal

(continued)

Table 2.5 **Continued**

Measure	Goal	Tool	Origin	Time Horizon	Impact on Federal Employment
18. "Bulge Project" to Reduce Grade 11–15 Positions, 1984	Set fixed numerical targets	Reductions in force	Executive	Two years	Minimal
19. Base Closure and Realignment Commissions, 1988–2005	Established base closure system	Reductions in force	Congress	Five rounds, 1988–2005	Major
20. Executive Order 12839 for a Reduction of 100,000 Federal Positions, 1993	Set fixed numerical targets	Reductions in force	Executive	Three years	Major
21. Federal Workforce Restructuring Act of 1994	Set fixed numerical targets	Ceilings & buyouts	Congress & Executive	Five years	Major
22. Presidential Memorandum on Government Hiring Controls, January 20, 2001	Prohibited hiring until agency heads were confirmed	Freeze	Executive	Very short term	Minimal
23. Executive Action to Senior Executive Service Hiring, November 2016	Suspended Senior Executive Service appointments	Freeze	Executive	One month	Minimal
24. Presidential Memorandum Regarding the Hiring Freeze, January 23, 2017	Prohibited hiring	Freeze	Executive	Three months	Minimal

the House Committee on Post Office and Civil Service to explain his work in 1954, Whitten described his amendment as little more than a simple member's effort to make government a little bit better:

> I had no ax to grind, and have none now, except to do what I can for orderly government. Sometimes I think politically it would be much wiser to get a staff and keep count of federal employees and release it to the press complaining about the total number now and then. Had I followed that course, I might have gotten an award of merit, and things of that sort, which I notice that others do.[114]

Whitten also told the committee he had never intended any harm, and certainly never expected President Truman to freeze federal hiring and promotions. He just wanted to save some money:

> I did not try to limit the total number of people that we might need to have in Government to meet the jobs which might arise. But I thought 2 million permanent folks ought to be enough to have on a permanent basis, and I thought those ought to be protected in it. So what I did was fix appropriately 2 million as all the permanents we are going to have.[115]

As Figure 2.2 shows, presidents have remained close to the two-million line ever since it took full effect and long after its repeal. It is now firmly established as a measure of excess.

How Whitten's Cap Survived

By most accounts, Whitten was not the most likable member of Congress, whether during the 1950s when he signed the *Southern Manifesto* opposing integration, in the 1960s when he defended pesticides in the wake of Rachel

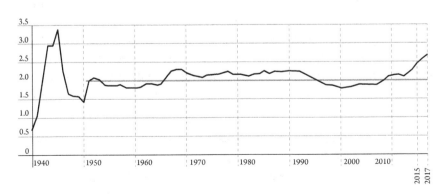

Figure 2.2 Federal Government Employees, 1940-2017

Carson's *Silent Spring*, and other episodes in his career as when he fought to keep the cotton subsidy alive, stocked his state with pork barrel projects such as the Tennessee-Tombigbee canal, and took on the postal unions to protect his cap. He may have moved toward the Democratic median, but he was still difficult to persuade. "He'll give you an ulcer," former Rep. Silvio O. Conte (R-MA) told the *New York Times* a decade before Whitten died in 1995. "Dealing with him is like throwing putty at a wall."[116]

Repealing the Whitten Amendment also turned out to be like throwing putty at a wall, indeed. It even returned to life after being repealed not once, but twice in the mid-1960s. The first repeal was restricted solely to the US Postal Service, while the second removed the cap on the federal government as a whole.

However, both repeals were based in part on the notion that Whitten's amendment was undermining economy and efficiency by forcing the federal government to hire thousands of "temporary substitutes" who stayed on the payroll year after year as if permanent, and even distracting the nation from war as the Defense Department redeployed combat-trained military personnel and contract employees to do work once done by federal employees.[117] Having been pilloried as an anachronism, a straitjacket, a violation of labor rights, vicious, and a source of instability, waste, and mass resentment, the amendment was repealed by voice votes on August 5, 1965, and again on October 11, 1967.[118]

As if to prove its resilience as Congress entered a tough election year, the amendment returned to life by another voice vote on June 28, 1968. This time the amendment covered full-time and temporary employees alike, and reset the clock on total allowable employees to sixty days before the first repeal passed. Whitten's original amendment may have been an anachronism, but someone on the Appropriations Committee designed the new cap to erase any hiring that had occurred after the 1965 repeal. This someone was the future committee chairman, Jamie Whitten himself.

The repeals and counter-repeals continued into the early 1970s, took a breather during Watergate, and returned in full under Jimmy Carter and in the final compromise on the 1978 Civil Service Reform Act. Facing resistance in the House, the Carter White House agreed to limit total federal employment to the number employed on September 30, 1977.[119] Rep. Jim Leach (R-IA) authored the amendment, arguing that indirect employees should have been constrained. He even used what appear to be the first estimates of contract employees ever developed:

> Frightening statistics recently presented by HEW Secretary Califano to the Senate Appropriations Committee indicate that at the same time the U.S. Government is paying salaries to 144,000 regular HEW employees, HEW is indirectly paying the salaries of another 980,000

who work for private think tanks, universities, State and local government, and related programs. Thus, the equivalent payroll for this one Federal Department alone exceeds 1 million.[120]

By this point, Whitten's amendment was no longer needed, not because Congress and the president abandoned caps, cuts, and freezes, but because it had become an inviolable campaign pledge. Whitten never explained his cap as good acquisition policy—it created many of the obstacles to rightsizing discussed above—and it did not survive because he outlasted every member who had questioned him in the early 1950s, kept a tight rein on government employees from his seat on the Appropriations Committee, or doled out so many favors as chairman of the Appropriations subcommittee on agriculture that colleagues called him the "Permanent Secretary of Agriculture."

Rather, Whitten's amendment stood because Congress and presidents supported it. Despite occasional complaints about the freeze, members rarely put themselves on the record lest they be accused of favoring big government.

Members may have wanted to grow their departments and agencies as the Cold War deepened, but they never questioned the need to control the size of the federal workforce. Nor did they worry that contract employees might produce the products and services. Congress and the president had established the Atomic Energy Commission in 1946 knowing that it would rely on contract firms for much of the work in harnessing the atom, and created the NASA in 1958 knowing that the agency would rely on a "surge tank" of contract and grant employees that would rise during each phase of the lunar program, and fall during the down times.

In fact, NASA was the very model of the contract-centered agency. As Guttman writes, NASA has been dependent on contract firms from its establishment:

> NASA marked the creation of an entirely new agency on the publicly declared premise that it would depend on contractors for the bulk of its workforce. It soon combined the deployment of systems managers, the reliance on support services, and the use of contract. The support service model was now well in evidence, complementing the project management contractors. From the start, NASA employed aerospace manufacturers (such as Rockwell and Boeing) to manage rocket building, called on contract research centers (such as the Jet Propulsion Laboratory), and supplemented its own staff with cadres of support service contractors.[121]

Even the time cards at the Kennedy Space Flight Center were color-coded so that the contract employees could be easily separated from the federal employees.

Whitten also understood, or perhaps even calculated, that it would be easier to spend money if the public measured the size of government by the number of employees, not the federal budget. Even though trust in government was much higher in the 1950s and 1960s, a vote against the Whitten Amendment was tantamount to a vote for big bureaucracy. Whitten's amendment lasted because Americans understood the calculus.

Almost everyone who could have fought the cap understood the politics, too, including presidents who wanted big endeavors at home and big victories abroad, political candidates who needed campaign contributions to win elections, presidential appointees who must implement prized programs such as healthcare reform, senior executives who must faithfully execute the laws during fiscal crises, federal managers and supervisors who need to hire quickly, and even federal employee unions who need presidential support for new labor-management partnerships.[122] Even new federal employees can find good reasons to support a cap if it produces faster promotions and a chance to learn. After all, one employee's hiring delay is often another employee's chance to take on more responsibilities.

Despite its occasional positives, Whitten's cap continues to disrupt the faithful execution of the laws. It has not only changed the basic shape of government but has also exposed critical missions to uncertain delivery and potential breakdowns. With little room to maneuver above the original two million cap, the federal government has little choice but to use contract and grant employees to achieve its goals. The combination is imperative to government's overall success but is fixed on one side of the boundary and almost fully open on the other. The result is what might be labeled "imperative vulnerability." There are few options beyond higher prices for retaining contract and grant talent, and even fewer if inherently governmental functions require large infusions of new federal employees. The two-million barrier can only be stretched so far before it breaks.

Moreover, as Donald Kettl argues, "proxy government" by the states, nonprofits, contract firms, and grantees is here to stay: "The strategy has been attractive to many liberals because it has allowed them to expand government's reach without making government bureaucracy bigger. It has been attractive to many conservatives because they have been able to swallow a larger government as long as the private sector delivered it."[123] Without action either one way or the other, government will grow—it is just that the growth will be hidden from public view.

Proxy government is not without costs, however. Despite decades of argument about federal pay, the recent evidence suggests that proxy employees often cost more than contract and grant employees. Moreover, proxy networks appear to be less reliable in producing intended results. John Dilulio has made the point repeatedly over the past decade in opinion pieces and articles arguing for more federal hiring. A *Washington Post* opinion article titled "Want a Leaner Federal Government? Hire More Federal Workers" notes:

> Members of Congress and blue-ribbon panels calling for cuts in the federal workforce are missing the real problem. We don't need fewer federal workers; we need more of them—a lot more. More direct public administration would result in better, smarter, more accountable government.
>
> Big government masquerading as state or local government, private enterprise, or civil society is still big government. And privatization that involves "acquisition workforce" bureaucrats contracting out work to entrenched interests is not really privatizing. The growth of this form of big government is harder to constrain, and its performance ills are harder to diagnose and fix, than they would be in a big government more directly administered by an adequate number of well-trained federal bureaucrats.[124]

The case for more federal hiring is far from settled, especially given the lack of hard numbers on the true size of the government-industrial complex and its associated costs. "We don't know for sure how much government would save if it did more of its work itself, if it would save any money at all," Kettl concludes. "But it is at least plausible that, regardless of its size, government will decide to bring more of its work back inside government."[125]

Dilulio and Kettl have been optimists about reducing the number of federal proxy employees, and I, a harsh the piecemeal reforms that preoccupy Washington. Whereas they argue forcefully for the insourcing of one million proxy jobs, I focus on the need for radical reform of the federal systems and operations. Whereas they argue that outsourcing is wasteful and unreliable, I focus on the recent cascade of government breakdowns rooted in policy design, budget cuts, failed leadership, dense hierarchies, and weak accountability.

However, Dilulio, Kettl, and I agree that the federal government needs help. "Government increasingly is everywhere, because we want it do more," Kettl writes early in his book *Jurassic Government*, "But we've worked hard to undermine its capacity and to wipe its fingerprints, because we don't trust government to do it."[126] Much as Kettl and his colleagues make the case for one million more federal employees, I see no chance of success without addressing Whitten's cap. More might be better in the abstract, but not without removing the obstacles that have created the cavities, vacuums, blind spots, and so forth that has kept the cap in place.

The federal workforce is always going to be part of a government-industrial complex, the question being how to make sure that each side is engaged in the right work. Although the ratios of industry to government do change over time with events and presidential politics, the best way to reset Whitten's cap without a storm of familiar invective is to embrace the imperative nature of the government-industrial complex as a whole. Federal, contract, and grant employees may get their checks from different accounts, but the dollars always track back to the public. As such, all three have an obligation to create public benefit. They are all public servants whether they like the term or not.

Unanticipated Consequences

Whitten may have described his work as a simple tool for reducing federal spending, but its greatest impact has been to imbalance the government-industry workforce. In fact, the available research, dated though it is, suggests that caps, cuts, and freezes undermine productivity, increase costs, and create long-term dependencies that weaken government's ability to faithfully execute the laws. In short, no one benefits from a government hiring cap, cut, or freeze. Moreover, even celebrated caps, cuts, and freezes such as the 1994 reinventing government targets serve more as a lagging indicator of what was already in train.

In fact, the most frequently cited report on cause and effect is now more than twenty-five years old and was based on a quick analysis of the four Carter and Reagan hiring freezes between 1977 and 1981. Pushed by Congress to provide its analysis as quickly as possible, GAO drew on a handful of interviews with personnel and budget specialists in just ten departments and agencies to reach its conclusion:

> While the Government-wide hiring freezes reviewed by GAO provided an illusion of control on Federal employment and spending, they had little effect on federal employment levels, and it is not known whether they saved money. Because they ignored individual agencies' missions, workload, and staffing requirements, these freezes disrupted agency operations, and in some cases, increased costs to the Government.[127]

House Democrats described GAO's conclusion as "seminal" in fighting Trump's hiring freeze, but would have made an even stronger case with GAO's 1977 report titled *Personnel Ceilings—A Barrier to Effective Manpower Management*.[128] The report started with a summary of negative effects such as reduced services, increased backlogs, uneven staffing, excessive overtime, and the use of contract and grant employees to perform essential jobs, segued into a history and evaluation of hiring freezes dating back to 1942, and ended by describing personnel ceilings as "an inferior substitute for effective management."[129]

GAO also warned its readers about the underlying dependencies on contract and grant employees discussed in this chapter:

> The Federal work force should be no larger than needed to do the essential work required to accomplish the programs and functions authorized by the President and the Congress. If agencies need more manpower than allowed by their assigned personnel ceilings, they must acquire the additional manpower by other means. Even though the Government ultimately bears the cost of all manpower used in Federal programs, reports on Federal employment give no recognition to manpower acquired through contracts for personal services or through grants to institutions and State and local governments.[130]

GAO's reports overshadowed a more speculative CRS analysis that deserves another read today. Meekly titled *The Relationship between Federal Personnel Ceilings and Contracting Out: Policy Background and Current Issues*, the report raised a series of questions that are still open.[131] CRS began the report by criticizing the lack data on the "alleged sub rosa relationship between ceilings and contracting out" but found enough circumstantial evidence to suggest personnel ceilings had increased the number of contract employees.[132] According to CRS, "what becomes most apparent in studying the relationship between personnel ceilings and contracting out is the lack of coordination between these two major areas of Government Personnel. . . . In essence, the Government maintains two systems of Federal employment, operating side by side, with no official coordination."[133]

More to the goal of putting the right people in the right positions for faithfully executing the laws, CRS made an unprecedented recommendation for a hybrid personnel system that considers federal and contract employees as members of a single workforce:

> It is arguable, for example, that if certain personnel records and employment standards are necessary for Federal employees, many of the same requirements should exist for others paid from taxpayer funds, even if technically they are privately employed. Conversely, if some of the employment records and standards maintained for Federal employees are unnecessary to the performance of the public's business or irrelevant to the expenditure, the requirements might be dropped for all personnel.[134]

Congress received the CRS report on August 5, 1980, but never mentioned it in any debate, forum, or hearing, nor did it ever reference the call for a unified personnel system.[135] Nevertheless, the report still stands as one of the earliest statements in favor of strategic workforce planning in government, and deserves a second reading among those who support a more rational system for sorting responsibilities across the dividing line between government and industry.[136]

The most candid assessment of impact in the CRS excerpt from a Senate Governmental Affairs Committee exchange between Sen. David Pryor (D-AR) and a private consultant:

SEN. PRYOR: How do the people in the consulting business respond when the Congress adopts personnel ceilings?

CONSULTANT: Joy.

SEN. PRYOR: Why?

CONSULTANT: Well, because the requirement is not going to get less or go away. The same amount of questions or more are going to be asked and agencies will have to respond. Now if they have fewer people to respond, then they have to get outside help to dig up the answers. So we respond with joy by knowing that, it is going to be a fruitful year.

SEN. PRYOR: There is going to be more business for consultants if we establish a personnel ceiling?

CONSULTANT: Yes.

SEN. PRYOR: Is the consultant business bigger and more powerful than the Federal Government?

CONSULTANT: Well, probably bigger, and yes, I guess I would say more powerful because if you would right now cut off the consulting business, I think the Federal Government would grind to a screeching halt, or at least many of the programs would.[137]

Joy is not a quantifiable measure of impact, of course, but is a powerful indicator of the rate of return of federal government caps, cuts, and freezes. As chapter 3 will suggest, the caps, cuts, and freezes are just one of many pressures on the dividing line between government and industry, but they set the overall frame in which federal departments and agencies must faithfully execute the laws with little room to recruit, manage, oversee, and direct their own employees.

3

Pressures on the Dividing Line

Just as the government and industry worked together on the front lines to help the nation win its independence in 1783, they worked together after the war to bind the young nation together in the years that followed. Federal contractors helped deliver the mail; take the census; build postal roads, bridges, and lighthouses; design new transportation systems; operate warehouses and repair depots; and advise government agencies. "Private contractors are as American as apple pie," one analyst at the conservative CATO Institute concludes, concludes. "Or, to paraphrase Genesis: In the beginning, God created private contractors."[1]

Working together in the public interest, the federal government-industrial complex now employs one out of every fifteen working Americans. The question for this chapter is not whether the total is too big or small, but whether the federal government has the right blend of employees to execute the laws faithfully. As noted below, the federal government cannot create this blend unless it has full authority to choose whichever sources it needs.

Although reasonable people can disagree about how to create a proper blending of government and industry, there are some things the federal government can, should, and must do, and other things that it cannot, should not, and must not do. By setting boundaries between government and industry, the nation avoids at least some of the misplaced influence that might arise at the intersections.

The essence of a proper blending involves its success in meeting the constitutional obligation to execute the laws faithfully toward the public's benefit. As one industry representative argued in 2002, "the true and most important measures of government's size lie in its overall mission, performance and budget, regardless of who is performing the work."[2] At the same time, Congress and the president must either give the federal government sufficient resources to achieve its broad mission or acknowledge what Eisenhower called "the temptation to feel that some spectacular and costly action could become the miraculous solution to all current difficulties."[3]

If there is no room for temptation, there is no room for false accounting, undisclosed campaign cash, and political posturing. Nor is there room for yet another round of bureaucrat or contract bashing, clever cost comparisons, or job guarantees on either side of the government-industrial dividing line.[4] Congress and the president must always remember that the nation should take nothing for granted in the effort. Eisenhower made the argument early in his farewell address:

> A huge increase in newer elements of our defense; development of unrealistic programs to cure every ill in agriculture; a dramatic expansion in basic and applied research—these and many other possibilities, each promising in itself, may be suggested as the only way to the road we wish to travel. But each proposal must be weighed in the light of a broader consideration: the need to maintain balance in and among national programs—balance between the private and the public economy, balance between cost and hoped-for advantage, balance between the clearly necessary and the comfortably desirable, balance between our essential requirements as a nation and the duties imposed by the nation upon the individual, balance between actions of the moment and the national welfare of the future.[5]

Congress and the president cannot create this balance without authority to adjust and discipline the government-industrial complex. They must have the authority to raise the headcount even if doing so violates a cap, cut, or freeze that favors one side or the other. They also must have the authority to move government functions across the government-industrial dividing line without fear. A proper blending is possible only if Congress and the president take care to mix and match the workforce to deliver on the promises they make.

However, Congress and the president cannot embrace this strategic workforce planning if they cannot act strategically.[6] They must also have a clear sense of mission, a point Representative Danny K. Davis (R-IL) made in quoting his mother on just what "right" means in rightsizing government:

> I remember my mother used to tell us that right is right if nobody is right, and wrong is wrong if everybody is wrong. And so, trying to figure out what would be the right size of government it seems to me begs the question, because the first question that has to be answered is what do you view as the role and function of government? What is the purpose? What is the mission? What are you are trying to accomplish? And if we can answer those questions, then it gets easier to decide what the right size would be.[7]

This chapter will examine the time, bureaucratic, and political pressures that often undermine a proper blending of federal, contract, and grant employees.[8] Some of these pressures reflect the natural accidents created by a personnel system created for a workforce that no longer exists and jobs that are no longer needed; other pressures emerge from bureaucratic stagnation, false comparisons of costs and benefits, and persistent attacks on the oversight that might undermine effective blending, and still other pressures involve the inevitable political contests over who gets what, when, and how.

Even though these pressures may create an undue dependence on contract and grant employees to perform functions that should be reserved solely for federal employees, the contract and grant employees who are called over the dividing line still deserve recognition for their shared commitment to the public benefit. Their costs may be excessive, their loyalties divided, and their engagement improper if not illegal, but the federal government cannot honor its promises without their help. The government-industrial complex must be properly blended to ensure the highest benefit, performance, and accountability, but it must always put the faithful execution of the laws first.[9]

An Inventory of Pressures

The federal government cannot faithfully execute the laws without help from contract and grant employees, but neither can it deliver on the promises it makes without the help of its own employees. If the federal government is to do its job, it must hire the right people for the right positions at the highest benefit, performance, and accountability. However, it cannot deploy the right people if it must favor one workforce over another.

There are many reasons to use contract and grant employees to execute the laws faithfully, but convenience is not one of them. In theory and regulation, for example, federal employees should perform inherently governmental functions even if a commercial source is available at lower cost. Also in theory and regulation, contract and grant employees are allowed to perform other functions deemed appropriate for outsourcing.[10] In practice, however, there are three sources of pressure on the dividing line between government and industry—a first that involves time pressures that weaken the federal government's ability to manage its own workforce, a second that reflects bureaucratic pressures that limit the federal government's agility in monitoring its blended workforce, and a third based on political pressures that frustrate action to put the right people in the right jobs.

Time Pressures

Time creates five pressures that favor industry over government in the recruitment and deployment of government-industrial employees: (1) competition for scarce talent, (2) an aging workforce, (3) high promotion speed, (5) inflated performance appraisals, and (5) easy access to the hidden bureaucratic pyramid of contract and grant employees who fill the mid- and lower-level jobs once held by federal employees.

The Trump administration featured many of these pressures in a 2018 budget appendix titled "Strengthening the Federal Workforce."[11] The appendix began by celebrating federal employees as essential to "the smooth functioning of our democracy" before turning to a broad attack on employee pay, retirement benefits, union interference, poor performers, and civil service regulations. "Today's Federal personnel system is a relic of an earlier era," the administration argued. "The competitive personnel system that Civil Service Commissioner Theodore Roosevelt envisioned to elevate the country has fallen into disrepute, criticized from most quarters as a compliance-oriented regime that ill-serves Federal managers, employees, or the Nation at large."[12]

The appendix made the case by mixing soaring rhetoric about the government's "untold selfless employees" with a stinging indictment of its poor performers, union meddlers, bloated retirement plans, and "low-value" work. The mixed messages prompted the *Post*'s Joe Davidson to ask if Trump was joking about strengthening the federal workforce when he signed off on the message. As Davidson reported, the administration's true intent was clear: "Improved hiring procedures, as the administration wants, would strengthen the workforce. But the central thought in Trump's plan to improve an 'increasingly incomprehensible and unmanageable civil service system' is firing feds faster."[13]

His conclusion gained credence over the spring and summer as the Trump administration moved ahead in 2018 with a series of shallow repairs designed more to create a body count of disciplinary actions and employee firings than deep reforms in government systems and leadership. The administration also abandoned its initial interest in counting the federal government's "indirect workforce" in part because it was so difficult to measure.[14]

As this chapter shows, the Trump administration was wise to join good government organizations such as the National Academy of Public Administration, Partnership for Public Service, and Volcker Alliance in calling for civil service reform. However, once past the familiar paen to innovation and comprehensive reform, the appendix moved quickly to budget cuts, poor performers, union interference, and the president's demand for more firings. It was an agenda destined to reduce the number of federal employees, while pushing more work over the government-industrial divide.

Waiting for Arrival

The federal hiring process was designed to select employees on merit, not hidden influence, and has succeeded in doing so for more than a century. However, the system has become so cumbersome that endurance, not merit, is often its core test. Despite decades of promised improvement, the federal hiring process is still complicated, slow, and discouraging. It is little wonder, therefore, that federal departments and agencies might call on contract and grant employees when they need to fill a job quickly.[15]

There are many ways to measure hiring effectiveness, not the least of which is the quality of the workforce it produces. Quality being infinitely subjective, however, the easiest way to track effectiveness is time to hire, shorter being generally better than longer. In theory, applicants should move from application to "onboarding" without delay. In practice, the federal government continues to impose time penalties at every step of the process.[16] Hiring speed increased during the Obama administration, but still trailed private and nonprofit employers in industries such as accounting, aerospace, biotechnology, energy, health, higher education, logistics, telecommunications, and transportation.[17]

The Senate Committee on Homeland Security and Governmental Affairs focused on time to hire when it pressed the new Obama administration to fill most job vacancies in eighty days or sooner:

> Those seeking federal employment have long faced an opaque, lengthy, and unnecessarily complex process that ultimately serves the interests of neither federal agencies nor those seeking to work for them. . . . Weak recruiting, unintelligible job announcements, onerous application requirements, an overly long hiring process, and poor communications with applicants deter potential candidates from applying and cause many of those who do apply to abandon the effort before a hiring decision is made.[18]

The Obama administration deflected the legislation by launching the first of three hiring reforms in May 2010. "I understand the frustration of every applicant who previously has had to wade through the arcane Federal hiring process," Obama's personnel director, John Berry, said of the president's decision to create a plain-language application for most jobs and allow résumés and cover letters in lieu of essay questions. "If qualified applicants want to serve our country through the Federal service, then our application process should facilitate that."[19] The commitment was strong enough to convince Congress to shelve the Senate's bill, but not strong enough to move the federal hiring model from its a "post-and-pray" system to "post-and-pursue."[20]

The administration refused to abandon the effort, however. Indeed, it or-dered a final round of reforms on November 1, 2016, just six days before Trump won the presidency. Although the guidance acknowledged the administration's previous efforts, it offered an unvarnished critique of barriers to effective recruit-ment: one in five hiring actions failed, three in five federal managers did not par-ticipate in recruiting their new employees, and the government's chief human capital officers listed hiring reform ahead of employee engagement and training as their top priority for 2017.[21]

Despite recent congressional hearings with hopeful goals such as "Jobs, Jobs, Jobs: Transforming Federal Hiring" and "Uncle Sam Wants You: Recruitment in the Federal Government," comprehensive reform remains a distant goal. Even the federal government's ongoing overhaul of its sluggish one-stop-shopping USAJobs hiring platform is unlikely to have an impact if its "human-centered design" does not lead to good jobs.

At least for now, USAJobs is more a disappointment than a shining success. As one expert told a Senate roundtable in 2016, "USAJobs has become home to a seething group of confused and angry job seekers and fulfills a main purpose for a limited set of people desperately seeking any kind of employment or those who don't really know what job they seek."[22] Other witnesses showed more con-fidence in the eleven million USAJobs account holders, as did Davidson, but all agreed the system had to change.[23]

It is little wonder that a harried federal manager or supervisor might prefer contract and grant employees to meet urgent needs.[24] "Hiring contractors is much easier, especially when it can be done on a sole-source basis," the RAND Corporation's Bernard D. Rostker explains:

> With money and a contract in hand, managers can give new tasks to an existing contractor without competition. The contractor, unen-cumbered by having to compete for the task or to meet employment standards, can supply a qualified worker in short order, sometimes within hours—though usually at a substantial premium, by some ac-counts as large as 50 percent.[25]

Aging Upward

The federal workforce is aging ever closer to a demographic crisis created by the simple passage of time. In September 2018, there were five federal employees over fifty years of age for every one employee under thirty. Translated from ratios into headcounts, the number of federal employees under thirty held steady between 2001 and 2017 at about 115,000, the number over fifty-five also held steady at about 850,000, the average employee was 47.5, and 30 percent of the workforce was eligible to retire.[26]

This trend confirms what many experts describe as an unavoidable "retirement tsunami" as federal employees move closer to exit. "The rapid shift of the workforce profile is significant and a bit shocking," federal personnel expert Jeff Neal writes. "This rapid demographic shift is unlike what we have seen in the past and it is safe to say no one knows when current employees will retire. Societal trends are moving in the direction of longer careers, both for lifestyle and economic reasons. If this continues, we are likely to see a retirement bubble at some point in the future."[27]

The exact timing of the retirement wave is unknown, but its effects are predictable. First, the federal retirement wave is expected to create a "brain drain" as the government's intellectual capital and institutional memory decline. These assets are not easily created through the federal government's weak career development systems. Moreover, much of the nation's intellectual capital has been shaped by repeated budget and hiring freezes that teach younger employees how government does not work. The best way to secure these assets has often been through contract and grant employees who often acquired their skills inside the corridors of government.[28]

Second, the retirement wave will also likely increase employee shortages at the middle levels of government where so many contract and grant employees work. Service contract employees rarely reach the top of the federal hierarchy but often perform tasks that would have been reserved for federal employees in the past. Absent a steady pipeline of committed employees, federal managers and supervisors have little choice but to call for help. The contract and grant employees who fill the gaps are often highly qualified for the work, but they cannot take the higher-level posts without crossing the dividing line. They also create dependency that managers and supervisors cannot easily break.

At the same time, the wave could create the opportunity to strengthen the career paths that are essential for recruiting the next generation of federal employees. According to the federal government's own personnel surveys, younger and older federal employees share the same desire for constructive performance conversations, career development and training, work-life balance, an inclusive work environment, involvement in decisions, and open communication, but younger employees are less likely to believe their talents are well used in the workplace, know how their work relates to their organization's goals and priorities, say their work gives them a sense of accomplishment, or know what is expected of them.[29]

Older employees did not discourage their younger colleagues on purpose, but they may have created the sense that there is no room at the top nonetheless. Indeed, even though older employees are obviously closer to retirement, younger employees say they are more likely to leave their jobs for other government work or another sector. Higher job and pay satisfaction would reduce these intentions, as would greater fairness, career development, and work-life balance. However, the federal government cannot create these incentives without the resources and career opportunities that are now pinned down by older federal employees.

If the federal government does not accelerate the wave to full impact by giving its older employees incentives to leave, it may lose the younger employees who will eventually lead the federal workforce. Yet, even if it does accelerate the wave through incentives such as voluntary buyouts and phased retirement, the younger employees may leave anyway.[30]

Speeding toward Promotion

Time on the job drives advancement for most federal employees through nearly automatic promotions up the formal career ladder. Departments and agencies can reduce promotion speed during funding crises, but the career ladder guarantees promotions across the federal government's ten-step pay system and up its fifteen-grade classification ladder. Federal employees can also rise through reclassification into higher-level jobs or promotions into vacancies created as other employees move up ahead of them.

Promotions also depend on performance. Much as federal employees themselves question the relationship, there is at least some evidence to suggest a link between annual performance appraisals and advancement. According to a recent study of federal personnel records between 1988 and 2003, white-collar employees who received an "outstanding" performance rating during the period were half again as likely to receive promotions than employees who received a "fully successful" rating.[31] Because employees tend to receive the same ratings from year to year, high performers advance faster than their fully successful peers over the long term.

Education and the experience that goes with it also matter to promotion speed—educational advancement is almost always required for moving up from lower-level support jobs into higher-level technical positions. Indeed, many higher-level jobs require a college degree or more. Age and federal support give current employees the opportunities to gain more education, as does the ongoing recruitment of new employees.

Employment caps, cuts, and freezes also increase promotion speed, as do the associated retention wars with contract firms and grant agencies. As former federal personnel executive Henry Romero recently recalled, the movement of talented employees to contract and grant posts increased promotion speed as a retention strategy, much of the speeding having come from supervisors who use promotions as a retention strategy and back-door bonus system:

This pressure comes not only from employees but from management as well. Supervisors use constant upgrades as a retention strategy, especially for employees in technical and hard-to-fill positions. Three years of pay freezes, increased oversight of awards programs and elimination of promotion opportunities due to senior people who have delayed retirement, means that the only avenue for getting a raise (other than a periodic step increase) is to get your position reclassified to a higher grade, regardless of whether the job has changed and thus deserves a higher grade.[32]

Faster promotions may be the logical response to hiring cuts, caps, and freezes, but contribute to the erosion of accountability and the confusing chain of command that has resulted in so many government breakdowns since 2001.[33] It also gives managers and supervisors a reason to favor contract and grant employees as a lower-cost, easier-to-manage alternative to federal employees.

All above Average

The federal government's annual performance appraisal system creates temporal pressure on the dividing line in two ways. First, it fuels the promotion speed that moves federal employees ever upward. Second, it contributes to the anti-government portrait of federal employees as overpaid, poorly supervised, and immune to discipline.

In theory, an accurate employee appraisal system should create a measureable "line of sight" between individual performance and organizational performance.[34] In practice, the federal government's line of sight has been distorted by years of grade inflation. Between 1986 and 2013, for example, the number of employees who were rated "outstanding" rose from just 21 percent to 52 percent, while the number of employees rated "fully exceeds satisfactory" and "satisfactory" dropped from 50 percent to 36 percent and 20 percent to 12 percent respectively.[35]

This appraisal inflation eventually led GAO to warn federal managers to remind employees that a fully successful rating is not average or ordinary, but rather a "high bar" to be rewarded and valued as a significant level of accomplishment.[36] It is always possible that federal employees are almost all above average, but even the employees have their doubts about the system. In the 2017 federal employee survey, just 41 percent of employees said awards depended on how well employees performed their jobs, 34 percent of federal employees said differences in performance with their work units were recognized in a meaningful way, and 29 percent said steps were taken to deal with a poor performer who cannot or will not improve.[37]

This does mean federal employees are free from disciplinary action. Contrary to the myth of the unaccountable civil servant, the federal government laid off or discharged about 6 percent of its employees in 2017. Although the private sector laid off or discharged more than 15 percent of its employees the same year, the rate varied from layoff-discharge rate exceeded 15 percent the same year, it varied from a high of 47 percent in arts and entertainment to a low of 8 percent in education and health services. The question is not whether federal employees are impossible to fire—after all, almost 160,000 lost their jobs in 2017—but whether they are essential to keep in good economic times and bad.[38]

The more serious threat to credibility exists in the length of the disciplinary process. According to GAO, the process can take 80–200 days of formal monitoring just to reach the intention to dismiss, another 50–110 days to document an employee's performance and give frequent feedback, and 40–60 days more to issue a notice of proposed dismissal.[39] Even this timeline is uncertain, given the potential for further delay if an employee requests an accommodation, files a grievance, or registers an equal-opportunity complaint. As noted earlier, the Trump administration focused on this disciplinary tangle in its February 2018 management agenda and followed through in May with an executive order shortening the time employees have to both respond to a disciplinary notice and demonstrate improvement, while reminding managers that probationary periods provide a perfect chance to remove poor performers early.[40]

The challenge in future reform is to balance the demand for accountability with protection against the arbitrary action and political, racial, and sexual harassment that continues to affect federal performance.[41] At the same time, federal employees must also face sure consequences for poor performance. "The civil service needs to find a way to do an honorable discharge," one federal human capital officer told the nonpartisan Partnership for Public Service in 2014. "More than hiring reform, we need firing reform. In that reform you need to one, address poor performers and two, address skills that become outdated from otherwise good performers. There are just simply way too many hoops."[42]

The inflation is unlikely to abate until the federal government learns how to impose grade limits using curves and quotas, both of which are forbidden under existing personnel regulations. Even if such tools could survive congressional and judicial scrutiny, they could cost more in employee dissatisfaction, lost productivity, and high-risk turnover than they could ever gain in accountability and fiscal savings. The same might be said of the president's demand for a faster firing process. Much as he celebrated the 1,500 Veterans Affairs employees fired under the 2017 Veterans Affairs Accountability and Whistleblower Protection Act, the total was in line with recent history.[43]

If performance is the goal, the Defense Department may yet accomplish much greater effects and increased productivity by streamlining the annual performance process with its ongoing "New Beginnings" initiative. However, the success is unlikely to come from the department's decision to drop the "exceeds fully satisfactory" categories, which will likely migrate upward to little effect. Rather, the salutary effects will likely come from the shift from one performance discussion per year to three, and new links between the ratings, promotions, and automatic increases.[44]

The Hidden Pyramid

Time worked its will on the basic shape of the federal hierarchy as generation after generation of federal, contract, and grant employees moved through the government-industrial complex over the decades. Just before World War II, for example, the federal structure resembled Max Weber's bureaucratic pyramid: highly specialized, rule-bound employees topped by a small number of presidential appointees and senior-level career executives and supported by a rapidly expanding federal mission.

In the 1950s, for example, more than half of federal employees worked at the bottom of government as typists, couriers, sorters, filers, and counters. By 2010, more than half worked in the higher levels as analysts, economists, engineers, planners, and designers. Many of the lower-level jobs went the way of the typewriter, but some of the routine tasks still exist and are delegated to service contract employees.

As the distribution of federal employees changed, so did the basic distribution of federal employees.[45] In 1960, for example, the hierarchy still resembled a traditional bureaucratic pyramid—more federal employees worked at the bottom of the hierarchy than the middle or top, while contract and grant employees delivered their products and services to government from the outside.

By 1980, the federal hierarchy resembled a four-sided trapezoid—more federal employees still worked at the bottom of the hierarchy than the middle or top, but the number of federal employees at the professional and technical levels of the hierarchy was growing rapidly, as was the number of contract and grant employees who delivered their products and services to the government from the inside.

By 2000, the federal hierarchy resembled a pentagon—more employees worked at the middle and top of the hierarchy than at the bottom. The number of federal professional and administrative employees rose steadily from 31 percent of the workforce in 1985 to 61 percent in 1985. The number of clerical employees dropped a third over the decade, while the number of blue-collar employees fell by a quarter.[46]

By 2030, the federal hierarchy is almost certain to look like an ellipse, with far more federal employees at the middle levels and even more federal supervisors, managers, and executives at all levels. Concealed behind the changing shape of the federal bureaucracy, this hidden pyramid will hold the uncounted contract and grant employees that Dilulio has called "de facto feds" and "administrative proxies."[47]

Public administration scholar Donald Kettl tracks this change using the average employee grade, or level, which has risen from 6.7 on a scale from 1–15 in 1960 to 10.3 in 2014. Kettl rightly attributed the rise to a growing federal mission and the associated dependence on contract and grant employees:

> The big story overall is that federal employment has hovered around two million workers, but spending, after inflation, has risen sharply. The same number of federal employees is leveraging an ever-growing amount of money. . . . This is a direct result of the federal government's increasing use of proxies, as more of its work was done outside the federal government—and by the accelerating underinvestment in the people needed to do the work.[48]

This change is an illusion of a sorts. The federal hierarchy looks like it is rising largely because contract and grant employees are filling positions that are no longer counted within the civil-service pyramid. The couriers and stenographers may be gone, but the data suggest that the federal government still employs plenty of cafeteria workers, cartographers, groundskeepers, mechanics, security guards, and statisticians under contract. These employees may not carry federal government identification cards, but they help the federal government execute the laws far nonetheless. They are just hidden from view in contract firms and grant agencies.

The federal government may not know precisely how many employees work in this hidden pyramid, but it does know that millions of employees show up for work every day to do work once performed by federal employees. The decision to separate these employees from the federal headcount perpetuates the conceit that government can do more with less ad infinitum, and encourages departments and agencies to create their own systems for managing the workload. As the National Academy of Public Administration has concluded, the absence of reform has produced chaos:

> Among its many problems, the current civil service system is no longer a system. It is mired in often-arcane processes set up after World War II, in the days before the Internet, interstate highways, or an interconnected global economy. Pursuit of those processes, many now largely

obsolete, has become an end in itself, and compliance with them has
tended to come at the expense of the missions they were supposed to
support. As a result, the federal civil service system has become a non-
system: agencies that have been able to break free from the constraints
of the outmoded regulations and procedures have done so, with the in-
dulgence of their congressional committees.[49]

The hidden pyramid is the logical product of the caps, cuts, and freezes discussed
in chapter 2. As a team of senior federal employees wrote at the end of the
Clinton downsizing, the bottom of the federal hierarchy may be invisible, but it
raises questions about potential self-dealing nonetheless:

> First, locating contractors in the same government office with Federal
> employees means the contractors have access to information about
> the government that will give them an advantage in future contracting
> solicitations. Second, there is a question of contractors' involvement
> in core and essential functions of the Federal government where the
> government's own interests should be represented. When contractors
> representing their own private firms play important roles in key
> functions, such as strategic planning and other areas of management
> decision making, it is difficult to believe that the government's own in-
> terest is being fully represented.[50]

The federal government may not know how many employees work in this
hidden pyramid, but it does know that there are millions of employees who
show up for work every day, paid or unpaid, to do work once performed by federal employees. Some of this work disappeared as new technologies took over,
but some shifted to service contract and grant employees.

Bureaucratic Pressures

The federal government's bureaucratic routines create five pressures that
can favor contract and grant employees over their federal peers in faithfully
executing the laws: (1) skill gaps in mission-critical occupations, (2) barriers to
federal employee engagement, (3) disagreements on how much federal and private employees cost, (4) weakened oversight, and (5) the sluggish presidential
appointments process.

Hollowing Out

The federal government depends on its blended workforce to cover an increasingly complex agenda that demands deep expertise in highly competitive

fields. Although many mission-critical jobs can be filled by contract and grant employees, some positions are deemed to be so intimately related to the public interest that the work must be reserved solely for federal personnel. There is some dispute about scientific and technological skill gaps across the US economy writ large, but little doubt that the federal government has been losing skills in high-risk occupations such as auditing, cybersecurity, economic analysis, telecommunications, project planning, and the STEM fields of science, technology, engineering, and mathematics.[51]

The gaps are the logical result of the other pressures discussed in this chapter, including the sluggish hiring process and aging effects discussed above, and sui generis disruptions such as the National Security Administration's recent "NSA-21" reorganization and the Department of State turmoil that have been blamed for significant employee turnover.[52] The causes may vary by occupation and agency, but the result is simple: too many skilled employees are leaving, too many senior employees are standing pat, and not enough talented replacements are joining the workforce.[53] Lacking an effective planning process that puts mission at the top of the federal government's internal recruitment and retention agenda, the hollowing produces a natural, but urgent incentive to fill the gaps with contract and grant employees. Mission must come first.

The skill gap has been more than a quarter-century in the making. Indeed, GAO was actually late to the crisis when it added the gap to its high-risk list in 2001.[54] According to GAO, the cascade of agency-by-agency personnel problems finally crossed the threshold from one-off instances to government-wide crisis: "The combined effect of these challenges serves to place at risk the ability of agencies to efficiently, economically, and effectively accomplish their missions, manage critical programs, and adequately serve the American people both now and in the future."[55]

GAO's decision to list the skill gaps as a government-wide risk confirmed what former Federal Reserve Board chairman Paul A. Volcker and his first National Commission on the Public Service called a "quiet crisis" in 1988. According to Volcker's preface to the commission's final report, the crisis was easy to pinpoint at the intersection of workforce supply and demand:

> Simply put, too many of the best of the nation's senior executives are ready to leave government, and not enough of its most talented young people are willing to join. This erosion in the attractiveness of public service at all levels—most specifically in the federal civil service— undermines the ability of government to respond effectively to the needs and aspirations of the American people, and ultimately damages the democratic process itself.[56]

Even under pressure from a second Volcker Commission in 2003 and rising congressional concerns, most departments and agencies barely passed the planning stage by 2017.[57] Although GAO acknowledged OPM's commitment to action, it also noted that skill gaps were contributing causes to fifteen of the thirty-four other items on its high-risk list: "Regardless of whether the shortfalls are in such government-wide occupations as cybersecurity and acquisitions, or in agency-specific occupations such as nurses at the Veterans Health Administration, skills gaps impede the federal government from cost-effectively serving the public and achieving results."[58] The collateral damage is almost certain to increase as federal retirements increase in coming years.

The cybersecurity gap is a case in point. Cybersecurity professionals are difficult to hire under the best of circumstances, but the federal government's circumstances are far from the best.[59] According to recent studies of the cybersecurity skill gap, the federal government is saddled with a low-speed, uncertainty-plagued, salary-capped recruiting system in a high-speed, volatile market of budding wars, salary competitions, and on-the-spot hiring.

The result is an inevitable increase in use of contract employees. As RAND noted in its 2014 report, *H4CKER5 WANTED*, the federal government has little choice but to use contract employees to fill the gap even at much higher cost: "Over the last 20 or more years, the government has finessed the problem of recruiting really skilled individuals by outsourcing the work they would have done to private contractors. The outsourcers can then pay market prices to deliver from qualified individuals services otherwise unavailable from direct employees."[60]

The Office of the Director of National Intelligence acknowledged the higher costs in response to the *Washington Post*'s 2010 "Top Secret America" series cited earlier in this book:

> The growth in contractors was a direct response to an urgent need for unique expertise post-9/11. The surge in contractors allowed the IC [Intelligence Community] to fill the need for seasoned analysts and collectors while rebuilding the permanent, civilian workforce. It also allowed agencies to meet required skills, such as foreign languages, computer science, and electrical engineering.[61]
>
> It is true that core contract personnel are, on average, more expensive than their government counterparts. However, in some cases, contractor personnel are less costly, especially if the work is short-term in nature, easily available commercially, or requires unique expertise for immediate needs. Overall, core contractors enable the Intelligence Community to rapidly expand to meet short-term mission needs or

fulfill non-recurring or temporary assignments, and then shrink or shift resources as the threat environment changes.[62]

The federal government has taken steps to address the gap, including the use of expedited hiring authorities for mission-critical jobs. In January 2018, for example, the Department of Veterans Affairs launched accelerated searches in fifteen occupations that had produced what it called a "severe shortage of candidates." The list reflected gaps in high-tech posts such as biomedical equipment support, crisis line specialists, information technologists, and histopathology technicians, but also included more mundane occupations as boiler plant operators, personnel security specialists, police officers, and utility system operators.[63]

As the list suggests, the gaps appear to be expanding well beyond the familiar STEM inventory, which merely confirms the rising pressure on the dividing line. "If the 'cool jobs' are given to contractors, then extant and even prospective federal employees will have that much less motivation to stay or to join the federal government to work on cyber problems," RAND concludes. "This then reduces the quality of the federal labor pool, which then reinforces the initial tendency to assign the 'cool jobs' to contractors."[64]

The Engagement Gap

Federal employees are often pilloried as overpaid security cravers, while private employees are not only advertised as less expensive, but harder working on an hour-to-hour and even month-to-month basis.[65] Although this critique is anchored in the flawed cost data discussed later in this chapter, it also reflects the federal government's own employee viewpoint surveys.[66] Federal employees may come to work each day motivated by the chance to make a difference for their country, but they work in organizations plagued by political and fiscal uncertainty, appointee turnover, media scrutiny, antiquated technologies, and public distrust.[67]

The 2017 Federal Employee Viewpoint Survey (FEVS) offers ample evidence of threats to engagement. Although OPM celebrated the survey results as proof that departments and agencies were "empowering employees" and "inspiring change," the 485,000 federal employees who completed the web-based survey expressed doubts about both claims.[68] Despite positive movement in sixty-one of the eighty-four survey questions and a 2 percent gain in OPM's employee engagement index, majorities of federal employees still gave their work units poor grades on recruitment, discipline, rewards, and innovation. The responses were moving ever so slightly in the right direction but still fit the same pattern that led the *Washington Post* to headline its story on the 2015

FEVS, "Good News: Federal Worker Morale Has Finally Bottomed Out. Bad News: It's Still Terrible."[69]

Start with the FEVS questions about empowering employees. According to the 2017 survey, less than half of respondents were satisfied with the information they received from management (48 percent), had sufficient resources to do their jobs (47 percent), felt personally empowered with respect to work processes (45 percent), believed their organization recruited people with the right skills (43 percent), worked in units where employee performance was recognized in a meaningful way (34 percent), thought their work units took steps to deal with poor performers who could not or would not improve (29), and said pay raises depended on how well employees do their jobs (22 percent).

Turn next to the FEVS questions about inspiring change. According to the 2017 survey, less than half of respondents said they were recognized for providing high-quality products and services (48 percent), acknowledged for doing a good job (48 percent), satisfied with the policies and practices of their senior leaders (42 percent), worked for leaders who generated high levels of motivation and commitment (41 percent), were rewarded for their creativity and innovation (38 percent), believed they had the opportunity to get a better job in their organization (36 percent), and thought promotions were based on merit (32 percent).

Despite their concerns, the respondents were generally positive about their own performance on the job. Substantial majorities said they were ready to put in the extra effort to get the job done (92 percent), were held accountable for results (82 percent), were judged fairly on performance (70 percent), had a sense of personal accomplishment at work (72 percent), were satisfied with their jobs (66 percent), would recommend their organization as a good place to work (64 percent), and were encouraged to come up with new and better ways of doing things (58 percent). In a sentence, federal employees believe they create impact everyday but that they must do so against the odds.

These negatives were echoed in a recent Vanderbilt University survey of more than 3,500 federal executives. Although a majority of executives said they would recommend a career in public service to young Americans, 39 percent said that a poorly skilled workforce was a significant obstacle to fulfilling their agency's core mission, 42 percent said their agencies were unable to recruit the best employees, and 70 percent said that under-performing employees are rarely or never reassigned or dismissed.[70]

There is little research on how these attitudes affect government performance, in part because the US Bureau of Labor Statistics stopped measuring federal employee productivity in the 1990s.[71] However, there is some evidence that suggests employee engagement affects the decision to retire, which can contribute to hollowing out. According to a recent analysis of employee attitudes, the effect may be modest, but any delay in a mission-critical retirement is a small victory: "Although direct supervisors do not seem to play a significant role in the retirement decision, their efforts to ensure that older employees are priorities may pay off. Offering older employees ways to improve their skills—training workshops and seminars, for example—could keep them satisfied enough to remain on the job for a bit longer."[72]

According to the Partnership for Public Service, there is also significant evidence that private-sector employees were more positive than federal employees on many of the 2017 FEVs questions.[73] According to the Partnership's side-by-side comparison of the two workforces, federal employees were slightly more satisfied with their pay (57 percent versus 55 percent) and much more likely to say they were willing to put in the extra work to get a job done (95 percent versus 83 percent). At the same time, they trailed their private-sector peers by 14 percentage points or more on 10 other questions:

1. I can disclose a suspected violation of any law, rule or regulation without fear of reprisal: -14 percent
2. My supervisor provides me with constructive suggestions to improve my job performance: -14
3. I have trust and confidence in my supervisor: -15 percent
4. My training needs are assessed: −18 percent
5. I feel encouraged to come up with new and better ways of doing things: −18 percent
6. Employees are recognized for providing high quality products and services: -19 percent
7. My talents are used well in the workplace: −20 percent
8. Awards in my work unit depend on how well employees perform their jobs: −23 percent
9. I have sufficient resources (for example, people, materials, budget) to get the job done: −24 percent
10. I believe the results of this survey will be used to make my agency a better place to work: −31 percent

Tempting though it might be to use these findings to favor private-sector employees at the government-industrial divide, it impossible to know how contract and grant employees view their jobs as part of the much larger workforce represented in the Partnership for Public Service comparisons. After all, contract and grant employees often face the same uncertainty, political intrigue, media scrutiny, and public distrust as their federal peers. Nevertheless, the notion that work is easier and employees more manageable on the industry side of the government-industrial complex creates temptations and opportunities to move jobs to a putatively more responsive side of the labor market.

Compensation versus Cost

Contract and grant employees are often advertised as a low-cost alternative to federal employees, but the data suggest quite the opposite. Federal employees may seem more expensive than contract and grant employees on average, but may be much less expensive than contract employees when compared occupation-by-occupation.[74]

POGO made this case in its 2011 report, *Bad Business: Billions of Taxpayer Dollars Wasted on Hiring Contractors.* The research was designed to challenge the long-standing assumption that the federal government saves money when it hires contract employees in lieu of federal employees. According to POGO's comparison of thirty-five occupations such as auditor, groundskeeper, statistician, and technical writer, the assumption was based on a false equivalency. POGO's data showed that federal employees had higher compensation in twenty-six of the thirty-five occupations but that private sector employees cost more than federal workers in thirty-three.[75]

The explanation is in billing rates, not paychecks: Contract employees are less expensive until indirect costs such as supplies, equipment, materials, and other costs of doing business enter the equation. Add this overhead to the totals, and contract employees can cost two times as much as federal employees. If the question is how to put the right employees in the right jobs for the highest benefit, federal employees appear to be the better choice:

> POGO's findings confirm the basic premise that government employees are *compensated* at a higher rate than private sector employees. However, in the 35 occupational classifications and 550 specific jobs POGO analyzed, reliance on contractor employees costs significantly more than having federal employees provide similar services. As a result, taxpayers are left paying the additional costs associated with corporate management, overhead, and profits that the government has no need to incur.[76]

The confidence in contracting out was not shaken. To the contrary, the contract lobby poured fire on the report, including one point-by-point rebuttal from the technical and professional services industry. The report was "a smear on industry," the Professional Services Council said, and built on the "irrelevance of averages."

> POGO's conclusions are based on data purporting to show that "on average" contractors are more expensive than government performance of the same or similar work. Yet as a decision-making tool, averaging has little value or relevance since it offers no perspective or insight. Even if one assumes the baseline data is complete and accurate, all the

POGO report shows is that sometimes contracting is more expensive than government performance and sometimes not. It does nothing to aid in the government's determination of where and how best to perform a given requirement.[77]

Ironically, the anti-averaging argument strikes at the traditional comparisons of government and private wages. Writing for the libertarian Cato Institute in September 2017, Chris Edwards reported that federal employees averaged $88,809 in wages during 2016, compared with private-sector employees at $59,458, and that federal employees had also received an additional $38,450 in benefits, compared with private-sector employees at $11,306.

Edwards data do show important differences across the nation's many workforces but are often misused to claim that federal employees are overpaid compared to other employees in the same jobs that demand the same education, experience, and pressure. Although Edwards sees the hidden impact of steady promotion, grade inflation, and job security on federal pay, he also acknowledges that "federal pay should be reasonable, and we need competent people in federal jobs."[78]

These sector-to-sector comparisons face many of the same criticisms the contract industry made against the POGO report. According to CBO's 2017 analysis of federal pay and compensation between 2011 and 2015, federal employees with no more than a high school diploma earned 21 percent more per hour on average than private-sector employees with the same amount of education, while employees with a bachelor's degree earned about the same wage per hour and federal employees with a doctorate or professional degree earned 23 percent less on average.[79]

The contract industry also uses in its claim that job competitions between federal and contract employees could save between 10 and 40 percent in total cost.[80] The competitions were used by the George W. Bush administration to test its theory that any federal job that could be found in the Yellow Pages phone directory can be done for less by a contract employee.[81] Although federal employees won a significant majority of the Bush-era competitions, the contract lobby continues to use the percentages to argue that the competitions produce significant savings regardless of who wins.[82]

Monitoring Government

The federal government's internal management and oversight units are essential for policing the boundaries between government and industry. They also make and enforce the rules governing the blended workforce, and are responsible for promoting economy and efficiency in the administrative process. They are generally invisible until they are called to investigate a national scandal, enforce new management protocols, or check a president who is testing the limits of executive authority. They can be a source of delay during fast-moving events and are rarely popular within their own departments and agencies, but are generally given the resources and freedom to do their jobs and are occasionally applauded for their work.[83]

The Clinton administration was an exception to this embrace, though the Trump administration may soon launch its own attack as the number of independent investigations rise. Convinced that federal management and oversight offices stifled creativity and innovation at excessive cost, the Clinton staff promised to focus its budget and personnel cuts in what it called "the structures of over-control and micromanagement that now bind the federal government," meaning federal supervisors, headquarters staff, personnel specialists, budget analysts, procurement specialists, accountants, and auditors.[84]

The reinventors targeted the management and oversight units at every step of the downsizing. One former reinventor remembers calling these units "forces of micromanagement and distrust," while estimating that one out of three federal employees had the job of interfering with the other two. Another former reinventor continues to call these units part of the "fear industry" of oversight agencies, watchdog groups, and even members of Congress that relies on "criticism and attacks to beat down employees or managers, and scare them into shape."[85]

The reinventors had a long list of targets, but focused most heavily on the Offices of Inspector General (OIGs). Congress created the first OIG in 1976 to unify the scattered audit and investigatory functions within the Department of Health, Education, and had created forty-two by the time Clinton entered office. The OIGs used their broad investigatory authority to build impressive totals in what they called "funds put to better use," but also earned a reputation for padding their statistics with small-scale, "gotcha" investigations. "The OIGs are not doing a bad job," I wrote in 1992, "but they may be doing the wrong job."[86]

The reinventing campaign was far less generous:

> When we blame the people and impose more controls, we make the systems worse. Over the past 15 years, for example, Congress has created within each agency an independent office of the inspector general. The idea was to root out fraud, waste, and abuse. The inspectors general have certainly uncovered important problems. But as we learned in conversation after conversation, they have so intimidated federal employees that many are now afraid to deviate even slightly from standard operating procedure.[87]

The reinventing government campaign never published statistics on its attack, but the yearly OIG budget requests confirm the general downsizing during the reinventing. Having activated its own "fear industry" against the OIGs and other control offices, the Clinton administration may have encouraged future administrations to continue the campaign.[88]

The management and oversight offices have recovered somewhat since the campaign ended, but they are still fighting to regain full capacity. As acquisition scholars Steven Schooner and Daniel Greenspan wrote in 2008, the effort "not only left the government woefully understaffed to manage its omnipresent cadre of service contract firms, but also—through an absence of succession planning manifested by more than a decade of cuts and hiring freezes—ensured that fixing the damage could not feasibly be achieved in the foreseeable future."[89] Recent surveys by the Association of Government Accountants suggest that the OIGs were still struggling to regain headcount two decades after the first wave of the Clinton downsizing, and were particularly concerned about the skills gaps in their auditing and investigatory staffs caused by the sluggish hiring process.[90]

Nasty, Brutish, and Not at All Short

Presidential confirmation delays appear to create a surge in industry employees as vacancies cascade down the chain of command. According to appointments expert Anne Joseph O'Connell, the top jobs in government are vacant 15 to 25 percent of the time, creating uncertainty down the chain of command.[91] Although second- and third-tier presidential appointees fill some high-level vacancies, career members of the Senior Executive Service are the default appointees. As such, these career officers are the key policymakers in government.[92]

Turnover after elections is not the only source of vacancies, however. A surprisingly high percentage of nominations are either withdrawn, rejected, or simply set aside once they reach the Senate. According to O'Connell, one in five of the executive nominations sent to the Senate between 1981 and 2017 were withdrawn or rejected, including 20 percent of nominations for White House positions at agencies such as the Office of Management and Budget (OMB), 20 percent of nominations for executive branch agencies such as the Environmental Protection Agency, 15 percent of nominations for cabinet secretaries, and 26 percent of nominations for Inspectors General.[93] O'Connell's analysis shows that 96 percent of agency nominations failed in 1981, compared with 72 percent in 2016.

These long vacancies not only break the president's chain of command, but can elevate senior executives and their assistants ever higher to fill and support empty positions in an acting capacity. The vacancies also confirm the continued damage created by a process that G. Calvin Mackenzie described in 2001 as "nasty and brutish without being short":

The nation's presidential appointments process is a national disgrace: It encourages bullies and emboldens demagogues, silences the voices of responsibility, and nourishes the lowest forms of partisan combat. It uses innocent citizens as pawns in politicians' petty games and stains the reputations of good people. It routinely violates fundamental democratic principles, undermines the quality and consistency of public management, and breaches simple decency.[94]

O'Connell measures the disgrace today by average number of days between nomination and confirmation of the president's top officers. According to her data, the interval rose from 60 days under Reagan to 122 days under Obama, and is well on pace to a higher mark as Trump struggled to complete his first class of Senate-confirmed officers in 2018.[95]

These intervals only cover the post-nomination process, however. As such, they do not count the extended delays between the president's selection and the formal nomination. Once identified, each advise-and-consent nominee, White House aide, and other high-level officers must enter the executive-branch screening and ethics process, including forms for every facet of their lives, personal, financial, and professional.

They must complete a national security form that forces them to look back over the years and list up to five addresses where they lived and a neighbor's name for each one, up to five jobs and their supervisor's name for each one, foreign countries that they have visited and the purpose of the trip, the names of at least three people who can speak to their character, and all their relatives and their places of both. They must also answer some of the most convoluted, logic-defying questions in investigatory memory, including whether anyone, fairly or unfairly, overtly or covertly, will oppose their nomination.

They must also answer dozens of questions that explore the intimate details of their personal lives, including queries about drug use, illegal employees, mental health counseling, and variations whether anyone, fairly or unfairly, covertly or overtly will oppose their nomination.[96]

Finally, as the Trump administration's Senate-confirmed nominees quickly discovered, potential nominees must also fill out a detailed financial disclosure form and offer cures for their financial conflicts. This time-consuming process is confidential and hidden from public view, which means that the amount of time from saying "yes" to the president to formal nomination cannot be tracked.

It is little wonder that presidential appointments expert Terry Sullivan has called this "murky fen" of forms, entanglements, and "gotcha" politics a "Fabulous Formless Darkness" that the White House itself may not fully understand.[97]

Political Pressures

Despite intense demographic and bureaucratic pressures, five political pressures create even greater incentive to call contract and grant employees across the dividing line and thus weaken the government's ability to make a thoughtful "who-does-what" choice: (1) the thickening of the leadership hierarchy, (2) the need to protect government achievements and fix breakdowns, (3) public anger toward government, (4) high levels of political polarization, and (5) cabal, intrigue, and corruption.

Thickening Government

The slow but steady thickening of the federal hierarchy also creates pressures on the government-industrial divide as departments and agencies struggle to monitor performance through dense chains of command. Even as thickening pulls federal employees upward with promises of new responsibilities and higher grades, it reduces oversight of the unwarranted influence that may produce unjustified outsourcing. As such, thickening is both a cause and a symptom of the hollowing discussed above.

The addition of new layers of leaders and leaders per layer is easiest to identify and count in the cabinet departments. John F. Kennedy inherited seven cabinet departments from Eisenhower in 1961, while Donald Trump inherited fifteen from Obama. In turn, Kennedy's departments had seventeen layers from top to bottom, while Trump's departments had seventy-one. In turn a final time, Kennedy's federal phonebook listed 451 political or career occupants at the top of government, while Trump's first phonebook listed 3,265.[98] From 1961 to 2017, the number of layers grew 318 percent, while the number of leaders per layers grew 624 percent.

This thickening starts at the very top of government in the five leadership compartments headed by Senate-confirmed presidential appointees: (I) secretaries, (II) deputy secretaries, (III) undersecretaries, (IV) assistant secretaries, and (V) administrators. About 300 of these positions are subject to Senate confirmation, another 400 are filled through presidential appointments of noncareer members of the Senior Executive Service, 1,000 are occupied by lower-level presidential appointees who serve at the will of the president, and the rest work their way into the positions as career members of the Senior Executive Service or high-level federal employees. Congress reduced the number of presidential appointments subject to Senate confirmation in 2011, but has shown little interest in ways to improve the flow of information up and down the chain of command.[99]

The evidence of increased thickening comes from this author's inventory of the number of layers (titles) and leaders (titleholders) between 1960 and 2016. The inventories are based on a careful coding of the federal telephone books at six-year intervals.[100] The directories contain the titles, names, addresses, and phone numbers of all senior appointees in the federal government's departments and agencies, but the thickening is particularly troublesome at the very top of the fifteen cabinet departments.

The thickening occurred in every cabinet department, but large, older departments with broad missions such as Defense and Treasury had more layers and leaders in 2016, while small, young departments such as Commerce and Labor had fewer. However, regardless of this variation, the thickening continued across the fifteen cabinet departments. Table 3.1 shows the remarkable variety of titles open for occupancy across the entire cabinet in 2016, while Table 3.2 shows the rising number of layers and leaders at four points in recent history.

Some of the titles may challenge credulity, but the March 2016 federal phonebook included all of them—an Associate Principal Deputy Assistant Secretary for Regulatory and Policy Affairs at Energy, Associate Assistant Deputy Secretary for Innovation and Improvement at Education, Principal Deputy Associate Attorney General and a Principal Deputy Assistant Attorney General at Justice, and Associate Deputy Assistant Secretaries for Logistics and Supply Chain Management, Human Resource Systems and Analytics, and Acquisition and Logistics at Veterans Affairs. Past patterns suggest that these relatively new titles will spread to other departments as lower-level officers move up to match titles with their peers.[101]

Even though the total number of leaders is often described as being an insignificant fraction of total federal employment, it creates a significant percentage of the layers between the top and bottom of federal departments and agencies.[102] In 2002, for example, veterans hospital nurses reported upward through nine formal layers of command, including five at the Veterans Affairs Department's Vermont Avenue headquarters, while air traffic controllers reported upward through twelve, including six at the Federal Aviation Administration's headquarters on Independence Avenue in Washington.[103]

The number of layers includes more than managers, supervisors, and Senate-confirmed appointees, however. Once regional, district, and local layers of gatekeepers such as chiefs of staff are counted, Veterans hospital nurses reported upward through eighteen formal and informal layers, including nine in Washington, while air traffic controllers and park rangers reported through nineteen.[104]

Trump seemed to recognize the potential cost of the layers in February 2017 when *Fox & Friends* asked him to explain the slow pace of presidential appointments barely one month into the term:

Table 3.1 **Titles Open for Occupancy, 2016**

I

1. Secretary
2. Chief of staff to the secretary
3. Deputy chief of staff to the secretary

II

4. Deputy secretary
5. Deputy secretary with portfolio
6. Chief of staff to the deputy secretary
7. Deputy chief of staff
8. Principal associate deputy secretary
9. Associate deputy secretary
10. Deputy associate deputy secretary
11. Assistant deputy secretary
12. Associate assistant deputy secretary

III

13. Undersecretary
14. Chief of staff to the undersecretary
15. Deputy chief of staff to the undersecretary
16. Principal deputy undersecretary
17. Deputy undersecretary

IV

26. Assistant secretary
27. Chief of staff to the assistant secretary
28. Deputy chief of staff to the assistant secretary
29. Principal deputy assistant secretary
30. Associate principal deputy assistant secretary
31. Deputy assistant secretary
32. Chief of staff to the deputy assistant secretary
33. Principal deputy deputy assistant secretary
34. Deputy deputy assistant secretary
35. Associate deputy assistant secretary
36. Deputy associate deputy assistant secretary
37. Chief of staff to the associate deputy assistant secretary
38. Deputy associate assistant secretary
39. Assistant deputy assistant secretary
40. Principal associate assistant secretary

V

48. Administrator
49. Chief of staff to the administrator
50. Assistant chief of staff to the administrator
51. Principal deputy administrator
52. Deputy administrator
53. Chief of staff to the deputy administrator
54. Associate deputy administrator
55. Deputy associate deputy administrator
56. Assistant deputy administrator
57. Deputy assistant deputy administrator
58. Principal assistant deputy administrator
59. Associate assistant deputy administrator
60. Senior associate administrator
61. Associate administrator
62. Chief of staff to the associate administrator

18. Chief of staff to the deputy undersecretary
19. Principal associate deputy undersecretary
20. Associate deputy undersecretary
21. Principal assistant deputy undersecretary
22. Assistant deputy undersecretary
23. Deputy assistant deputy undersecretary
24. Associate undersecretary
25. Assistant undersecretary

41. Associate assistant secretary
42. Chief of staff to the associate assistant secretary
43. Deputy associate assistant secretary
44. Principal assistant assistant secretary
45. Assistant assistant secretary
46. Chief of staff to the assistant assistant secretary
47. Deputy assistant assistant secretary

63. Deputy chief of staff to the associate administrator
64. Deputy executive associate administrator
65. Deputy associate administrator
66. Senior associate deputy administrator
67. Assistant administrator
68. Chief of staff to the assistant administrator
69. Deputy assistant administrator
70. Associate assistant administrator
71. Associate deputy assistant administrator

Table 3.2 **Trends in Titling, 1964–2016**

	Number of Layers of Leaders						Number of Leaders in Layers					
	1960	1992	1998	2004	2010	2016	1960	1992	1998	2004	2010	2016
Total	17	33	51	64	61	71	451	2,409	2,385	2,592	3,123	3,265
Absolute Increase	–	16	18	13	–3	10	–	1,958	–24	207	531	142
Percent Increase	–	94%	55%	26%	–5%	16%	–	434%	–1%	9%	21%	3%

Well, a lot of those jobs, I don't want to appoint, because they're unnecessary to have. You know we have so many people in government,
even me, I look at some of the jobs and its people over people over
people. I say what do all these people do? You don't need all those jobs.
There are hundreds and hundreds of jobs that are totally unnecessary
jobs.[105]

Trump repeated the claim six months later when he told *Fox & Friends*, "I'm the
only one that matters: We don't need all the people they want."[106]

Trump had good cause to ask whether all the posts were needed, but was
wrong to suggest that presidents can merely ignore vacancies and expect faithful
execution of the laws. Presidential appointments are governed by constitutional
procedures, created through statute, and hardwired into the chain of command
that links the top of the federal government to the bottom. These connective
positions link the heads of government to the career workforce that must execute the laws and executive actions. With of hundreds of positions still vacant as
of the end of its first year, the Trump administration was so much headless, but
also neckless.[107] The administration was still far behind recent presidents in July
2018.[108]

Contrary to it sluggish pace in filling Senate-confirmed posts, the administration was one of the fastest in recent history in filling its lower-level political positions such as chiefs of staff, staff assistants, and public affairs officers.
As of March 7, 2018, the administration had yet to nominate candidates for
200 Senate-confirmed positions, but had filled almost 2,500 "at-will" positions.
According to the nonpartisan *ProPublica* news group, 250 of these appointees
had worked for Trump campaign groups, 200 were former lobbyists, and 125
had worked at conservative think tanks. Although *ProPublica* decried the penetration of ideologues and operatives, Trump was well within normal in salting
the lower levels of the hierarchy with campaign aides, former lobbyists, "beach-
head" advisers, and confidants. Trump was merely following the title-creep
that preceded him into office, but was adding people over people nonetheless,
while giving them significant authority to act as the more visible presidential
appointments process stalled.[109]

However, Trump was anything but normal in the rate of White House staff
turnover. According to tracking data collected by Kathryn Dunn Tenpas, 43 percent of Trump's senior staff exited during his first year, including six of the
president's twelve "Tier One" positions such as chief of staff, press secretary, and
White House counsel. "Trump's turnover is record-setting, more than triple that
of Obama and double that of Reagan," Tenpas wrote in late January 2018. "If history is any guide, retaining senior staff members in year two will be an even more
daunting task. All five of Trump's predecessors experienced a large uptick in

second-year staff turnover."[110] Instability at the top of the chain begets instability below, as both weaken discipline at the government-industrial dividing line.

Achievements and Breakdowns

Name a domestic or international challenge since World War II, and odds are that the government-industrial complex helped address it, often to great success. There is still much to do in converting Hamilton's arduous and extensive enterprises into lasting achievements, but the nation can be proud what the federal government has accomplished.

Yet, just as the complex has created great achievements, it can be fairly implicated in a recent cascade of large-scale breakdowns. According to public opinion surveys of public news interest, the federal government generated 1.6 breakdowns per year that reached the public agenda in the fifteen years between 1986 and 2001, but 3.3 in the fifteen years from 2001 to 2017, including several of the most visible events recorded in the post–World War II era. The federal government often recovered quickly as events unfolded, but contributed nonetheless to national tragedies such as the September 11 attacks, Shuttle *Columbia* explosion, 2008 financial collapse, the healthcare.gov failure, veterans waiting list scandal, the failure to anticipate the rise of the Islamic State in Iraq and Syria, and the data breaches that have compromised national security and individual privacy.[111] (Table 3.3 provides short descriptions of the fifteen most visible federal breakdowns since 2001.)

It is important to note that many of these breakdowns involved errors of omission, not commission. The federal government did not hijack the aircraft that killed so many Americans on September 11, 2001, but did not imagine the possibility in time to prevent the tragedy. It did not breach the levees when Hurricane Katrina came ashore in 2005, but did not have the leadership or plans to respond quickly. And it did not design the Byzantine instruments that triggered the banking collapse in 2008, but had little capacity to stop the risk.

It is also important to note that there was no single cause of failure. Staffing shortages and skill gaps in mission-critical occupations contributed to 36 of the 53 breakdowns, antiquated technology to 31, broken chains of command to 28, funding shortages to 24, duplication and overlap across agencies to 19, and contract failures to 17. Even as inflated expectations, ambiguous direction, conflicting statutes, and unattainable deadlines produced impossible policy, funding shortages, skill gaps, miscommunication, poor decisions, duplication and overlap, and misconduct undermined effective management. As the 9/11 Commission concluded, these problems framed the much broader "failure of imagination" that exposed the nation to the devastating attack.[112]

Table 3.3 **The Most Visible Federal Government Breakdowns, 2001–2017**

Description	Year	Public Interest in Story[1]
1. Despite early warnings, al-Qaeda operatives were able to hijack four commercial airliners and use them as missiles to attack the World Trade Center's Twin Towers, in New York City, and the Pentagon.	2001	96%
2. After years of making high-risk investments with little regulation, the banking system collapsed under the weight of toxic assets created by risky mortgage loans, poorly understood financial instruments, and a credit crisis that froze the economy.	2008	92%
3. Hurricane Katrina made landfall in Louisiana on August 29, breaching the levees that protected New Orleans; stranding thousands of residents on rooftops, in the Superdome, and on bridges; and overwhelming the Federal Emergency Management Agency and state agencies.	2005	91%
4. The federal government failed to detect safety lapses that were partly to blame for an explosion on British Petroleum's Deepwater Horizon offshore drilling platform that killed eleven workers and created a massive oil leak far below that went on for eighty-seven days.	2010	88%
5. Aided by his younger brother, a known terrorist—who had been lost by at least two federal intelligence agencies— detonated improvised pressure-cooker bombs near the Boston Marathon finish line, killing three spectators and wounding 250 others.	2013	85%
6. A breach of the space shuttle *Columbia's* heat shield on reentry after a sixteen-day mission killed its seven-member crew and involved many of the same problems that had caused the *Challenger* disaster almost two decades earlier.	2003	82%
7. The Obama administration acknowledged the Taliban's resurgence in Afghanistan by halting the further withdrawal of US troops. The decision was made after an unrelated and mistaken US bombing of a Doctors Without Borders hospital in Kunduz that involved failures in the air force chain of command.	2015	82%[2]

(*continued*)

Table 3.3 Continued

Description	Year	Public Interest in Story[1]
8. Twelve miners were killed when methane gas exploded inside a West Virginia mine; soon after, six were killed inside a Utah mine when the walls collapsed. Other mine disasters occurred in the interim.	2006	80%
9. Thirteen people were killed and ninety injured when an interstate-highway bridge perched over the Mississippi River in Minnesota collapsed during rush hour, partly because of a repair project designed to fix a flawed design.	2007	80%
10. The US government missed a long list of opportunities to monitor and intercept suspected terrorists who later engaged in violent attacks.	2015	79%[3]
11. Army Major Nidal Hasan shot and killed thirteen people and wounded another forty-three while shouting, "Allah is great," in a terrorist attack at Fort Hood, Texas. Hasan later described himself as a "soldier of Allah."	2009	78%
12. The Consumer Product Safety Commission issued 473 recalls during a surge in Chinese imports that entered the United States without adequate inspection, but it could not keep up with the flood of cheap and often toxic toys.	2007	77%
13. US forces were unable to confirm Iraq's possession of biological, chemical, or nuclear weapons of mass destruction (WMD) that created momentum for the Iraq War. Specially trained US troops spent two years in the search before giving up.	2003	76%
14. Prisoners at Iraq's infamous Abu Ghraib prison were abused and humiliated by US guards and contractors, leading to widespread publication of photographs from the incidents and later reports of similar abuse at the Guantanamo Bay detention camp.	2004	76%
15. The Ambassador to Libya and three other Americans were killed during an attack by heavily armed forces that launched what appears to have been a coordinated attack on the US Special Mission in Benghazi.	2012	76%

[1] Percent of Americans who followed each event very or fairly closely.

[2] Based on a Kelley Blue Book October 5, 2015, showing that 64% of Americans had heard about the Volkswagen scandal.

[3] Based on a CBS News December 2015 survey showing that 79% of Americans believed that a terrorist attack on the United States was very or somewhat likely.

Achievements and breakdowns both create pressure on the government-industrial complex. The easiest way Congress and the president can make grand achievements even grander is to call upon the same contract and grant employees who helped create the success in the first place. In turn, the fastest way to repair a breakdown is to call upon the same contract and grant employees who may have contributed to the mistakes. Expertise is the coin of the realm for scaling achievements and fixing breakdowns, and contract and grant employees are often the ones who have the needed skills.

What Americans Want from Reform

Americans hold seemingly irreconcilable views about the federal government and its mission. Just as they tend to hate Congress, but love their member of Congress, Americans tend to hate the federal bureaucracy, but love their soldiers, postal carriers, cancer researchers, weather forecasters, and social security representatives, and are even surprisingly positive toward the agency that collects their taxes. This ambivalence creates incentives to hide the true size of government whenever possible, even if it involves higher cost.

The Pew Research Center's trend lines show this effect. Trust has rallied from time to time over the past seventy years, but has never fully recovered from the sharp declines following the Vietnam War and Watergate. After hitting a post–World War II high at 77 percent in 1964, the percent of Americans who said they trusted the federal government to do the right thing just about always or most of the time fell on a mostly straight line to 30 percent in 1980, recovered to 47 percent during the Persian Gulf crisis in 1991, dropped to 20 percent in 1994, steadily recovered to 49 percent just after 9/11, and eventually dropped to just 18 percent in December 2017.[113]

Distrust is just one of many signs of growing anti-government sentiment over the decades. The disaffection also shows up in public anger and frustration toward government and beliefs that government is almost always wasteful and inefficient, run by a few big interests looking out for themselves, needs "very major" reform, and is so poorly led that ordinary Americans could do a better job of solving the nation's problems than elected officials. Interviewed in December 2017, for example, 56 percent of Americans said the federal government is almost always wasteful and inefficient, compared with 40 percent who said government often does a better job than people give it credit for, while 79 percent said they were either frustrated or angry with the federal government, compared with just 17 percent who were basically content.[114]

Despite these concerns, Americans want the federal government to protect the nation from international and domestic threats. Interviewed by Pew in

December 2017, majorities said the federal government should play a major role in keeping the nation safe from terrorism (94 percent), responding to natural disasters (89 percent), ensuring safe food and medicine (80 percent), managing US immigration (80 percent), and protecting the environment (75 percent). Americans also gave the federal government good marks on most priorities, including terrorism (66 somewhat or very good), natural disasters (64 percent), and ensuring safe food and medicine (61 percent). Although they also gave the federal government much lower marks on ensuring basic income for older Americans (41 percent), strengthening the economy (53 percent), managing the immigration system (32 percent), and helping people out of poverty (26 percent), they still wanted the federal government to play a major role on each issue.[115]

Most Americans are also favorable toward most departments and agencies. Interviewed in February 2018, they gave the Postal Service their highest favorability rating (88 percent), followed by the Centers for Disease Control (78 percent), the FBI (66 percent), the CIA (64 percent), EPA (60 percent), and the Department of Justice (69 percent).[116] Even the often-disparaged and understaffed IRS earned a 57 percent favorability rating in 2018, perhaps confirming Vanessa Williamson's conclusion that Americans believe paying taxes is part of being a good citizen:

> The idea that "Americans hate taxes" has become a truism without the benefit of being true. Instead, Americans see paying taxes as a civic obligation and a political act. To be a taxpayer, Americans believe, is something to be proud of. It is evidence that one is a responsible, contributing, and upstanding member of society, a person worthy of respect in the community and representation in the government.[117]

Despite these high marks for individual departments and agencies, Americans remain sharply divided when asked how much government should deliver and whether it needs major reform or not much change at all. Asked about the size of government in June 2018, 46 percent of Americans said they favored a smaller government that provides fewer services or a bigger government that provides more services, while 45 percent said they favored a bigger government that provides more services. Also asked about the need for government reform in the same survey, 60 percent said the federal government needed very major reform, while 31 percent said the federal government is basically sound and needs only some reform.[118] Finally, asked about the federal government's performance in running its programs, just 2 percent said the federal government was doing an excellent job, 22 percent said it was doing a good job, 47 percent said it was doing an only fair job, and 27 percent said it was doing a poor job.

Combined into a two-by-two measure, these views create four distinct images philosophies of reform: (1) the dismantlers who said government needs very major reform, favor a smaller government that provides fewer services, and were the most likely to rate government performance as poor, (2) the rebuilders who said government needs very major reform but favor a bigger government providing more services, and were the second most likely to rate government performance as poor, (3) the expanders who said government is basically sound and favor a bigger government that provides more services, and were the most likely to rate government performance as good, and (4) the streamliners who said government is basically sound but favor a smaller government that provides fewer services and were the most likely to rate government performance as only fair.[119]

As Figure 3.1 shows, the past twenty years have witnessed the almost complete collapse of the reinventors as a force for modest reform. Between 1997 and 2018, the number of dismantlers rose from 17 percent to 43 in 2016 percent in 2016 before falling back to 35 percent in 2018, while the number of rebuilders increased from 16 percent to 25 percent before pushing up to 31 percent in 2018, the number of reinventors fell steadily from 43 percent to 20 percent in 2016 before hitting bottom at 17 percent in 2018, and the number of streamliners drifted

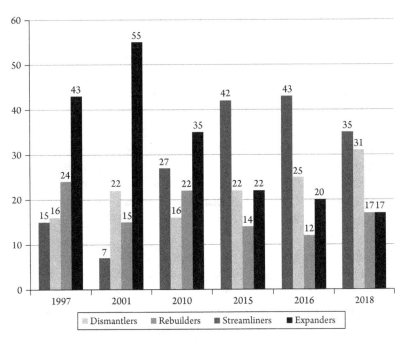

Figure 3.1 Views toward Government Reform, 1997–2018

mostly downward from 24 percent to 12 percent before a slight recovery to 17 percent in 2018.[120]

The sharp decline in the number of expanders is tied to demands for major government reform. Although the percentage of respondents who favored smaller government varied modestly over time between 40 percent in 1997 and 50 percent in 2018, the percentages of respondents who said the federal government needed very major reform rose from 37 percent in 1997 to 60 percent in 2018 as the percentage who said the federal government was basically sound fell from 58 percent in 1997 to 29 percent twenty years later. Although much of this shift toward rough parity between the dismantlers and rebuilders reflects sharp differences on the economy, health care access, and immigration reform, Figure 3.1 also suggests a growing battle between two competing views of government reform that favored Trump in 2016, but that reached rough parity in 2018.

Further analysis also reveals deep divisions by political ideology, party affiliations, race, and sex. Whereas more than half of the dismantlers described themselves as very or somewhat conservative, more than half of the rebuilders described themselves as them as somewhat or very liberal, and whereas more than 40 percent of the dismantlers described themselves as Republicans, more than 50 percent of rebuilders described themselves as Democrats; whereas more than 80 percent of dismantlers described themselves as white, 5 percent as Hispanic, and 3 percent as black, just 50 percent of the rebuilders described themselves as white, 20 percent described themselves as black, and 15 percent as Hispanic. Finally, whereas 64 percent of the dismantlers identified themselves as male, 54 percent of the rebuilders identified themselves as female.

Much of the movement toward very major reform appears to reflect a general sense among Americans of all persuasions believe their side is losing more than winning on the issues they care about. As Pew reported in 2015, Republicans of all educational levels had come to believe their side was often on the losing side of the policy debate during the Obama administration, but even a slight plurality of Democrats also felt they were losing more than winning. Both groups also shared similar doubts about their ability to influence the government in Washington and were more likely than college-educated Americans to believe that ordinary people could do a better job solving the country's problems than elected officials.[121]

Federal employees tend to be the only employees that count when Congress and presidents pursue major reforms in how government works. As noted in chapter 2, the Trump administration focused entirely on federal employees in its government reform agenda, while Democrats stood against any cuts in the number of federal jobs. Although Democrats continued to argue against outsourcing, they fought the Trump agenda by protecting federal jobs where they could, while promoting traditional reinventing government themes about the need to give federal employees the tools and support to succeed on the public's behalf. If doing so meant using contract and grant employees to plug potential threats to federal performance, Democrats seemed ready to acquiesce, but their general preference in reform appears to involve a traditional view of the career civil servant.

Polarization

Industry learned long ago that profitability depends on planning for the future, but the federal government cannot even plan for the present given the deep political polarization that imposes endless delay at every turn of the budget cycle. Given the lack of closure and the potential for deep cutbacks of the kind faced during the 2013 budget sequester, departments and agencies were forced to rely on contract and grant employees to fill the gaps created by the de facto caps, cuts, and freezes.[122] With uncertainty at every turn in the legislative process, federal departments and agencies often hedge against failure by creating "surge tanks" of contract and grant employees that can be filled or emptied quickly.

The uncertainty is driven in part by polarization. The rise in hostage-taking, political tribalism, and win-at-all-costs legislating is not only "worse than it looks," as Thomas E. Mann and Norman J. Ornstein recently argue, but it also is more destructive than might be imagined.[123] Experts may disagree on who and what caused the bitterness, but the Partnership for Public Service is certain of the impact on government performance:

> The end result has been a disservice to the American people, leaving federal agencies to cope with leadership vacuums that impede decision-making as well as funding uncertainties that disrupt services for the public, create inefficiencies, increase costs and make it difficult to plan and innovate. The current climate also has often left federal leaders without constructive congressional partners to oversee their work or provide legislative authority to change or drop underperforming programs or embark on new initiatives.[124]

The polarization has equally significant impacts at the government-industrial divide. Testifying before Congress on the "insidious" effects of budget uncertainly only months before the October 2013 shutdown, budget expert Philip Joyce warned the Senate Homeland Security and Governmental Affairs Committee that even a "normal" year of budgeting would not be particularly normal. As Joyce told the committee at the time, Congress had not adopted its annual budget resolution on time in seven of the last fifteen years, completed its appropriations process by the start of the new fiscal year for sixteen years in a row, and had been forced to enact more than 150 short-term continuing resolutions over the years to keep government afloat. "Any organization—whether it is the federal government, a state or local government, or a business—needs to plan for the funds it is going to have available in order to effectively budget and management," Joyce told the committee. "And my message to you is that late appropriations not only create negative consequences for federal agencies, but also for people who get money from the federal government."[125]

Joyce's message did not change history, of course. Between 2012 and 2018, Congress added five more years of missed budget deadlines, nineteen continuing resolutions, and three government shutdowns to its inventory of budget uncertainty. The congressional hearing record shows Congress knew what it was doing to government performance with the stopgap measures and shutdowns. Only days after Congress ended a three-day government shutdown with a two-week continuing resolution, GAO warned the Senate Homeland Security and Governmental Affairs Committee of the "legislative anomalies," unsteady contract and grant cycles, hiring slowdowns, costly workarounds, and spending distortions that lay ahead. Ironically given the desire for certainty, GAO told the committee that the longer the continuing resolution, the more the damage.[126]

GAO did not tell Congress that even the threat of a shutdown causes damage, but Brookings Institution scholar Kathryn Dunn Tenpas had made the point with force in 2015 as follows:

> I am not naïve to the pressing electoral needs in Congress, the siren call of big donors who relish the ideological mud-slinging, or the permanent campaign ethos that pervades our government. . . . However, the fact remains that threatening to shut down the government, let alone actually shutting it down, severely harms executive branch operations in both the short and long term. Practically speaking, the mere mention of a budget shutdown sparks numerous meetings, memos, and subsequent OMB reviews of contingency plans—an enormous checklist to work down in preparation for the government closing, plans that divert resources (work hours and funding) from agencies' missions.[127]

Daredevil budgeting clearly affects the government-industrial complex as federal, contract, and grant employees consider their options, but continuing resolutions, not shutdowns appear to create the greater damage. Turning the power back on after a shutdown is a difficult, but far less of a burden than the repeated, incremental tasks needed to adjust operations as continuing resolutions disrupt operations. Contract firms and grant agencies must also adjust to the uncertainty—they must maintain their capacity, but cannot deliver their products and services. "Contractors also feel the sting," an information industry lobbyist wrote as Congress hurtled toward the January 2018 shutdown:

> That's operational investment that is lost to companies and small businesses that they cannot get back. The result is that this annual funding instability drives greater risk into the federal market and increases taxpayer costs. Is it any wonder that we see fewer and fewer companies willing to invest in the government as a customer and we find it harder and harder to convince cutting edge technology developers to bring their products and services to bear on government challenges?[128]

Polarization also undermines legislative ambition to improve government performance. Although Congress continues to enact two to three major government reform statutes each year, polarization has affected the size and scope of the statutory ambition. According to this author's analysis of recent legislative action, Congress passed twenty-one reform laws from 2005 to 2018, including ten that created or repaired administrative systems; four that attacked fraud, waste, and abuse; five that strengthened government transparency; and two that streamlined government rules of some kind.[129] This recent contribution to the tides of reform is meager when compared to the forty reform statutes enacted from 1975 to 1984, but it still demonstrates at least minimal congressional interest in government reform even during an era of intense polarization and budgetary uncertainty.

Polarization even has a visible effect on the actual the size (government-wide versus agency-specific) and scope (new policy versus small-scale revisions of the status quo) of the reform effort. As Table 3.4 shows, the number of large-scale government reforms dropped steadily from a high of 50 percent in the first decade following World War II to just 5 percent in the period 2005–2017, while the number of new reforms dropped from 64 percent in the years 1955–1964 to just 18 percent from 2005 to mid-2017. When combined into a single measure, the percentage of large/new ideas fell from 20 percent in the period 1985–2004 to just 5 percent in the period 2005-2018. Although there were two large-new and one small-new reforms between 2005 and 2017, Congress spent its time on more-limited efforts.

This is not to diminish smaller-gauge reforms such as the Serve America, Government Performance and Results, Inspector General, or Whistleblower Protection and Enhancement Acts. Nor is it to dismiss the importance of new initiatives such as the Veterans Affairs Accountability, Federal Funding Accountability and Transparency, Post-Katrina Emergency Management Reform, or Presidential Appointment Efficiency and Streamlining Acts. Rather, the recent history suggests that large/new reforms such as the Dodd-Frank Wall

Table 3.4 **The Scale of Government Reform, 1945–2017**

Decade	New Idea Not Old	Large Idea Not Small	Large/New Idea	Small/Old Idea
1945–1954	27%	50%	10%	41%
1955–1964	65	47	17	29
1965–1974	34	34	12	46
1975–1984	50	30	17	43
1985–1994	48	33	20	40
1995–2004	55	29	20	38
2005–2017	18	29	5	71
Average	44	35	13	43

N=195

Street Reform and Consumer Protection and the Digital Accountability and Transparency Acts are the large/new exceptions to a more limited rule during a period when calls for major government reform go unanswered.

This decline in large/new reform confirms broad changes at both ends of Pennsylvania Avenue.

At the White House, recent presidents initiated fewer reforms over time, and fewer of the reforms they produced were comprehensive. Presidents initiated 60 percent of all reforms before Watergate, compared with just 24 percent after. Presidential interest in large-scale reforms also fell from 55 percent of their statutes before Watergate to 40 percent after.

On Capitol Hill, Congress picked up some of the slack in the number of reforms as presidents stepped away, but showed even less ambition. Although the congressional share of activity surged from 41 percent of all reforms before Watergate to 76 percent after, its interest in large-scale reforms fell from 47 percent to just 24 percent during the period.

These patterns suggest that presidents and Congress have both lost the capacity and opportunity to produce comprehensive reform. The Office of Management and Budget no longer has the staff to generate deep management analysis, while personnel cuts at GAO have weakened that agency's ability to develop comprehensive reforms. Although both offices are still able to focus attention on major management problems, it is not clear whether presidents or Congress are interested in deeper analysis. Nor is it clear that either institution has the political will to drive comprehensive reform forward in an era of intense partisanship. The question, therefore, is how to help presidents and Congress develop and enact the kind of comprehensive reform needed to reduce the peril to performance.

Cabal, Intrigue, and Corruption

A proper blending of government and industry is impossible without controlling cabal, intrigue, and corruption that Hamilton called the "most deadly adversaries of republican government."[130] At least according to recent reports and investigations, all three appear to exist within the government-industrial complex, the only question being to what extent and effect.

As noted above, most Americans do not know much about the government-industrial complex. However, they do know something about scandal. Indeed, asked in 2015 to name in their own words the biggest problem in Washington, Americans put special interests first on their list at 16 percent, followed by a mix of lying, dishonesty, broken promises, and immorality at 11 percent, being out of touch with regular Americans and caring only about their political careers at 10 percent each, not being able to work together at 9 percent, violating the Constitution at 4 percent, and a mix of being unqualified, bad managers, and just plain "idiots" at 3 percent. No one used the phrase "cabal and corruption" in their answers, but the term easily fits the list.[131]

Dark money is an example of how all three adversaries work together to create public disquiet. Defined as a form of support for political action committees (PACs) that are not required to disclose their donors, dark money has come under fire from a host of public-interest groups that are working to expose the potential link between federal contract firms and campaign contributions. As New York University's Brennan Center for Justice argues, dark money creates both the perception and potential for pay-to-play by contract firms and grant agencies:

> With so much money at stake, the imperative to court those in power is obvious. As of 2011, federal contractors made up 33 of the 41 largest disclosed corporate campaign contributors over the previous two decades. In the 2014 cycle, the top 25 federal contractors all made disclosed contributions through their PACs; in total, they gave more than $30 million. Contributions by the top five corporate contractors have more than doubled since 2004.
>
> There is nothing to stop these same companies, along with the various individuals and entities affiliated with them, from contributing unlimited amounts to dark money groups who do not disclose their donors. Such secret election spending can foster a hidden pay to play culture, in which

awards go to those best able to play the political money game, rather than those offering the best, most cost-effective product or service.[132]

Obama committed himself to curing the problem in his 2016 State of the Union address. As he acknowledged, most members of Congress do not like raising money. "I know," he then said. "I've done it."[133] His rhetoric was clever for sure, but also revealed the bipartisan support for at least some elements of the status quo. Members and presidents may not like raising money, but they do like spending it on re-election efforts.

Obama could have easily made the spending more visible by requiring disclosure from government contract firms, but he never signed the order. Although a simple stroke of the pen would have required disclosure by as many as 70 percent of the Fortune 100 companies that held at least $130 billion in federal contracts at the time, it never left the president's desk despite intense lobbying from more than 100 members of Congress.[134]

Obama never gave a formal explanation for his decision, but he no doubt understood that Republicans and Democrats both benefit from dark-money contributions. After all, campaign contributors are notorious for backing incumbents on both sides of the aisle to hedge their bets in the hunt for future support. Obama may have favored executive action, but also had to know that his party would be affected by at least some of the $160 million spent undisclosed contributions in 2016.[135]

Gifts to presidential campaigns, favorite charities, and family brands are not the only adversaries of good government. So is the hidden fraud, waste, and abuse that has plagued government since Valley Forge. "Nepotism and favoritism were common means of awarding contracts," writes procurement expert Sandy Kenny of the Revolutionary War. "Deliveries of spoiled meat, axes without heads, one-quarter size blankets, and shoes and saddles that fell apart were commonplace. Congress tried to eliminate fraud through regulation, but the resulting red tape was so burdensome and complex that it paralyzed the system."[136]

Thus do the three deadly adversaries increase the pressure to substitute contract and grant employees for federal employees. Contract firms and grant agencies have ample incentive to resist full disclosure of their campaign spending and lobbying activity even as they claim proprietary rights to information on how they compensate and deploy their employees. They rarely complain about the lack of federal oversight and administrative capacity, of course, but nonetheless benefit from the cascade of breakdowns rooted in the demographic, bureaucratic, and political pressures that create demand for their help.

The Prospects for Reform

Democrats and Republicans create their own pressure on the government-industrial dividing line through one-sided rhetoric. Republicans rarely miss an opportunity to attack federal pay and extol the market, while Democrats rarely miss an opportunity to attack contract waste and highlight government achievement.

The current inventory of one-sided reforms undermines this sense of shared service. Recent reforms in how government and industry behave have produced little more than passing effect, if any effect at all. Congress and the president have removed one problem from the high-risk list only to find one in another form at another agency, while the underlying pressures have increased. As Volcker argued in 2015, the government still needs help:

> We depend on government in so many ways, often unseen and unrealized. But one can't help but conclude upon seeing our institutions at work—or, more accurately, not working to their fullest potential—that we need to make some fixes. These institutions, from the UN and the World Bank, to our federal, state, and local governments for that matter—are tools that can improve people's lives. We need them to run well. We have seen what happens when insufficient attention is given to understanding and mastering the basics of execution—the botched launch of healthcare.gov, the gaming of the veterans' medical scheduling system, and, of course, the failure of the financial regulatory system to prevent unacceptable levels of private sector risk-taking at the expense of the stability of the economy.[137]

This revival will not come from one-sided reform or tinkering. There are simply too many relationships within and across the demographic, bureaucratic, and political realities to expect comprehensive impacts from small-scale action. Reblending the government-industrial complex is not unlike reforming the navy, which President Franklin Roosevelt described as like punching a featherbed: "You punch it with your right and you punch it with your left until you are finally exhausted, and then you find the damn bed just as it was before you started punching."[138]

As chapter 4 argues, the greatest barrier to a proper meshing of government and industry is the failure to accept the imperative role that federal, contract, and grant employees share together. They may work under separate rules in separate sectors, but they must pull as one to faithfully execute the laws. Toward this end, chapter 4 outlines a "reset and reinforce" system for moving functions back and forth across the government-industrial dividing line as needed for faithful execution of the laws. If a job is inherently govern-mental, it must be filled by the right government employee; if it is not inher-ently government, it can be filled by the right employee from either side of the complex based on agreed-upon rules and expectations toward the greatest public benefit, accountability, and performance. Such a sorting puts the onus on Congress and the president to ensure the proper blending to assure liberty and performance can prosper together.

4

A Proper Blending

Congress knows a great deal about the government-industrial complex. After all, it has held thousands of hearings on parts of the whole, and occasionally the whole itself. Indeed, the first great congressional investigation focused largely on the role of contract fraud on the disastrous 1791 Battle of the Wabash.[1] According to the congressional hearings database, the past 114 congresses have added an additional 1,450 hearings on this one government-industrial topic alone, including contract misconduct during and after every war and major engagement in American history.[2]

Congress has also shown persistent interest in the federal government's many workforces. Between 1791 and 2018, for example, the House and Senate have held 18,300 hearings on different groups of federal employees, including the armed forces, civil servants, contractors, contract employees, consultants, federal employees, government employees, postal workers, mail carriers, and military peronnel.[3] Ninety percent of these hearings were held after 1933 as the federal budget and organization chart expanded with war and economic calamity.

As these workforces grew and caps, cuts, and freezes became common practice, Congress began asking when and how jobs and functions should and should not move the two sides of the government-industrial complex. Between World War II and 2018, for example, the House and Senate held 355 hearings on tools for moving jobs and functions back and forth across the government-industrial divide.[4] Three quarters of these hearings were held between 1975 and 2001 as Congress fought about who gets what from government through downsizing, insourcing, outsourcing, and methods for protecting competing groups of employees.[5]

Congress continued to argue over the relative strengths of the federal, contract, and grant workforces after 2001, but also opened a new vein of bipartisan work on the tools for a proper blending of the government-industrial workforce. Between 1975 and July 2018, the House and Senate held 41 hearings on the federal government's multisector workforce, rightsizing, strategic human capital, and workforce planning.[6] All but eight of these hearings took place between

2001 and 2009 after Rep. Tom Davis (R-VA) and Sens. Daniel Akaka (D-HI) and George Voinovich (R-OH) introduced rightsizing to the hearing agenda.[7]

GAO's decision to put federal human capital management on its 2001 high-risk list was central to the surge. "We felt compelled to designate it high risk primarily because of the pervasiveness and the serious nature of it," the comptroller general told the Senate Governmental Affairs Committee in February 2001. "At many agencies, human capital issues have contributed to serious programmatic problems and risks, and in most cases, these risks are increasing rather than decreasing."[8]

The GAO hearings produced two streams of oversight, one that focused on the workforce problems facing a long list of individual departments and agencies, and the other that focused more broadly on the blended workforce as a fact of life.[9] Most of the House and Senate hearings were rooted in a general belief that Congress had to move away from what Davis called the traditional "black and white discussion of outsourcing" and toward what Voinovich and Sen. Daniel Akaka (D-HI) described as a "balancing act" in 2010.[10] Democrats and Republicans continued to promote their favored workforces, but their committee leadership focused more on the whole.

This bipartisan consensus began to dissipate after the Tea Party movement helped Republicans reclaim the House majority in the 2010 midterm elections and partisanship increased with demands for new rounds of government downsizing. As the partisanship increased, the number of hearings on the blended federal workforce plummeted. Whereas Congress averaged six hearings on the blended workforce per year during George W. Bush's first and second terms and seven per year during Obama's first term, it held just three hearings per year during Obama's second term.

The consensus also dissipated in part because Congress and the president could not find a reasonable methodology for a proper blending of the government-industrial workforce. "The question is, are we getting our best value," House Government Reform Committee chair Darrell Issa (R-CA) said in 2011. "And until we have a system so that we can get the best value, we are not going to rightsize the federal work force in-house or get the best value from our contractors out of house."[11]

Issa's call for balance was represented in the Reducing the Size of the Federal Government through Attrition Act of 2011 that came before his committee after the 2010 Republican takeover of the House.[12] The act would have imposed a one-for-three replacement ratio for every federal job vacancy, while mandating a 10 percent reduction in total federal employment by October 1, 2015, and a full-stop federal hiring freeze if total attrition fell short of the target. Although the bill also contained a parallel reduction in service contract spending, CBO cautioned that the actual impact was "very uncertain," especially if the spending was shifted to other contract vehicles.[13]

Freedom Caucus founding member and future Trump administration budget director Rep. Mick Mulvaney (R-SC) sponsored the bill, calling it essential for reining in the "explosive growth of the public sector."[14] The committee sent the bill to the House floor on a party-line vote in December 2011, but it was never scheduled for debate. Mulvaney cosponsored the bill again in 2013 and 2015, but the moment for downsizing the federal and contract workforces together had passed. There is no evidence, for example, that Mulvaney pushed for balanced cuts in the 2017 hiring freeze or his 2018 workforce strengthening package, nor did he show any interest in building an apples-to-apples process for balancing the direct and indirect workforces highlighted in the fiscal year 2019 budget.

This chapter will outline a "reset and reinforce" process that Mulvaney and other reformers might use to assure best value based on rigorous annual headcounts and workforce planning. Assuming that rigorous headcounts are within reach, Congress and future presidents would set an annual workforce cap for federal, contract, and grant employees; adjust each workforce total based on the federal mission and performance; allocate functions and associated jobs across the government-industrial dividing line; and monitor the value, performance, and accountability of the whole through ongoing oversight, the budget and appropriations process or a Base Closure and Realignment Commission (BRAC) model in setting multiyear targets.[15]

Before turning to this process, it is helpful to consider the recent history of one-sided reforms in the government-industrial complex. Congress and presidents may know that the nation depends on a blended workforce to execute the laws, but they have yet to embrace a comprehensive agenda for blending federal, contract, and grant employees for maximum effect. Democrats and Republicans may have agreed on a proper blending, but not a rightsizing tool.

The President's Agenda

Presidents have made their own mark on the government-industrial complex through their policies and promises. Like Congress, they rarely talk about the federal government's many workforces and share the long history of one-sided promises to cut government or restore the federal workforce:

- Carter embraced love for "the poor, the aged, the weak, and the afflicted" in accepting the 1976 Democratic presidential nomination, but also attacked "the complicated and confused and overlapping and wasteful federal bureaucracy."[16] Once in office, he signed the first of three hiring freezes on March 3, 1977, and turned to comprehensive civil service and ethics reform.

- Reagan promised "a government that will not only work well, but wisely" and rarely missed an opportunity to repeat his favorite joke about the nine most terrifying words in the English language. He launched his war on waste in the Capitol with an immediate hiring freeze, fired all the inspectors general appointed by Carter, and prepared to appoint a government reform commission that would produce forty-seven separate reports published in thirty-eight volumes of single-spaced typescript.[17]

- George H. W. Bush reassured the nation that he did not hate government but also promised to discipline its growth. He pursued benign government reform in celebrations of the Senior Executive Service, worked with Congress on a sweeping federal salary increase, approved two rounds of base closures, streamlined the government ethics process, and later created an advisory commission to help implement the recommendations of Paul A. Volcker's 1988 National Commission on the Public Service.

- Clinton promised to "streamline the federal government and change the way it works," balance the budget, control the special interests and lobbyists, and cut 100,000 federal jobs. Clinton gave Gore the keys to the National Performance Review less than a month after his inauguration, signed the Government Performance and Results Act a year later, and celebrated the end of the era of big government in 1996.

- George W. Bush accepted his party's nomination with a broad attack on government as a barrier to compassionate conservatism. "It can feed the body," he said, "but it cannot reach the soul." He shared his father's commitment to public service, but started his presidency with a standard hiring and regulatory freeze before Iraq and Afghanistan. Despite the wars, the administration still worked to identify and repair the federal government's "most apparent deficiencies" through a five-tiered "green-light/red-light" performance rating tool and a wave of competitive sourcing that entered thousands of federal employees in "yellow-page" job competitions against contract firms. Bush also created the Public Service Loan Forgiveness Program for future public servants.

- Barack Obama argued the 2008 financial crisis and continued economic strain was "not all of government's making" but also remarked "government should work for us, not against us, help us, not hurt us." Obama started his presidency with a White House pay freeze, an attack on no-bid contracts, a promise to insource inherently governmental jobs that had migrated to the private sector, and a commitment to expanding Americorps and social innovation.

- Donald Trump told his supporters he had "no tolerance for government incompetence" and embraced downsizing for all but a handful of federal departments and agencies. He started the downsizing three days after taking office with his ninety-day hiring freeze, soon revoked Obama's executive order on contractor compliance with federal labor laws, limited access to Bush's public service loan program, launched a sweeping government reorganization plan in mid-2018, and embraced deep federal personnel cuts at Housing and Urban Development (15 percent), Agriculture (15 percent), State (20 percent), and EPA (25 percent) as part of his 2019 budget.

Whose Side Were They On?

As these quick summaries suggests, six of the seven presidents focused primarily on government-side reform, in part to reduce the number of federal employees and agencies from needless rules and oversight. Several presidents also stretched their agendas to include new acquisition systems; better financial management and performance measurement; ethics reform; and attacks on fraud, waste, and abuse. However, their agendas simply generated greater demographic and bureaucratic pressures on the government-industrial divide.

Carter and Clinton deserve credit for their commitment to reform, but they worked at cross purposes. What Carter tightened through the Civil Service Reform, Ethics in Government, and the Inspector General Acts, Clinton tried to unwind through reinventing government, acquisition streamlining, and workforce restructure that sought to unravel Carter's reform.

Both presidents left a mark on the govenrment-industrial complex, but George W. Bush may have produced greater effect through continued demands for outsourcing. His President's Management Agenda (PMA) contained many salutary planks, including improved financial performance, expanded electronic government, and limited personnel reform.[18] However, it also called for new rounds of job competitions over commercial activities such as shelf stocking, custodial services, housing maintenance, animal caretaking, ground maintenance, missile repair, and cafeteria services.

The Bush administration hoped contract employees would win the head-to-head competitions, but did not put its political thumb on the outcome. Rather, the competitions gave federal employees the chance to prove they could do the jobs better, and they did 83 percent of the time. According to OMB deputy director Clay Johnson, the competitions also produced $1 billion in savings through increased efficiency.[19]

Despite intense opposition from federal employee unions, the competitions gave Congress good reason to question contracting out for commercial activities that federal employees were already performing. The competitions also gave presidents equally good reason to enroll contract employees in similar competitions. What was good for saving money on the government side of the complex could be equally productive on the industry side.

Obama's Two-Sided Agenda

Obama never mentioned the need to protect industry from government when he announced his multi-sector initiative only six weeks after inauguration. He had criticized what he once called "big" and "outdated agencies" when he accepted the Democratic nomination in 2008, but was the first president since Eisenhower to call for a proper meshing of government and industry. He had already embraced Hillary Clinton's 2007 campaign promise to cut 500,000 contract employees, albeit without setting a specific target.[20] Obama's campaign also reported his concerns about outsourcing in an August 2008 response to a *Washington Post* candidate questionnaire:

> Obama is concerned by the rising number of government contractors that are often unaccountable and often less efficient than government workers. As president, Obama will restore effective oversight of the government contracting process and reduce our nation's increasing dependence on private contractors in sensitive or inherently governmental functions. Obama will eliminate the Bush administration's ideological bias towards outsourcing of government services and abandon initiatives, like the inefficient use of private bill collectors to collect federal taxes that are a demonstrated waste of taxpayer money.[21]

The Obama campaign deepened this position only weeks before the general election in its "Change We Need in Washington" online booklet.[22] According to the inventory of promises, the administration intended to cut contract spending by 10 percent, strengthen protections for contract employees, ban cost-plus and no-bid contracts, and prohibit contracting with "tax cheats." Obama referred to the promises from time to time as part of his broader attack on government waste, including promises to harvest billions in savings.[23]

Obama focused on the government side of the complex, too. He promised to appoint chief performance officers in every department and agency, create SWAT teams to "set tough performance targets and hold managers responsible for progress," move workers from "bloated bureaucracies" to the frontlines, thin the ranks of middle managers, and give government agencies the right infrastructure for the twenty-first century.[24] Most of the promises were set aside in Obama's shorter campaign speeches, but he often referenced Whitten's cap when he promised to "fire government managers who aren't getting results."[25]

Obama moved first on a highly publicized effort to reset and reinforce the government-industrial dividing line. He mentioned no-bid contracts in his first congressional address at the end of February 2009, outlined his reforms in early March remarks after a meeting with Senate Armed Services Committee chairman and ranking member, Carl Levin (D-MI) and John McCain(R-AZ) at his side, and made his case for action in a prime-time news conference two weeks later still. Having promised to save $40 billion a year through contract reform, Obama said he would make sure the federal government stopped fattening defense contractors.[26]

Obama also affirmed his commitment to government-side reform just three weeks later still by appointing Jeffrey Zients as the first chief performance officer of the United States. Obama embraced Zients' reorganization proposals in his 2011 State of the Union address when he told Congress, "We shouldn't just give our people a Government that's more affordable, we should give them a government that's more competent and more efficient."[27] He restated this commitment to a "leaner, smarter and more consumer-friendly" government in 2012 and asked Congress to revive the president's reorganization authority as the first step toward abolishing the Commerce Department.[28]

Obama pursued these contract-side reforms even after Republicans won the House majority in 2010 and the Senate in 2014. "We sure could use Congress' help particularly at a time when Congress is saying they want more efficient government," he barked at reporters in July 2013. "They give a lot of lip service to it—and we're operating under severe fiscal constraints."[29] He asked Congress to approve the Commerce reorganization in his 2016 and 2017 budgets but had lost his chance three elections earlier when Republicans recaptured their House majority in 2010. Despite his obvious frustrations, Obama's government-industrial agenda still stands as the first sustained effort to honor Eisenhower's call for a proper meshing. He could have done more through executive orders to expose dark money but did more than any recent president to prevent the disastrous rise of misplaced power on both sides of the complex.

Reset and Reinforce

As noted in Chapter 2, Jamie Whitten's cap on total federal employment established a political litmus test that still exerts great force to this day. Its repeal did not weaken its impact on the politics of headcount, nor did it open the gates for comprehensive workforce reform. Whitten's amendment has been erased from the statute books, but his ghost will haunt the government-industrial balance until Congress and the president reset the cap. The two-million-employee target is now so deeply ingrained in the political discourse that it cannot be ignored.

The first way to reset Whitten's cap is to amend the budget process to create an annual federal personnel ceiling that includes the estimated contract and grant workforce. Congress could set the target on an agency-by-agency basis or establish a broad total to be allocated as needed. This government-industry focus would give Congress and the president an opportunity to consider the appropriate blend of federal, contract, and grant employees, but would also create new opportunities to attack big government.

The second and more appealing way to reset the cap is to create a formal, even statutory blending process that includes all federal, contract, and grant employees as part of a single workforce. The first challenge in such a reset is preventing Congress and the president from favoring one workforce over another for political gain, while the second is to make sure they maintain a tight focus on putting the right people in the right positions based on clear-eyed analysis of rigorous metrics. As the following pages suggest, this proper blending involves six steps: (1) strengthen workforce accounting systems, (2) encourage the government-industrial workforce to take social responsibility for its work, (3) track movement across the divide between government and industry, (4) sort functions based on careful definitions of which workforce should do what, (5) monitor and reset caps on the true size of the total workforce, and (6) reinforce the dividing lines between government and industry.

Account for Work

The first step toward reblending is to acknowledge the information asymmetries, conflicting motivations, and false premises embedded within the government-industrial complex. Although the complex plays a central role in faithfully executing the laws, the lack of rigorous workforce accounting undermines careful analysis needed to secure the highest benefit, performance, and accountability.

The federal government's contract and grant databases may be adequate for generating broad estimates of the number of contract and grant employees, but Congress and the president need more than headcounts to create a proper blending of the federal government's workforces. They must also know what federal, contract, and grant employees produce and whether their work crosses the line to inherently governmental responsibility that must remain on the government side of the blend.

However, Congress and presidents have yet to establish an ironclad divide between government and industry. Whether enunciated in statutes such as the Federal Activities Inventory Reform (FAIR) Act of 1998, OMB guidance such as Budget Circular A-76, policy letters, executive guidance, or presidential press gaggles, the line remains very much in the eye of the beholder and bidder. The ambiguity is not for a lack of detail. Rather, it is the product of constant change in the mix of products and services needed to execute the laws faithfully. The line cannot be so porous as to invite unwarranted influence, but not so dense that it threatens urgent action.

The concept of an inherently governmental function is easy to grasp in the abstract, but it is currently surrounded by what procurement expert Thomas J. Laubacher calls a "hodgepodge of definitions, lists, and instructions" that has done more to undermine clarity than enhance it, while tending toward what former OMB senior executive Jonathan Breul calls the "rigid pursuit of sterile, ideological orthodoxy."[30]

The Federal Activities Inventory Reform (FAIR) Act is an example of the need for greater precision. The statute was introduced in 1997 as the Freedom from Government Competition Act. As the title suggests, the 1997 version was designed to protect industry from government encroachment. Not only did Congress declare that private business was the strength of the American economic system and the most productive, efficient, and effective source of products and services, but it also declared that government competition was detrimental to all businesses, especially when the government acts beyond its core mission to engage in unfair competition.[31] Every sentence and declaration in the bill after the enacting clause was jettisoned en route to final passage as the FAIR Act the next year, but the demand for sorting remained. Departments and agencies were ordered to generate annual public lists of "not inherently governmental functions" and to subject the activities to reasonable cost comparisons in pursuit of competitive sourcing.

On the notion that agencies need help drawing lines between what federal, contract, and even grant employees can and cannot do, the FAIR Act was broadly designed to provide a simple action-forcing definition of the term, "inherently governmental function." According to the act, the term refers to a "function that is so intimately related to the public interest as to require performance by Federal Government employees."[32]

The standard definition may be brief, but it comes with a long list of examples. The word "intimately" implies a judgment, of course, as does the associated description of "functions included" that "require either the exercise of discretion in applying Federal Government authority or making of value judgments in making decisions for the Federal Government," and "the interpretation and execution of the United States so as (1) to bind the United States to take or not take some action; (2) to determine, protect, and advance United States economic, political, territorial, property, or other interests; (3) to significantly affect the life, liberty, or property of private persons; (4) to commission, appoint, direct, or control officers or employees of the United States; or (5) to exert ultimate control over the acquisition, use, or disposition of the property of the United States." The statute also contains more than enough adjectives and adverbs to dim even the brightest of lines.[33]

The act had an immediate impact on federal workforce accounting. OMB revised its coding system for monitoring commercial activities and ordered departments and agencies to organize their inventories of full- and part-time positions into four categories: (1) inherently governmental and should be reserved for federal employees only, (2) commercially available, but specifically exempt from competition, (3) commercially available and should be opened to competition, or (4) commercially available, but must be reserved for federal employees.

If the differences among the second, third, and fourth categories seems uncertain, it is not because of a lack of accompanying examples, lists, and tests. Rather, it is because the differences involve difficult interpretations of where to draw the lines between "should" and "may," and whether the interpretation is being used to push or pull functions back across the government-industry divide through insourcing or outsourcing.[34]

Early in Obama's 2009 attack on outsourcing, for example, Congress and the Obama administration ordered all departments and agencies except for Defense to give "special consideration" to calling back any function that was then being performed by a contractor and had been performed by federal employees at any time during the previous ten years, and/or was a function closely associated with the performance of an inherently governmental function, and/or was being performed under a contract that had been awarded without competition, or had been poorly performed.[35] Similar directions can be found regarding the decision to push activities outward through public-private competitions, most of which give the benefit of the doubt to commercially available sources.

Where one stands in these debates depends on where one sits institutionally and politically, and the time has come to embrace simplification over further specification. As Laubacher argues, the current definition of inherently governmental will never be usable—it is "overbroad" and "lacks any concrete aspects" that can be used to force decisions:

> When examining previous definitions of inherently governmental functions for specific aspects capable of guiding the analysis of a function, one aspect stands out: the use of discretion. The more discretion a contractor (an agent) enjoys—that is, the more leeway the contractor has and the more serious the potential impact of contractor's decisions and actions—the more likely the contractor's function is "inherently

governmental" and should not be outsourced to a private actor. . . . But discretion alone cannot be enough to classify a function as inherently governmental. There must be a link between the use of discretion and the government needing to retain control over that function. Such a link can be found by focusing on the application of that discretion.[36]

Laubacher's simple alternative focuses on the control of federal resources and the possible denial of rights and liberty: "any exercise of discretion that (a) directs, controls, or obligates funds, resources, or employees of the United States; or (b) that deprives citizens of rights or liberties."[37] Laubacher's tests show that his simple definition is broad enough to capture most of the activities currently used to illustrate inherently governmental functions, and he argues that federal courts would be better suited than Congress to resolve disputes over administrative decisions.[38] As such, Laubacher's definition would eliminate the need for more than a handful of examples in case federal courts became the destination for resolution.

The definition could be tested easily and formalized as part of the federal government's effort to create rigorous inventories of its contracted services.[39] As detailed in chapter 1, Congress ordered the Defense Department to create the first inventory in 2008 to track the surge in service-contract spending during the Iraq and Afghanistan wars, and expanded the concept all departments and agencies two years later under the 2010 Consolidated Appropriations Act. Also note that it is still unclear whether departments and agencies will ever use the data for sorting their blended workforces. GAO highlighted the issue in its 2016 analysis of the Defense Department's system, was responsible for more than half of all federal service contract spending at the time:

> As we noted almost a decade ago, critical to being more strategic is knowing what you are spending today and what you intend to spend in the future. In that regard, DOD programs have data on not only what they intend to spend next year on services, but, within reason, how much they anticipate spending beyond the budget year. Despite the availability of this data, senior DOD leadership has limited insight on future spending because DOD and the military departments' guidance governing the programming process do not require that it be provided. In other words, data on planned spending on contracted services do not get shared beyond the program office. As a result, DOD may be missing an opportunity to make more strategic decisions and improve the management and oversight of more than half its contract dollars.[40]

Laubacher's definition would expose these issues to the sunlight, thereby exposing the false premises embedded in regulating the government-industrial relationship, while forcing Congress and the president to make the trades discussed later in this chapter. As Guttman argues, the federal government continues to believe that there is one set of rules that governs federal employees, a second that governs contract employees, and, by implication, a third that governs grant employees. Guttman also argues that the federal government continues to believe that it has the capacity to oversee the rules with the "presumption of regularity," meaning the information and expertise to enforce the rules.[41]

Guttman argues that both premises are wrong. Federal, contract, and grant employees may have different motives, but the revolving door between the three destinations creates at least some shared interest, as do shared commitments to public service. At the same time, Guttman challenges the one-sided focus on government as the problem: "What, for example, if the rules that protect us against official abuse are not applied to those who, in fact, increasingly do the government's work? What if, for example, the presumption that officials have the capacity to oversee contractors runs against the reality that they do not and, indeed, that the work of contractor management is itself often contracted out?"[42]

Acknowledgment is both impossible and dangerous without clarity, but clarity may be unattainable without sunshine.[43] New York University's Brennan Center for Justice has been particularly aggressive in promoting disclosure and publicity to expose dark money. Obama could have created the sunshine through another in his long list of executive orders on contracting:

> Such disclosure would not bring all dark money to light, but it would expose a type of dark money that should be especially troubling: campaign contributions that could have been given to influence a contract awarded by the government. The federal government spends hundreds of billions of dollars on such contracts every year. Disclosure would protect the integrity of the contract award process, and provide the public with confidence that taxpayer money is not being misused to reward big donations.[44]

As noted earlier, partisans on both sides of the aisle appear to be equally conflicted on disclosure because dark money helps both parties. According to Center for Responsive Politics, dark-money PACs donated $1.1 billion to candidates and causes between 2008 and July 2016, including almost $320 million in the 2012 presidential election year and almost $50 million even before the Democratic and Republican nominating conventions.[45] Although it will take time to tally the total amount of dark money spent in the 2016 campaign, most of the undisclosed spending of the funding almost certainly found its way to incumbents in both parties—super PACs tend to invest in guaranteed winners rather than long-shots.

Accept Social Responsibility

The federal government began World War II with an acquisitions system built on full competition through sealed bids but ended it with a much more flexible system that allowed negotiated sole-source, cost-plus-fixed-fee contracts with little oversight. Whereas the prewar process was considered democratic, the postwar system was considered fast and efficient.[46] Competitive bidding was not dead, but the Armed Services Procurement Act of 1948 listed seventeen exceptions to using a competitive bidding process nonetheless. The result was a dramatic rise in sole-source contracts that allowed maximum flexibility in both choosing the contractor and altering the specifications as needed.

Congress turned to reform as its wartime profiteering investigations came to a close after the war. Overpricing, price gouging, cost overruns, and corruption prompted a series of visible investigations and calls for acquisition reform. By the end of the 1950s, the federal government was moving back toward the more structured prewar process and began building a professionalized acquisitions workforce to administer a growing inventory of rules.[47]

The system had become so complicated by 1974 that Congress created the Office of Federal Procurement Policy (OFPP) to explain the rules. Housed within OMB, the office was given even more authority five years later when it assembled the Federal Acquisition Regulation as the "go-to" source for questions and guidance on every aspect of the acquisitions process.[48]

The same argument holds for ethics regulation. Although many president enters office promising to "drain the swamp," restore trust in government, or re-create the most ethical administration in history, efforts to "scandal proof" government rarely produce the desired results.[49] Many are never implemented, others are poorly designed, and still others are ignored as other priorities take over. As Dennis F. Thompson argues, ethics regulation is often ignored because it is difficult to understand:

> Ethics regulation is intended not to prevent crimes (that is what the law is for), and not merely to promote favorable public relations (that is what political operatives are for). Its main purpose is to create and sustain confidence in government—to give the public reasonable assurance that public officials are making decisions on the merits for the right reasons. To be sure, ethics regulation is also supposed to create incentives to make decisions on the merits, but for that purpose other methods are available and more effective—making sure that honest and qualified people are appointed, for a start. Ethics regulation assumes that most officials are honest. It would not be sustainable otherwise. The rules are to provide reassurance, not to instigate recriminations.[50]

This reassurance depends on voluntary acceptance of the same calls for social responsibility that currently echo through the private sector. The federal government began promoting social responsibility in 2007 by ordering contract firms to develop codes of conduct, train their employees on violations, disclose improper conduct, and take prompt corrective action.[51] Contract firms followed the rules with fill-in-the-blank templates but showed little commitment to corporate social responsibility. Many firms promised to do well by doing good, but their embrace has often been peripheral to their operations.[52]

The federal government is partially to blame. Its "Contractor Code of Business Ethics" sets minimal expectations and is easy to finesse. Whereas the movement asks corporations to do the right thing because it sells, the contractor code dates to the Reagan-era procurement scandals and the effort to ferret out fraud, waste, and abuse in government contracting. The Packard Commission examined the "increasingly troubled relationship between the defense industry and government" and reached a familiar conclusion:

> Though government oversight is critically important to the acquisition process, no conceivable number of additional federal auditors, inspectors, investigators, and prosecutors can police government fully, much less make it work more effectively. Nor have criminal sanctions historically proved to be a reliable tool for ensuring contractor compliance. We conclude there is an urgency in dealing affirmatively with contractor practices.[53]

Having rejected calls for tougher laws, the Packard Commission focused on deregulation, professionalism, streamlining, government-industrial collaboration, innovation, and even a more flexible personnel system. In short, the commission provided an outline for reinventing government a decade before Gore entered office as vice president.

This affirmative approach led to new rules for ethics and codes of conduct inside the government-industrial complex. Like the corporate social responsibility and shared value movements, the federal government makes the case that contract firms should be ethical but does not provide the definition of the "satisfactory record of integrity and business ethics" or conduct "with the highest degree of integrity and honesty" embedded in the new directives.[54] Indeed, the entire regulation occupies less than two pages in acquisition regulation, which explains another ambiguity in federal contract management.

Moreover, some departments and agencies appear to be "teaching to the test" when outlining their expectations. The Federal Highway Administration even provides a cut-and-paste cover letter companies can use to announce their programs; definitions of key terms such as "code," "corporate compliance program," "program," and "employee;" the specific standards that meet its requirements; a list of consequences; and a signed acknowledgment of receipt from each employee of the "X Company."[55]

GAO expressed its concern about compliance in a 2009 assessment of Defense Department contract firms.[56] Contract firms had filled out the ethics reports and posted information but commitment looked peripheral. The department did not have the capacity to verify implementation, while some companies exposed employees to potential harassment.[57]

Track the Movement

As noted earlier in this book, federal government's current tracking systems suffer from a variety of problems that lead to confusion, deception, and inaccuracy. Even if these deficits were to be closed, the data would still pour into an "alphabet soup" of competing databases that defy thoughtful analysis and broad analysis of the contract workforce.[58]

In theory, the Federal Awardee Performance and Integrity Information System (FAPIIS) solved the problem when it came online in 2011. The system promised to give government and the public a full profile on every contract through an integrated platform.[59]

In practice, the FAPIIS may turn out to be another disappointment. The system has become easier to use over time but still contains gaps and errors. The system also suffers limits on public access to information on contractor performance. The congressional arbiters of FAPIIS transparency remain convinced that contract firms must protect proprietary information, but even simple summaries of data elements and evaluation methods would create a check on unwarranted influence.[60]

The standard answer to these problems has been more data and tighter rules, which produce more bad data, poor decisions, and public confusion.[61] Instead of adding another layer of integration, the federal government would be well advised to turn to recent breakthroughs in big-data analysis, crowdsourcing, "data exhaust" management, and visualization to achieve Woodrow Wilson's promised transparency:

> Light is the only thing that can sweeten our political atmosphere—light thrown upon every detail of administration in the departments; light diffused through every passage of policy; light blazed full upon every feature of legislation; light that can penetrate every recess or corner in which any intrigue might hide; light that will open to view the innermost chambers of government, drive away all darkness from the treasury vaults.[62]

The Recovery Accountability and Transparency Board that monitored the 2009 stimulus package could supply this disinfectant today. Working with a small staff, the Recovery Operations Center (ROC) managed to build the analytic capacity to examine contracts and grants to 1.7 million entities in 2012 and 2013 alone, and helped the OIGs monitor potential sources of fraud, waste, and abuse. Supported by barely three dozen federal and contract employees, the Center developed a suite of powerful predictive tools for identifying high-risk, high-value targets for further investigation that included link analysis and data mining.

Although these methods were still evolving as the effort came to an end, GAO encouraged Congress to reconstitute the ROC as a "proven resource" as a source of contract and grant accountability.[63] According to the study, a separate and centralized source of data analytics would add significantly to the federal government's ability to track and reduce risk, including improper encroachment across the government-industrial divide.

Dennis Thompson argues that the federal government already has more than enough agencies to monitor the government-industrial complex, but he also believes that ethics oversight requires a "body devoted to ethics policy" that would be modeled on the White House Council of Economic Advisors, National Economic Council, or even the National Security Council. Thompson's Council of Ethics Advisors would be housed in the Executive Office of the President and would advise the administration on policy, not prosecution:

> The Council would advise the president and his staff on the broad range of ethics issues. The Council would normally not deal with individual cases but would concentrate on general policies. Specifically, the Council would review current procedures and policies, examine the effectiveness of enforcement, report on trends and patterns in compliance and violations, explore best practices in the states and other countries, and provide opinions on relevant congressional legislation. It would make recommendations to the president for new policies and procedures and try to ensure that they are consistent across the government as far as reasonable, taking into account the different circumstances of various agencies and branches.[64]

Sort the Functions

Congress and presidents frequently struggle to define clear boundaries between commercial activities that can be performed either by federal or contract employees and inherently governmental functions that can be performed only by federal employees. The Eisenhower administration was the first to define commercial activities, while the Carter administration was the first to define inherently governmental activities in 1979.[65]

Despite further refinements over the decades, the definitions and weights assigned to the two key terms have moved back and forth over the decades. Even the use of seemingly simple adjectives such as "substantial," "critical," "near," or "close" can ignite a political firestorm.

Like so many decisions in government, the line between federal, contract, and grant employees often depends on who is holding the pen. Moreover, as CRS argues, the debate about where to draw the line is as old as the Constitution and the continued struggle over shared powers.[66] Ever was it thus perhaps and certainly ever has it been since the 1920s when the fight between public and private contracting broke out. As Don Price wrote of the government's scientific estate in 1965, much of the debate about government and industry does not involve elegant theory and analysis but "the grubby level of law enforcement and legislative investigations."[67]

OBAMA'S ORDER. Obama put these conflicts at the top of his government reform agenda when he ordered his staff to develop a new sorting system for rebalancing the government-industrial complex by 2011. Although the administration's ardor for acquisitions eventually cooled as it turned toward the 2012 election amid heightened concern about the war on terrorism, it left behind a valuable template that can be refined for future legislative action. Indeed, as noted below, the Obama approach is almost perfect for the task, if only because it is just fuzzy enough to provoke support on both sides of the complex.

Led in part by 2008 legislation demanding a "single consistent definition" of terms even before Obama arrived, the administration's sorting campaign began on March 4, 2009, when the White House released the president's memorandum on federal procurement.[68] Speaking with reporters immediately after announcing the initiative, Obama highlighted the rough doubling of noncompetitive contracts during the Iraq and Afghanistan wars and offered his own history of the "blurred" line between government and industry:

> For decades, the Federal Government has relied on the private sector for necessary commercial services used by the Government, such as transportation, food, and maintenance. . . . However, the line between inherently governmental activities that should not be outsourced and commercial activities that may be subject to private sector competition has been blurred and inadequately defined. As a result, contractors may be performing inherently governmental functions. Agencies and departments must operate under clear rules prescribing when outsourcing is and is not appropriate.[69]

Having placed the blame on contractors, Obama showed little interest in the underlying pressures that had led government to release inherently governmental functions in the first place.[70] So noted, he deserves credit for putting reform high on the policy agenda and setting clear deadlines for action. The OMB was to develop guidance by July 1, 2009, for "appropriate corrective action" to modify or cancel contracts that were unlikely to meet government's needs, which was code speak for insourcing, while OFPP administrator Daniel J. Gordon would draft a formal policy letter providing guidance on "governmental outsourcing for services is and is not appropriate" by September 30.[71] These directives led directly to the development and final publication of OFPP's 2011 policy letter on "Work Reserved for Performance by Federal Government Employees."[72]

THE FINAL DRAFT. The letter was published for notice and comment on September 30, revised in response to 30,050 comments, and published as formal policy on September 11, 2010. Gordon's letter honored Obama's demand for formal guidance for reserving certain kinds of duties solely for federal government employees, but it also contained a sorting scheme that remains one of the most significant clarifications since the Eisenhower administration developed the first definition of inherently governmental and commercially available functions in 1955.[73]

As the Congressional Research Service later reported, Gordon's letter clearly embraced Obama's vision of "multi-sector workforce management" that put the onus on federal agencies to prove their reliance on contract employees was "not excessive." Whereas the first definitions of federal "sourcing policy" put the onus on federal agencies to prove they were not robbing industry of commercially available work, Gordon's focused on how to ensure that industry was not robbing government of inherently governmental work.[74] As Gordon later explained, the federal government had been moving toward industry since 1992 as it shifted from closed-ended contracts to open-ended indefinite-contracts (IDIQ), in part because of the "unconscious assumptions regarding optics" and the pressure to do more with less without looking like big government:

> But whatever the reason, the Federal Government had come to depend on contractors—at home, but also in Iraq, Afghanistan and elsewhere overseas. And dependence on contractors sometimes crossed the line from healthy use to unhealthy overreliance, especially with respect to services. . . . I remember a junior member of an agency's contracting office telling me, in a mix of frustration and regret, that in her agency service contractors told the agency what it needed, wrote up those needs as statements of requirements and then won contracts to meet those needs. At another agency, I was told that no federal employee

understood the agency's information technology system and that the contractors were in control.[75]

Gordon started his final letter by answering the president's demand for "tough new guidelines" on services that should be performed only by government employees. He deepened the definition of inherently governmental functions through new adjectives and examples, ordered departments and agencies to pay special attention to functions that support inherently governmental activity and are therefore closely related, and introduced the government-industrial complex to his new concept of critical functions.

Gordon defined critical functions as activities "necessary to the agency being able to effectively perform and maintain control of its mission and operations," while ensuring "that Federal employees have the technical skills and expertise needed to maintain control of the agency mission and operations."[76] The government-side of the complex could not perform its inherently governmental functions or outsource its closely related functions unless it had the capacity to deliver the products and services itself and/or oversee the contract and grant employees chosen to fill the gaps.

Defined as such, critical functions were as important, if not more so, as inherently government functions and were therefore exempt from cost/benefit analysis. Some experts even began talking about "critical-function thinking" as essential to workforce reblending. If Congress and the president could not protect critical functions, they could not support the close-to-inherently governmental functions that support the governmental functions at the top of the sorting pyramid.[77]

Gordon finished his discussion of his three-tiered sorting scheme by providing further details on activities that are "closely associated" with inherently governmental functions. As agencies identify inherently governmental functions, they should also bear in mind that "certain services and actions that generally are not considered to be inherently governmental functions may approach being in that category because of the nature of the function and the risk that performance may impinge on federal officials' performance of an inherently governmental function."[78] Although departments and agencies would have to decide who could perform these functions, Gordon stated that federal employees should be given "special consideration" in making the choice.[79]

NOT ENOUGH SAIL? Despite Gordon's definitional labor, the policy letter arrived just before Republicans regained control of the House. The letter has not been repealed, but it has no force. Whereas Schooner described George W. Bush's procurement agenda in 2004 as *more* sail than rudder, Obama's effort may have produced *more* rudder than sail.[80] The letter produced intense opposition and faded from the president's agenda as the president moved into re-election mode after Republicans reclaimed the House majority. POGO had described Gordon as a "procurement Superhero" when he took his post after seventeen years in GAO, but insourcing turned out to be a source of constant attack.

Gordon's letter resolved long-standing disputes about who should do what and where, but it also contained more than enough ambiguity to earn plaudits from both sides of the government-industrial complex. As POGO's general counsel Scott Amey said at the time, "the proposed rule establishes a target approach that will better ensure companies with a financial interest are not driving policies and programs," while the contract lobby was broadly supportive:

> Rather than focus on labels that serve only as code words for desired outcomes, the proposed policy offers a solid foundation on which agencies can make practical and necessary decisions about how best to execute their missions by appropriately capitalizing on the total suite of resources available to them. We appreciate that the proposed policy letter does not pick winners or losers and is sector neutral when highlighting agency management's responsibilities.[81]

Gordon understood the challenge, too, and admitted as much when he wrote of the complexities surrounding multiple activities or tasks, some of which may be inherently governmental, some of which may be closely associated with inherently governmental work, and some of which may be neither.[82] The only way to know what government and industry can, should, and must do is to check the examples, weigh the responsibilities, make the call, and wait for Congress and the president to fight it out. Hence, the sorting process is perhaps best described as an "inherently political function" where simplification provides the opportunity for debate and resolution.

Set the Cap

Whitten's two-million cap was deceptively simple. He did not require thickets of data, years of analysis, deep regulation, or even CBO guidance.[83] As he testified, all he needed was persistence:

> Each time I offered that resolution I got the support of all the minority members but lost the support of the majority, and that was true, whether the majority was Republican or Democrat. Whichever was in the majority was against me, but the minority was always for it at that time. "You have not got a chance to pass it," I have been told, "it is too simple and practical."[84]

Being true to Whitten's "simple and practical" method, it is time to let the government-industrial complex expand and contract without regard to Whitten's limits. The public should know just how big government broadly combined is at any given point. Congress and presidents will always be tempted to target one workforce or another, but they should be clear that the federal workforce included federal, contract, and grant employees. Setting targets for this combined workforce will require some mix of estimates, inventories of contract services, and easily accessible federal personnel records. Once in hand, Congress could cap the totals at a specific number and give the president authority to waive the target during emergencies.

Adding contract and grant employees to the discussion of federal workforce planning would simultaneously help the public understand the number of employees needed to execute the laws, while showing the movement of contract and grant employees into government to backfill the vacancies created by caps, cuts, and freezes. Although the figures presented in this book are best treated as an illustration of the true size of government, they do provide support for adding contract and grant employees to the total federal workforce. They also illustrate the need to examine the blended workforce regularly.

The effort could start with a small drafting group chaired by recent champions of reform such as Davis, Mary Landrieu (D-LA), Carl Levin (D-MI), Voinovich, Olympia Snowe (R-ME), Mark Warner (D-VA), Henry Waxman (D-CA), and former heads of OFPP, OMB, and OPM such as Mitch Daniels (George W. Bush), Janice LaChance (Clinton), Mitch Daniels (Bush), and Daniel Gordon (Obama), Steven Kelman (Clinton), Alice Rivlin (Clinton), and Linda Springer (George W. Bush). Working with data and options from POGO, the Partnership for Public Service, and other good-government groups, and credentialed by GAO, the group just might forge a bipartisan success.

However, the reset must start with head-to-head comparisons of the true size of the government-industrial workforce. Such comparisons require an injection of integrity and rigor into the current system, as well as a confrontation with political manipulation of the kind that infiltrated the Defense Department's inventories of contracted services during the Obama administration.[85] As POGO argued in a November 2014 letter to then Defense secretary Chuck Hagel, high-level Defense offices were engaged in a "concerted effort" to "willfully breach and congressional mandates." POGO also reminded the secretary that Congress had made its intent for headcounts quite clear: "Despite DoD's promises through the years, Congress has repeatedly expressed in statute, report language, and letters that it is dissatisfied with DoD's progress on providing service contract information. Unfortunately, Congress is justified in its frustration."[86]

The inventories are worth improving. They eventually could provide the kind of head count data needed to monitor and adjust the flow of functions across the government-industrial border. According to RAND, the data should eventually help Congress and presidents track the personnel cost of their decisions while promoting more attention to accountability and performance. For now, the inventories are not measuring up well to congressional expectations, while some of the data are based on little more than guesses by overworked and undermotivated contractors.[87]

Done well and consistently, these inventories could provide the backbone for blending the future workforce discussed in the next chapter.[88] However, as GAO concluded in 2016, it is unclear when the information will be able to withstand audit, especially regarding the use of service contractors to perform inherently government functions. More to the point of resetting Whitten's cap, GAO also reported that the department had not appointed any official to use the inventory for workforce planning or budget decisions. Reading between the lines, GAO seemed to indicate that the department viewed the inventories as another piece of paperwork to be satisfied.[89]

Nevertheless, the Defense Department's inventory was an important first step toward government-wide success in collecting precise data on the service contract workforce needed for rebalancing the government-industrial complex. Presented to the Senate Armed Services Committee on August 31, 2015, the department reported that it had employed 641,428 service contractors the previous year, including almost 240,000 at the navy, 190,000 at the army, and 125,000 at the air force. According to the Defense Department, the numbers were based on information from contractors, inferred from contract invoices, developed by the department's own contract offices, and based on an estimating algorithm or an internal cost-to-head-count formula.[90]

Some of these methods appear to be "sufficiently reliable," as GAO might say, for use in workforce planning, but an unknown percentage of the numbers came from contract firms and "guesstimates" that hardly seem rigorous. Nevertheless, the inventory does provide important insights on the true size of the service contract workforce in the largest department of government. According to the data, the department's service contracts covered a third or more of the federal government's 3.6 million contract employees. In addition, simple division shows that the department's service contract employees cost an average of $204,000 each in 2014.[91]

The contract lobby ignored the findings, as did members of the House Yellow Pages Caucus. Both groups demanded an end to a 2009 moratorium on federal job competitions. (Recall that the Bush administration believed that any job listed in Yellow Pages phone book should be contracted out.)[92]

The moratorium was imposed in response to the *Washington Post*'s Pulitzer Prize–winning investigation of the mistreatment of wounded Iraq and Afghanistan soldiers who returned for care at the Army's Walter Reed Medical

Center.[93] The scandal had many causes but occurred during a distracting job contest. The contest had already taken six years by the time the scandal broke and had a direct effect on the center's morale and overall capacity to conduct the study. As former Army Secretary Togo West later told PBS, the competition itself froze the department:

TOGO WEST: The A-76 procedure is a procedure by which a facility evaluates whether it should take governmental assignments and convert them into private contractor assignments. It almost freezes any hiring until that process is completed. It was a long process. Once it was done, Walter Reed was down by as much as 37 percent among its most important caseworker, nursing, and the like functions.

JIM LEHRER: In other words, the number of people available to do the work was going down while the number of patients was increasing, both of them dramatically, right?

TOGO WEST: That's right. That's exactly right.[94]

However, as if to prove that memories fade, the pressure to renew the job competitions increased as the Defense Department improved its contract data.[95] More accurate data means more accurate and presumably business-favorable cost accounting. "This is about finding the right balance in public/private competition through the A-76 process," Rep. Mark Meadows (R-NC) explained regarding the new bill. "Under current law, public/private competitions are prohibited. We want to learn from past efforts and hopefully begin anew the discussion in the lead-up to a new administration."[96]

Job competitions will always be attractive to the contract lobby, but remain a distracting, rule-bound, and wasteful tool for creating and maintaining a reliable supply of skilled employees. Instead of trying to shift employees from one side of the government-industrial complex to the other, Congress and the president should focus on federal, contract, and grant employees as part of a supply chain for faithfully executing the laws.

Whether called "strategic sourcing," "supply chain risk management," or even old-fashioned "logistics," the buyer (federal government) does not prefer any source of employees (federal, contract, or grant) until the task is set.[97] If the task is defined as "inherently governmental," the source is already defined as federal only. Once past this basic definition and associated "special considerations" given to federal employees, the supply chain opens to other sources. Without saying that job competitions are passé, the focus of this strategic sourcing is the goodness of fit between employee and mission.

The concept may be new to Congress and the president, but it has been at the leading edge in the private sector for several decades. As RAND explains, the rise of supply management systems that focus on a "systemic, strategic approach to the drivers of value" is based on simple realities of a changing world:

> Thirty years ago, true supply chain management was almost unknown within American industry. . . . As demands increased for better quality, faster delivery, and better overall value, a few visionary leaders began to deliberately distinguish between the things that created value and the things that did not. What they discovered was that the supply chain was a huge opportunity waiting to happen. Their companies adopted best practices such as supplier development, cost management, supplier in-tegration, strategic sourcing themselves and value engineering to stay ahead of competitors and position for future success.[98]

GAO made the same point: strategic sourcing was not only more reliable, also reduced costs. Its ongoing study of corporate giants such as Boeing, Dell, Delphi, Humana, MasterCard, Pfizer, and Walmart showed that strategic sourcing could save 4 to 15 percent per year. The savings did not come from downsizing, but from a mix of competition, simple designs, long-range planning, and the volume buying already practiced under the Defense Department's "Better Buying Power 3.0" initiative.[99] According to GAO's estimates, strategic sourcing could have trimmed the federal budget by as much as $12 billion in 2012 alone.[100] I would also argue this sourcing would have strengthened the faithful execution of the laws immeasurably.

Strategic sourcing would automatically reset the Whitten effect, especially if it produced budget savings, and could improve productivity and accounta-bility across the labor supply chain. It might even satisfy the House Yellow Pages Caucus by creating reasonable comparisons across the governmental-industrial complex. The tool not only would produce savings, but also would require max-imum transparency from all suppliers, including full disclosure of socially respon-sible practices, ethics compliance, and fair labor practices. These requirements would apply equally to federal suppliers and might force confrontations with the government's antiquated personnel system.[101]

The concept of strategic sourcing has yet to spark much enthusiasm in the federal government, although the Senate Homeland Security and Governmental Affairs Committee and the House Committee on Oversight and Government Reform have both held recent hearings introducing the topic to their members. When most members hear the term, if they hear it at all, they tend to think "stra-tegic budget cuts."[102]

Congress and the president will no doubt meddle in the process, especially in promoting small- and minority-owned businesses while encouraging more competition. But the basic system just might integrate the federal government's vast inventory of paperwork-heavy human capital, purchasing, budgeting, transportation, hiring, base closing, property management, inspections, and purchasing systems into a front-to-back, top-to-bottom system for deciding who should do what in faithfully executing the laws.

Reinforce the Divide

The contemporary discussion about federal employees has focused much more on preventing the movement of inherently governmental activities across the government-industrial divide than on moving them back. As noted below, insourcing not only carries an implied bias toward government service, but also activates instant opposition from the contract lobby. The question, therefore, is how to conduct a "big sort" of functions needed to reblend the government-industrial workforce without sparking a backlash and inevitable defeat.

MAP THE PROCESS. Making trades across the government-industrial divide requires clear guidance on when government must retain, release, or recall a given function to government or industry:

1. Departments and agencies *must* retain or recall any inherently governmental functions that they identify using OFPP's definitions and examples.
2. Departments and agencies *must* give special consideration to federal employees for performing functions that are "closely associated with" inherently governmental tasks.
3. Departments and agencies *must* ensure that they have "sufficient internal capability" to perform critical functions that are important for controlling their missions and operations.
4. Departments and agencies *must* employ and train an adequate number of government personnel to administer contracts and protect the public interest, especially when contractors are performing "closely associated with" or "critical to" the performance of inherently functions.
5. Departments and agencies *must* employ and train enough government personnel to administer contracts and protect the public interest when the nature of a contract itself creates potential confusion as to whether work is being performed by government employees or contractors.[103]

The federal government cannot follow these rules without the authority to recall functions back to government. However, this permission cannot be given without greater clarity on the definition and identification of inherently government functions that are on the wrong side of the divide. Even the most carefully designed workforce analysis cannot withstand dispute if the definition itself is laden with ambiguity. Consider the list of highlighted terms in Gordon's short definition of "sufficient internal capability" as a case in point:

> *Sufficient* internal capability *requires* that an agency have an *adequate* number of positions filled by Federal employees with *appropriate* training, experience, and expertise to understand the agency's requirements, formulate alternatives, take other *appropriate* actions to *properly* manage and be accountable for the work product, and continue *critical* operations with in-house resources, another contractor, or a combination of the two, in the event of contractor default.[104]

Terms such as "appropriate" may have legal standing when linked to inspection, analysis, and judgment, but they nonetheless provoke second-guessing and protest. At the very least, they may trigger endless efforts to quantify the unquantifiable through wrestling matches such as competitive sourcing. With an average of four "appropriates" per page, the policy letter seems to invite the kind of interpretation that has stymied action so often in the past while providing full employment for contract lobbyists.

There are times, for example, when federal employees *must* do the work because the activity "is so intimately related to the public interest as to mandate performance by government personnel," *should* do the work because the function is "closely associated with the performance of an inherently governmental function," or are the only employees who *can* do the work because they have the right skills and experience to outperform nongovernmental employees.[105]

In turn, there are times when federal employees *cannot* do the work because they do not have the needed skills or experience, when they *must not* do the work because it is (1) not deemed inherently governmental and (2) available from commercial sources at equal or lower cost, or when they *should* not do the work because it is unethical, illegal, or prohibited by statute or executive order.

APPLY THE TEST. Gordon's most important contribution to future sorting involved his revised test for determining what government can and might not do. Found late in his 2011 policy letter, the tests form the basis for a trading system. Gordon started his list with a reasonable assertion that every agency has at least some work captured under the intimately related definition discussed above. He then moved on to the following checks:

1. *The Nature of the Function Test*: Functions which involve the exercise of sovereign powers of the United States are governmental by their very nature.
2. *The Exercise of Discretion Test*: A function is to be set aside as inherently governmental if it involves the exercise of discretion, meaning that two or more courses of action exist, but only one can be chosen.

3. *The Functions Closely Associated with an Inherently Governmental Function Test*: As agencies identify inherently governmental functions, they should bear in mind that certain services and actions that generally are not considered to be inherently governmental functions may approach being in that category because of the nature of the function and the risk that performance may impinge on Federal officials' performance of an inherently governmental function.[106]

Each one of these tests involved deeper, often subjective judgments that nonetheless provided more than enough detail to spark caution. However, I believe the discretion test creates the greatest interpretive challenge. According to Gordon's policy letter, a function must be reserved for a government employee if "the contractor's involvement is or would be so extensive, or the contractor's work product so close to a final agency product, as to effectively preempt the Federal officials' decision-making process, discretion or authority."[107]

Acknowledging the inventory of similar tests and examples over the decades, it should not be a surprise that some contract employees might cross the line by helping manage the federal prisoners, writing testimony, providing diplomatic security, conducting cyber-surveillance, conducting interrogations, drafting requests for proposals, and sorting bidders for government contracts. Surely, some of these activities would violate OMB's definition of inherently governmental functions as any activities that "significantly affect life, liberty, or property of private persons."[108]

Much of the information on inappropriate cross-overs is anecdotal. However, GAO discovered at least $20 billion in defense spending for service contract employees covered by the seventeen product codes identified as most likely to include activities closely related to inherently governmental functions. The total vulnerability was just one-eighth of all defense service spending, but the air force, army, and navy all warranted suspicion. For example, one navy statement of work asked a contract firm to support Defense Department budget preparation and draft statements of work for other contract firms. The activities were clearly closely associated with inherently governmental functions and could have easily been classified off-limits.[109]

FIX THE ERRORS. If outsourcing is the obvious tool for transferring commercially available functions to industry, insourcing is the logical tool for recalling inherently governmental functions to government. However, it is more popular to push a function over the government-industrial divide to industry than to pull a function back.

Insourcing may make perfect sense but is easily caricatured as a victory for big government and inefficiency.

The politics of insourcing was so harsh that Obama never uttered the term during his March 4, 2009, press conference on government procurement reform.[110] Nor did he use the term in his order requiring federal departments and agencies "to review existing contracts and formulate appropriate corrective action such as modifying or canceling further spending," or his March 24 press conference on next steps.[111]

Obama did not mince words when he attacked contractors for "massive cost overruns," "outright fraud," "influence peddling," "skimming," "blank checks," and "delay after delay after delay," but he knew the contract lobby would fight back. He also knew that the initiative would increase the number of federal employees and provoke conservative criticism in the 2010 midterm elections. Indeed, liberal advocates of insourcing such as the liberal Center for American Progress (CAP) had reservations. Although CAP endorsed Obama's insourcing agenda as a source of budget savings, protecting inherently governmental functions, and closing skill gaps, it also highlighted the political and fiscal pitfalls:

> To be sure, the idea of expanding government and hiring more bureaucrats at a time when budgets are tight may seem wasteful, but it is more practical and simple than one might expect. Insourcing often results in the individual contractor being hired to do the same work in the very same office under a more direct chain of command. Eliminating the need to pay for the additional layer of corporate bureaucracy that comes with the hiring of a contractor not only saves money, but it can also improve services to the taxpayer if done wisely.[112]

Obama's first OMB director, Peter Orszag, met the president's deadline three months later with a memorandum titled "Managing the Multi-Sector Workforce." Orszag began the memo by recognizing the important role that federal employees and contract employees both play in executing the laws while referencing the need to "achieve the best mix of public and private labor resources to serve the American people." He then criticized federal agencies for following the "one-sided management priorities" of the prior administration, thereby "becoming experts in identifying functions to outsource," while eroding the "in-house capacity that is essential to effective government performance," ignoring "the costs stemming from loss of institutional knowledge and capacity" and tolerating "inadequate management of contracted activities."[113] Orszag ended by ordering departments and agencies to use a simple decision tree to reblend their workforces:

1. Does the fact that contractors perform the work cause the agency to lack sufficient internal expertise to maintain control of its mission and operations? If "yes," develop the capacity. If "no," go to question two.

2. Does preliminary analysis suggest that public-sector performance is more cost effective and that it is feasible to hire federal employees to perform the function? If "yes," develop plans for insourcing. If "no," do not insource unless risks associated with contract performance outweigh federal employee performance.[114]

Orszag's tree may have been short, but it contained a thicket of hidden braches. Departments and agencies were required to complete a series of discrete tasks that included a detailed analysis of cost and performance, a "gap analysis" of the organization's optimal balance of employees and contracts, a pilot recall program upon a multi-sector talent assessment, and further secondary reports and reviews. Given the persistent skill gaps already on GAO's high-risk list of troubled problems in 2010, most departments and agencies would need contract employees just to answer Orszag's questions.

The Defense Department had begun studying the insourcing process even before Obama entered office and issued its own directive two months before Orszag with a "cheat-sheet" for making choices.[115] Unlike Orszag's analysis-heavy process, the department's seven-step, "yes/no" decision tree was designed for speed and tough decisions:

1. Is the mission requirement valid and enduring? If "yes," move on. If "no," eliminate requirement immediately or, if not an enduring requirement, eliminate upon completion of work.
2. Is the function inherently governmental? If "yes," in-source function as expeditiously as possible. If "no," ask question 3.
3. Is the function exempt from private-sector performance? If "yes," in-source as expeditiously as possible. If "no," ask question 4.
4. Is the contract for unauthorized personal services? If "yes," in-source as expeditiously as possible. If "no," ask question 5.
5. Are there problems with contract administration? If "yes," in-source function as expeditiously as possible. If "no," ask question 6.
6. Can all legal, regulatory, and procedural impediments be addressed in the timeframe required and Department of Defense civilians used to perform the work? If "yes," ask question 7. If "no," retain services in the private sector.
7. Does a cost analysis show that Department of Defense civilian performance is more cost effective? If "yes," in-source function as expeditiously as possible. If "no," retain services in private sector.[116]

The Defense tree may have been taller than OMB's, but it put the questions in the appropriate order and demanded definitive answers. Why bother, it seemed to ask, with intense analysis if the mission is not valid? Why begin a legal slugfest if the odds of success are minimal? The department did not have time to waste. Paired with a symbolic three-year hiring freeze in the Office of the Secretary of Defense, the guidance pushed the department to act. As the RAND Corporation later concluded, the department reversed the burden of proof from showing that a function is inherently governmental to showing that a function is not.[117] Moreover, the Defense decision tree was much easier to use, largely because its terms were more familiar. As GAO would report in October 2009, departments and agencies were already three months behind schedule in implementing Orzag's guidelines because they could not make sense of the key terms such as "inherently governmental," "mission-critical," and "core competency.[118]

FOLLOW THE BRANCHES. The Defense Department's decision tree had three advantages over Orszag's approach: (1) it put mission first, (2) it produced quick knockouts of potential targets, and (3) it provided possibilities, not requirements. Orszag's approach pushes departments and agencies toward very expensive and time-consuming analysis before making a go/no-go decision, while the Defense Department's tree allows immediate terminations.

The Defense question tree also started with the issue missing in most other decision trees: is the mission requirement valid and enduring? If the mission is invalid, the requirement should be eliminated immediately; if it is not enduring, it should be eliminated at the end of the contract. Assuming "requiring officers" can define the terms "valid" and "enduring," they have no alternative but to suspend the contract.

The tree does start with a loose sorting of functions that should be performed by federal employees and should be converted, and then turns to the mission assessment. However, unlike other sorting mechanisms, the tree does not assume that all functions qualify for continuance. In contrast, Orszag's memorandum focused more on the workforce:

> Federal agencies must use both federal employees and private sector contractors to deliver important services to citizens. Agency management practices must recognize the proper role of each sector's labor force and draw on their respective skills to help the government operate at its best. Current policies and practices must be improved so that agencies consistently identify the proper role of each sector and achieve the best mix of public and private labor to serve the American people.[119]

Alas, neither Orszag nor the Defense Department ever defined their key terms. Terms such as "important services" and "valid missions" involve considered judgment and electoral consequences. They are not easy to define during a head count exercise. The next iteration of OFPP's definitional letter and the

Defense Department's insourcing directive might start with the same kind of review, if only to remind Congress and the president that the first question for insourcing or outsourcing is the validity of the mission at hand, whatever the term might mean.

PREPARE FOR HARDBALL. The few thousand positions subject to Defense review were trivial compared to the 3.1 million contract employees who worked at the department when the insourcing began, but even the hint of a trade provoked intense opposition. Whereas Obama described his plan as "not outsourcing," the contract lobby was quick to describe insourcing as fuel for big government: "Insourcing for the sake of insourcing is no more intelligent, no more effective and no more defensible than outsourcing for the sake of outsourcing," said a representative of the Professional Services Council; "Pulling jobs out of the private sector in this economy is not good public policy," said an official at the newly formed Small Business Coalition for Fair Contracting; "The federal government has gotten too big to succeed," said the president of the Business Coalition for Fair Competition; and "A better use of everyone's time would be to figure out how to better manage that contractor workforce rather than recreate the era of big government, which has implications not just for those of us working now but for people working for the next couple generations," said the head of Coalition for Government Procurement."[120] *Forbes* put these articles together in writing the obituary for insourcing in March 2011:

> When contractors fail to perform or the job they are doing is completed, the government can simply stop using them. Civil servants will continue to be a burden to the government for decades to come, first as employees and then as retirees. So replacing contract personnel with full-time government workers will tend to raise costs unless the government workers are substantially more productive. Higher productivity is a possibility given the federal worker's commitment to a career in public service, but there is scant research demonstrating such a linkage. In any event, the government loses much of its management flexibility in the bargain.[121]

Defense Secretary Robert Gates soon joined the doubters, too, albeit without the anti-government rhetoric. He had been an enthusiastic insourcer in May 2009 when he promised deep cuts in the number of support-service contract employees and a 30,000 increase in federal employees. However, he soon realized that unraveling decades of dependency with an antiquated procurement and personnel system would take longer than expected.

More important, Gates soon discovered that insourcing was not producing the promised savings. "As we were reducing contractors, we weren't seeing the savings," Gates told *Defense Daily* in August 2010. "You really don't get at

contractors by cutting people," he said, "because you give the contractor a certain amount of money and they go hire however many people they think they
need to perform that contract."[122] The secretary of the army was well on his way
to suspending the program in late 2010, contractors were mounting a campaign
against the effort on Capitol Hill, and rumors of congressional action spread
through the contract community as Republicans celebrated their midterm election victory.

Gordon continued to defend the effort against the growing backlash but
tapped the brakes in mid-December. He still believed in the concept for sure—
"No corporation would agree to have someone else running their entire operations," he said at a media breakfast. "There are far too many situations where we
have yielded control of our own mission to contractors. That needs to be fixed,
but it doesn't require massive insourcing." At the same time, he clarified that
the administration was committed to a targeted effort toward rebalancing the
workforce. "We do not view insourcing as a goal," he said.[123]

MAKE THE TRADES. The first step is managing the fight over who gets
what at the government-industrial divide is to acknowledge that federal agencies,
contract firms, and grant agencies all make mistakes in classifying functions.
Whether the errors are deliberate or benign, a consequence of unwarranted influence or data deficits, or a reflection of uncertainties about future missions or
budgets, there are plenty of examples of misclassification on both sides of the
government-industrial complex. However, most mistakes are made because of
one-sided questions about how much each workforce can deliver on behalf of
the public interest.

Writing of "placard-waving protesters and pontificating scholars" who fixate
on how much contract and grant employees deliver, public-policy scholar John
D. Donahue concludes that "how much" is the wrong question:

> The right question concerns not "how much" but rather, "how" the pri-
> vate sector should be involved. There is a vast, variegated and under-
> examined menu of options. For-profits can carry out cleanly specified
> tasks for an agreed-upon fee, or enter into messier forms of partner-
> ship with shifting goals and shared control. Community organizations
> can parlay grants into social services. Big nonprofits (the Salvation
> Army, Habitat for Humanity, major hospitals, universities and research
> institutions) take on pieces of the public agenda on various terms, from
> contracts to grants to pure charity.[124]

Federal departments and agencies can make two mistakes in sorting functions.
First, they can retain or recall functions that are permissibly and appropriately
assigned to grant-funded organizations—this misclassification often looks like
mission hoarding driven by self-preservation and even aggrandizement. Second,

they can release functions that must be retained under law and regulation—this misclassification often looks like a hedge against the sluggish hiring process and the costly uncertainty as Congress and the president wander from stalemate to stalemate. Better to release an inherently governmental function to a contract firm or grant recipient than to watch it starve.

More troubling is that at least some departments and agencies would rather would rather use contract and grant employees at higher cost than hire, train, advance, discipline, and manage employees in a delay-ridden, rule-bound, antiquated government personnel system. Whereas federal executives can hire and fire a contract employee in the same day, they are lucky if they can hire and fire a federal employee in 250 days.[125]

Hence, any sorting system for retaining or recalling inherently governmental functions must also contain options for releasing functions that are better performed by contract or grant employees. The same cost analysis that supports insourcing can promote outsourcing, for example, while the same mission question can apply to both. The federal government does not need more job competitions but does need to create two-way streets for retaining or recalling inherently governmental, closely associated, and critical functions back into government, while releasing non-inherently governmental, commercially available, and cost-effective functions out. Instead of giving the benefit of the doubt to one destination, managing the multi-sector workforce must be fair, transparent, and cost-effective.

Thus, if Congress and the president want to do the right thing for taxpayers, the sorting process must abandon expectations about how much federal employees cost, and focus on more realistic assessments about how to deliver the federal mission with precision and at a reasonable price. With grantees added to Gordon's original draft, the second paragraph of his 2011 policy letter could be easily adjusted to cover the entire industrial side of the government-industrial complex.

Who Delivers?

The insourcing debacle shows the futility of one-sided trades across the government-industrial divide. Obama may have embraced Eisenhower's call through his campaign and first months in office, but he eventually pursued a one-sided solution to reblending. Obama had always argued insourcing was about saving money and creating greater transparency, but he launched his reforms with a broadside against outsourcing, influence peddling, cost overruns, price gouging, and no-bid and cost-plus contracts that wasted 40 billion taxpayer dollars a year.

Democrats and Republicans will not agree on a new sorting process unless they both have an interest in the result. The public benefit of a government that works better and costs less are not enough to justify even tiny movements across the divide. They must first agree to fair trades and reform on both sides of the complex, focus on honest analysis, and agree from the start that reblending is an iterative process that yields imperfect outcomes.

There are ways to insulate a proper meshing from political pressure, but another national commission is not one of them. Blue-ribbon commissions can produce stellar results on government breakdowns such as the September 11 terrorist attacks, Shuttle *Challenger* accident, Hurricane Katrina, and Iraq wartime contracting, but are incapable of long-term oversight and policymaking.

Once past a commission, there are two devices available. The first is formal delegation of authority to an independent agency modeled on the Recovery Accountability and Transparency Board that provided credible monitoring of the 2009 stimulus package. As noted earlier in this chapter, the board's Recovery Operations Center could be easily retooled as a monitoring source.

The second option is a variation of the Base Realignment and Closure Commission (BRAC). The first BRAC commission was created in 1988 to help Congress and the president close or merge dozens of obsolete military bases, and was followed by four more in 1991, 1993, 1995, and 2005. Each commission was tasked to close or merge obsolete bases as the number of military and civilian personnel continued to fall after the Cold War. Members of Congress often objected to a commission's recommendation to close bases back home, but Congress was only allowed to reject the entire list within a relatively short period of time. If Congress could not pass a resolution of disapproval, the cuts were made, which is exactly what happened in one round after another.[126]

The allure of a similar process for sorting governmental functions and redistributing the numbers of federal, contract, and grant employees based on clear justifications should be obvious. The BRAC process was fast, hard to reject, anchored in careful analysis, independent of presidential and congressional interference, and successful. The BRAC commissions were called upon to make very difficult choices, and they did.

The BRAC commissions were not immune to criticism, however. Their data were often criticized, their memberships included retired military officers with obvious biases toward protecting their own services, and their final lists took intense fire from the contract lobby, members of Congress, and presidential staff.[127] Moreover, as political scientist Kenneth Mayer argues, there are democratic concerns in using a closed process to make very difficult choices:

> Automatic delegation comes at the cost of accountability, which as a policy value is at least as important as rationality and efficiency.

Delegating authority to an independent body, or governing via an automatic rule, is often a "blame avoidance" mechanism designed to obfuscate the ultimate responsibility and make it difficult for voters to connect cause and effect. As we have seen with BRAC, sometimes this works, at least in the sense of producing a preferred but politically difficult outcome that cannot be traced back to the actions of any legislator or group of legislators. But delegation, by itself, does not resolve underlying disagreement and controversies, and the electorate ought to have enough information to assign blame or credit. BRAC arose from an unusual set of circumstances, and it should be replicated with great caution.[128]

At the same time, the BRAC commissions generated enough credibility and operated with enough insulation to make the very difficult choices about whether to close, realign, restructure, or retain precious resources, which makes them particularly attractive as a model for making trades across the government-industrial divide. Even with BRAC-like protection, there will be tough trades and intense opposition, but a bipartisan, quasi-independent shield could reduce the sorting that Whitten's cap has blocked since the Korean War.

The result would not be a work of art, as former Rep. Barber Conable (R-NY) described the 1983 Social Security rescue package but would be the product of artful work.[129] There has not been much artful work on the government-industrial complex of late, but perhaps the effort to reset the Whitten cap might spark some creativity. Whitten just might appreciate the effort—he used plenty of creativity over the years to protect his cap.

5

Conclusion: The "Next Gen" Public Service

Eisenhower's farewell address did much more than simply introduce the nation to a new term. It also created a pairing that could be used to describe almost any intersection between government and industry. The term can also be amended to reference just about any confluence of industry and profit, historian Jeffrey Engle writes, and has been used over the decades to cover a host of troublesome engagements such as the organic-industrial complex, prison-industrial complex, polluter-industrial complex, and even the wedding-industrial complex. "The term is rarely invoked as a compliment," Engle concludes, nor does it reference a hopeful resolution of the problem at hand.[1]

As noted early in this book, Eisenhower gave little guidance on how to compel the proper meshing of the military-industrial complex. Earlier drafts of the address did seem to call on Congress and the next president to exercise "constant vigilance and a jealous precaution against any move which would weaken the control of civil authority over the military establishment" and special care "to avoid measures which would enable any segment of this vast military-industrial complex to sharpen the focus of its own power"[2]

It is not clear why Eisenhower put these burdens solely on an alert and knowledgeable citizenry. Perhaps he knew that a dividing line would be impossible to enforce without full-throated public demand. Indeed, he said as much in his very last press conference the morning after the address. "I know nothing here that is possible, or useful, except the performance of the duties of responsible citizenship."[3]

What is clear is that Eisenhower had concerns about the workforces on both sides of the government-industrial dividing line. This book suggests that Eisenhower's concern about the military-industrial complex applies to the government-industrial complex within which it now runs. The nation continues to depend on many federal, contract, and grant employees, the number of which expands and contracts in response to real world events such as wars and economic crises. The question is not whether the number of federal, contract, and grant employees is too big or small but whether the total is best for the faithful execution of the laws. The answer will still be elusive until Congress and the president close the data deficits needed to faithfully execute the laws about the blended federal workforce.

One conclusion is clear at the end of this journey: the nation will depend on a large and blended workforce far into the future. Congress and presidents may disagree about where to set the boundaries within the government-industrial workforce, but Eisenhower would almost certainly argue that the public benefit must be central to any balancing tests. At the same time, he would caution that both sides of the complex have a stake in protecting their share of the blended workforce. He saw the greatest threat at the intersection between interests and brought his own concerns about public service motivations to his final message.

Eisenhower's Public Service

Eisenhower had expressed deep concerns about his military leaders well before he reached his farewell. He took the military establishment to task early in his administration for opposing his "New Look" defense strategy, and saw the air force as a tireless promoter of increased defense spending. "I'm damn tired of Air Force sales programs," he said in spring 1954 after a particularly blunt meeting about the number of bomber groups. "In 1946, they argued that if we can have seventy groups, we'll guarantee security for ever and ever. . . . Now they have a trick figure of 141. They sell it. Then you have to abide by it or you're treasonous."[4]

Eisenhower also confronted intense resistance to the New Look from the army officer corps. As military historian Donald Carter argues, the New Look not only undermined the army's prestige and influence, but created what some officers saw as an existential threat to the branch's survival. The army's two representatives on the Joint Chiefs of Staff, Generals Matthew Ridgeway and Maxwell Taylor, soon resigned in protest and made their opposition clear to sympathetic members of Congress. According to Carter, Eisenhower considered the opposition to be "outright insubordination" and pushed against the armed forces more generally by sealing off presidential access:

> As the Army's vocal opposition to the New Look continued, Eisenhower took steps to distance himself from all the service chiefs and to limit their role in providing military counsel to his administration. The reorganizations of the Defense Department that he supported in 1953 and 1958 removed the service chiefs from any direct advisory role to

the President and limited their ability to provide military counsel to subsequent commanders-in-chief.[5]

Much of this resistance focused on Eisenhower's defense cuts, which former Reagan-era budget director David A. Stockman celebrated in 2014 as an example for the deficit-plagued Obama administration in an opinion article titled "Yes We Can: How Eisenhower Wrestled Down the US Warfare State." It was Eisenhower, Stockman said, who brought the Defense Department back under control after World War II, and Eisenhower who tamed the "warfare" state. In contrast, it was Obama, Stockman said, who had given in to the pressure for a budget that eclipsed even George W. Bush's final war budget from 2011. "This made one thing abundantly clear," Stockman argued: "Even an out-and-out 'peace' president is no match for the modern warfare state and the crony capitalist lobbies that safeguard the Moloch-like US defense industry's vast budgetary appetites."[6]

Eisenhower also expressed concerns about the senior civil service. Asked if civil servants should feel "jittery" about their jobs as his administration maneuvered to create a category of presidential at-will appointments, Eisenhower said he was a very strong supporter of civil service and merely wanted to protect that "great body of governmental services and competency" by removing them from harm's way:

> I know of no reason why any great number of these people should have the slightest concern about their jobs, because the only thing we have talked about, so far, is policy-making jobs, which must necessarily be subject to appointment by the people that the United States holds responsible for policy. You can't possibly put policy in the hands of a body that cannot be removed, if necessary, by the electorate. That is the way I see it. So there is no excuse whatsoever for the great body of people to believe that their jobs are in jeopardy.[7]

Eisenhower also had strong reservations about the underlying commitment to the public benefit at the top of the federal hierarchy, however. He once declared that that "almost without exception, these individuals reached these high administrative offices through a process of selection based upon their devotion to the socialistic doctrine and bureaucratic controls practices over the past two decades," and expressed frustration about corruption and disloyalty.[8]

Writing for the *American Political Science Review* in 1954, Herman Miles Somers reported that the president "genuinely believed that the executive branch had become contaminated with grafters, incompetents, political hacks, "socialistic thinkers," and even a not inconsiderable number of disloyal persons, and that a wholesale substitution of honest men with administrative ability would solve most of our problems."

Somers also reported that the administration had been giving federal employees "an unremitting psychological pummeling through a constant stream of press releases regarding future budget cuts and releases of personnel," and in doing so through its poor employee relations, had managed to make all employees feel that their jobs were at risk. Although Eisenhower's new Schedule C job pool would only rise to 1,500, it created the image of politicization nonetheless. As noted in chapter 3, it creates a similar image today.[9]

Like Republican presidents who served before and after him, Eisenhower showed an initial preference for the industry side of the government-industrial complex. As Allison Stanger writes in *One Nation under Contract*, Eisenhower's role cannot be understood without referencing the creation of the Defense Department under the 1947 National Security Act:

> Despite the dramatic demobilization of American forces, after World War II the federal budget would never return to prewar levels. The government's projected total outlays for 1947 were roughly four times what they had been in 1940, and they escalated exponentially from there. . . . Big government's shortcomings, the Eisenhower administration reasoned, could be circumvented by harnessing private sector energy, efficiency, and initiative to government ends. Outsourcing followed directly from core American values: faith in free markets and free trade, distrust of big and distant government, and the belief that individuals deserve to reap the benefits of their own striving.[10]

Much as he embraced market virtue during his first term, Eisenhower did not take significant action to rebalance the government-industrial complex until 1955, when his budget director, Roland Hughes, released Bulletin 55-4. The policy was framed by the simple principle that "the government shall not start or carry out any commercial activity to provide a service or product for its own use if the product or service can be procured more economically from a commercial source." Some key terms have been updated in subsequent versions of what is now codified as budget Circular A-76, and the "shall-not-start" clause was removed in a 2003 revision. So noted, the general directive to rely on commercial sources continues to shape the debate about the appropriate government-industry balance.[11]

Eisenhower did not embrace this policy to promote the defense industry or celebrate the number of jobs created through defense spending. Rather, he embraced the policy to help small business.

At the height of his 1956 re-election campaign, for example, Eisenhower sent a public telegram to the head of a small trade association called "Small Businessmen for Ike" to report that the administration had "done more for small business than any prior administration."[12] He began his case for support by reminding readers that he had created the Small Business Administration in 1953 and allowed the excess profits tax to expire at the end of the same year, but quickly turned to a long discussion of the small-business share of federal contracts, expansion of existing small-business set-asides to nondefense departments and agencies, the Federal Trade Commission's attack on unfair competition, and a quarter billion dollars in small business and disaster loans. Eisenhower also celebrated the administration's procurement reforms, new opportunities for small business subcontracting, elimination of what he labeled as 234 federal activities, and his success in getting the federal government "out of competition with cobblers, drycleaners, nurserymen, hotel operators, and other small enterprises."

It is not entirely clear why Eisenhower focused almost exclusively on small business contracting, though one can argue that he must have known that the new budget circular would have no effect on the battle over future defense contracts. Eisenhower also knew the federal government had already made the decision to privatize its once-formable arsenals and shipyards. Although the private sector had provided supplies and services in every American war in history, World War II opened a new era in commercial production of the weapons and ships.

As international relations scholar Aaron Friedberg argues, history did not dictate this "veritable revolution in peacetime procurement practices" that greeted Eisenhower in 1952. Rather, the postwar privatization was the result of a clash of ideas and interests that left private industry well positioned to corner the defense market as the federal government came under attack:

> During the opening years of the Cold War, the public elements in this system came under attack both from Congress and from the top levels of the executive branch. Although the differences were largely a matter of degree, congressional action was more obviously and immediately motivated by a desire to satisfy the demands of industry, while executive decision makers tended to place great emphasis on their desire for efficiency. Throughout the American government and, indeed, throughout American society, there was also a widely shared and ultimately decisive belief that placing primary reliance on the private sector to produce the nation's arms was good for reasons of political principle as well as of practicality.[13]

It is difficult to know whether Eisenhower would have supported this extensive commercialization, but he did express at least some concern about corporate virtue in his decision to abandon the industrial planning that preoccupied the Truman administration in the run-up to the Korean War. He also put defense spending on the cutting block in his "Chance for Peace" speech only months after Inauguration Day.

As Friedberg writes of Eisenhower's final address, the irony of the military-industrial complex circa 1961 was not that it was so big, but why it was not much bigger: "Left unchecked, the forces of expansion might have been expected to gobble up ever-larger portions of the national income and steadily to increase the range and depth of the government's directive powers. In the absence of countervailing pressures the United States might indeed have become a garrison state."[14] Eisenhower created much of the pressure through the budget process, including aggressive use of his impoundment power. As Friedman readily admits, the fact that US policy reflected a balance between ideas and interests is different from saying the result was optimal.

What Would Publius Say?

The Founders sought a similar balance in undertaking Hamilton's arduous enterprises for the public benefit. They recognized private firms had been essential to winning the Revolutionary War, but also knew there had been fraud, waste, and abuse. As Sandy Kenny writes, the corruption was often justified by the need for speed, but it was corruption nonetheless:

> Quartermasters regularly gave inside information on upcoming bids to cousins and colleagues. In a way, this practice could be justified with the arguments that the quartermasters were familiar with these peoples' past performance and so could be sure the government would be getting best value; and, that in the interest of getting supplies to the troops as quickly as possible, advance information was distributed to people the quartermaster knew in order to speed up the process.[15]

Given this experience, it seems reasonable to ask what the Founders would think about changes in the government-industrial complex over the past twenty years. What would they think of the contract lobby and its demand for a share of government work? Would they have agreed with Eisenhower on the potential for unwarranted influence? Would they have demanded tighter boundaries between government and industry? Would they have placed as much faith in an alert and knowledgeable citizenry to compel a proper meshing so that security and liberty could prosper together?

Hamilton laid the groundwork for an answer in the second paragraph of *Federalist*, No 70 when he called upon future presidents to take responsibility for government performance: "A feeble executive but another word for a bad execution; and a government ill executed may be in theory, must be in practice, a bad government."[16]

Hamilton did not provide a list of examples in his call for ratification, but did argue that unity, duration in office, adequate provision of support, and competent powers created energy in the executive. He later argued that safety in the executive depended in part on accountability and transparency. The public could not hold the executive accountable if they cannot detect or assign responsibility for "national miscarriage or misfortune." Nor could the public punish a pernicious measure if responsibility shifts "with so much dexterity, and under such plausible appearances, that the public opinion is left in suspense about the real author."[17]

However, Hamilton knew the contracting process well—he must have encountered fraud, waste, and abuse as army inspector general during the Revolutionary War, and he oversaw the fine details of the federal procurement process as the nation's first secretary of the treasury. He reviewed every contract for purchasing buoys and beacons, building lighthouses and piers, and transporting military supplies. No purchase was too small for Hamilton's review, including the contract for "timer, boards, nails and workmanship" for the Sandy Hook lighthouse in New York Harbor, and the exact number of muskets and cannonballs to be carried on each of the nation's new revenue cutters. According to Ron Chernow, Hamilton asked the president to approve most contracts and even recommended that the new cutters be built in different parts of the union to avoid regional favoritism.[18]

Despite this experience and his penchant for detailed assessments of his work, one might wonder imagine what Hamilton might say about the government-industrial complex. Janine R. Wedel engaged in just such a thought experiment in drafting an appendix to *Federalist*, No. 70 for a special issue of the *Public Administration Review*. Wedel began her journey in 1788 by describing today's dependence on contracts as "Swiss cheese" government before giving Publius a platform for exploring the "massive contracting out of government functions."[19] Writing in Hamilton's voice, Wedel made the case against a government "ill-contracted."

- PUBLIUS: We are now aware that public priorities and decisions are being driven by private actors who are duty-bound to shareholders and investors instead of government officials who are duty-bound to citizens and the national interest, which violated our core principles in drafting the constitution.
- PUBLIUS: Just as we warned against the consolidation of powers, the present fusion of state and private power poses a grave danger to the public and national interest.

- PUBLIUS: Given current events and the exponential increase in the use of private parties to deliver our promised guarantees, we support a fundamental redesign of the system.
- PUBLIUS: We must thoroughly rethink how government makes use of contractors and restore the adequate provision of support inside government.
- PUBLIUS: Government must fulfill its responsibility to administer what contemporary experts call "inherently governmental" functions.
- PUBLIUS: Laws and regulations must be changed to make the system for obtaining private support less susceptible to the influence of private and corporate interests.
- PUBLIUS: In essence, we urge the national government to reclaim its "soul," by which we mean its prominence in faithfully executing the laws.

The federal government cannot meet Publius' call for action unless it embraces four broad challenges: (1) it must streamline the federal mission to concentrate on the most important endeavors, (2) stop the cascade of government breakdowns, (3) strengthen public service motivation on both sides of the government-industrial dividing line, and (4) invite the next generation of public servants into the governemnt-industrial complex.

Reform under Pressure

These challenges do not exist in a vacuum, of course. They are framed by continued pressures at the government-industrial divide. As noted in chapter 3, the dismantlers and rebuilders are unlikely to shift toward comity in this period of deep polarization. Anti-government sentiment may be the only source of legislative progress, but it can only damage federal government performance without a full appreciation of the facts presented in this book.

First, as the Federal Employee Viewpoint surveys show, many federal employees are deeply concerned about the need to repair their own agencies after a wave of caps, cuts, and freezes. Recall that less than half of federal employees believe their work units can recruit people with the right skills, effectively link pay and promotions to performance, deal appropriately with poor performers, and provide needed information. Many federal employees are proud of the work they do and believe their organizations are accomplishing their missions, but less than half say creativity and innovation are rewarded within their work units.

Second, policymakers must reject the president's notion that the federal workforce has grown dramatically in the past several decades. The number of full-time-equivalent federal employees has been remarkably stable at around

2 million since Congress imposed a ceiling on total employment in 1951. The ceiling was removed in 1978, but presidents still hew close to the mark. Federal employment was 2.1 million when the cap took effect in 1952 and 2.1 million when Trump took the oath of office.

As noted in chapter 2, Trump's press secretary was technically correct when he said that number of federal employees jumped from 1.7 million under Clinton to 2.2 million under Obama.[20] But he was guilty of plotting his curve before collecting his data. The total number of federal employees had risen by almost 250,000 under George W. Bush and another 300,000, to just below 2 million, as hiring surged during the war on terrorism, and rose by 160,000 under Obama as he worked to restart the economy and repair understaffed agencies such as the Veterans Affairs Department.

Moreover, three-quarters of the Clinton cuts came from the Defense Department's Cold War downsizing. Recall that federal full-time-equivalent employment was just over 2.1 million when Ronald Reagan left office in 1989 and just under 2 million when George H. W. Bush left office in 1993. Bracketing the data to make the best case against big government is an alternative fact that merely fuels fake news, not good policy.

Third, it is time to acknowledge the government-industrial complex. It may not have been fourteen million strong in 2017 as Dilulio suggested, but he was right to conclude that the contract and grant workforce will continue to expand and contract in response to national priorities. Congress and the president must accept the reality that there is a government-industrial complex that demands careful oversight. They must also acknowledge that the combination of a relatively steady number of federal employees with seven to nine million contract and grant employees raises same concerns about "unwarranted influence, sought or unsought" that led Eisenhower to warn the nation that the potential for the disastrous rise of misplaced power not only existed, but would persist.

Members of both parties know that it is time to fix the system, but neither party appears ready reblend the whole rather than just the side they want to cut. The challenge is to find the shared purpose, reasonable data, and bipartisan leadership to push forward on long-overdue reforms. It is time to pull the federal government into the twenty-first century by acknowledging the government-industrial complex and its critical role in securing the blessings of liberty.

Four Challenges

The federal government cannot meet this call for action unless it embraces the four broad challenges discussed in this chapter: (1) streamline the federal mission to concentrate on the most important endeavors, (2) stop the cascade of government breakdowns, (3) strengthen public service motivation on both sides of the government-industrial complex, and (4) recruit the next generation of public servants.

1. Streamline the Mission

The most important threshold in securing the blessings of liberty is not to declare a given function inherently governmental, critical to an inherently governmental function, or closely associated with an inherently governmental function, but to decide whether the work itself is worth doing at all. This question reaches well beyond the boundaries of the traditional insourcing/outsourcing debate, but is nonetheless central for deciding whether a given function is valid and enduring in the first place.[21] If the mission is not valid, why should anyone do it at all?

The question is particularly important for sorting the federal government's greatest endeavors over the past half century. Congress and the president appear to have an almost unlimited appetite for launching great endeavors to change the world and strengthen the nation. The question is whether these endeavors remain relevant year after year, decade after decade. Congress, the president, and the Supreme Court would certainly deem their endeavors as valid and enduring over time, but the question is not about the past so much as it is about the present and future.[22]

Hamilton may have provided the simplest definition for sorting national missions in calling on presidents to engage in "extensive and arduous enterprises for the public benefit."[23] Hamilton did not define the term at the time, however, possibly because the phrase has a plain meaning as the opposite of limited and simple enterprise, and because he intended to define the specific missions in *Federalist*, No. 72:

> The actual conduct of foreign negotiations, the preparatory plans of finance, the application and disbursement of the public moneys in conformity to the general appropriations of the legislature, the arrangement of the army and navy, the directions of the operations of war—these, and other matters of a like nature, constitute what seems to be most properly understood by the administration of government.[24]

As Hamilton's list suggests, the federal government was not created to solve trivial, easy problems; it was created to take bold action to address the kind of important, difficult problems and equally important, difficult opportunities for growth that confronted a fragile republic in a rapidly changing world.

The federal government's commitment to an extensive and arduous agenda has ebbed and flowed over the decades as the nation has pushed for and against action. But there can be little question that the nation has often called upon the federal service to embrace a long list of seemingly intractable problems. To the extent a nation is known by the problems it seeks to solve and the opportunities it seeks to leverage, the United States has been very ambitious indeed.

Thus, six questions frame the outlines of a sorting system for deciding which enterprises the nation should pursue:

1. Is the endeavor important to the public benefit? This central question asks whether an endeavor is central to the national interest. If the answer is "yes," the endeavor should continue if the nation provides resources to succeed; if the answer is "no," the endeavor should be abandoned.

2. Is the endeavor arduous and extensive? Simply stated, the federal government should use its substantial resources to pursue difficult missions that create the greatest impact. If the answer is "yes," the endeavor should continue; if the answer is "no," the endeavor should be abandoned.

3. Is the endeavor achieving impact? This question puts publlic benefit to the test. If the answer is "yes," the endeavor is an achievement and should continue to create benefit; if the answer is "no," the endeavor should be abandoned.

4. Is the endeavor faithfully administered? This question focuses on administrative prowess as essential to success. If the answer is "yes," the endeavor should continue; if the answer is "no," the nation should stop until Congress and the president provide the resources to produce benefit.

5. Is the endeavor ambitious enough? This question addresses the potential for creating even more benefit through expansion, revision, and adjustment. If the answer is "yes," the endeavor should expand if the nation provides the resources to succeed; if the answer is "no," the nation should stop when it has achieved its initial promise.

6. Does the endeavor have the public's support? This final question asks whether an achievement has the social and political capital to continue until faithful execution is complete. The question also asks if the achievement is still accepted as an important contributor to public value. If the answer is "yes," the endeavor should continue; if the answer is "no," the endeavor should be abandoned.

Asked in this order, these six questions force tough confrontations with the federal government's current inventory of endeavors. It is one thing to launch an important, difficult, and ambitious endeavor, and quite another to convert it into an achievement. It is one thing to create an achievement, and quite another to protect, expand, revise, or even jettison it as other endeavors take precedence. Thus, the six questions create a sorting ladder that begins with two essential questions that must be answered "yes" to continue.

Endeavors that earn a "yes" to every question down through the decision tree are among *government's greatest achievements*. These endeavors would reflect appropriate effort for the public benefit, are expandable, well run, and still viable. Represented by endeavors that the Defense Department would call "valid and enduring" missions, these achievements would generate great public benefit in the past and present, and would be quite capable of generating important breakthroughs in the future. The question simply asked, therefore, would be: what more can be done to expand the impact? Although some of these endeavors would be a single groundbreaking statute, such as Medicare or the Civil Rights Act, many would gain impact through a cascade of significant statutes enacted by and expanded in their benefit through Congress after Congress, president after president, and Supreme Court after Supreme Court.

Endeavors that earn a "yes" for importance and difficulty, but a "no" on impact are among *government's greatest disappointments*. Despite their potential benefit to the nation, they would still demand action, but would provoke obvious questions about their future viability. The question simply asked, therefore, would be: what went wrong and can the endeavor be renewed? Represented by endeavors such as environmental protection, financial reform, and the war against poverty, these endeavors might be impossible to continue without substantial revisions and innovation, since they might survive long into the future with minimal momentum, but would never reach their promised impact.

Endeavors that earn a "yes" on importance, but earn "no's" on difficulty and impact are among *government's greatest frustrations*. Despite a clear path to success, these endeavors would be difficult to defend, operate, and sustain. The question simply asked, therefore, would be: how could government fail at something so important, and yet so easy? But for their importance, these endeavors would be particularly vulnerable to ridicule and attack, and might have few champions for renewed effort. Represented by endeavors such as veterans care and manned space exploration, these endeavors would suffer from operating failures, uncertain missions, dwindling demand, and even strong competition from private providers such as urgent care clinics and SpaceX. Without a restatement of purpose and needed repairs, these endeavors might simply fade from the agenda without regret.

Once past these "establishment" questions, Congress and the president must ask whether they are willing to allocate the resources to turn frustration into achievement. There are more than enough unimportant, easy, and low-benefit endeavors on the federal government's agenda to help balance the federal budget again, create space for needed expansions of existing achievements, and even convert many of government's greatest frustrations into achievements. Doing so requires more than a sorting system, however, just as reblending government involves more than good questions about valid and enduring missions. Sorting the federal government's mission requires the perseverance and will to confront sacred programs that are not important, not difficult, and not a source of public benefit.

2. Stop the Cascade of Breakdowns

According to an ancient Japanese proverb, vision without action is little more than daydreaming. Unfortunately, the federal government has too much vision and not enough action. As noted earlier in this book, the result has been a cascade of government breakdowns that doubled between 1986 and 2017. Whereas Reagan, George H. W. Bush, and Clinton confronted on average 1.5 highly visible administrative breakdowns per year between 1986 and 2001, George W. Bush and Obama faced 3.3.

This author's strongly suggests that the federal government could have minimized, if not prevented, every breakdown discussed in chapter 3. Congress and the president simply needed to consider implementation as part of the policy process. Congress and the president almost always know what caused the breakdowns long before they receive their blue-ribbon reports. The question, therefore, is stop the daydreaming. The answer involves at least five simple recommendations:

1. Congress should require implementation scores for all pending legislation, including the proper mix of government-industrial employees. Congressional committees already estimate the cost, paperwork burden, and state and local impact of every bill reported to the floor, and could easily add an assessment of feasibility. GAO has the expertise to do so if Congress and the president have the courage to ask.

2. Congress should assess the implementation costs of every legislative proposal before it receives a vote. Congress and the president could easily request a CBO or GAO estimate of the ongoing delivery costs associated with each new proposal, thereby pressuring both branches to set aside the support to avoid future breakdowns. Congress must also ask how much government must spend to put the right people in the right positions at the highest impact, performance, and accountability.

3. Congress should address the communication problems that have produced so many breakdowns in the post-2001 period. Communication continues to be a major source of failure, in part because information must flow up through multiple layers to reach the top of an agency, while guidance must flow down through the same over-layered chain. There is also plenty of bloat in the contracting community and the plethora of policies and organizations

that cover the same space. Although some duplication and overlap serves important goals such as tailored support for specific groups like veterans, much of it undermines delivery by dividing responsibilities and wasting dollars.

4. Presidential appointees should be selected for their governing skills. Policy views and political histories will always be an appropriate part of the appointment process, but governing must not be left to chance. As the 2005 Hurricane Katrina fiasco demonstrated, presidents are free to nominate whomever they wish, but political loyalty is no substitute for basic expertise, nor is venality a sign of effective leadership. Whatever the selection process, Congress and the president must guarantee that presidential appointees receive the training to make quick and effective decisions as new policy and delivery problems arise. They also must ensure that appointees stay around long enough to make a difference, even if that means limiting their own ambition for high-income lobbying posts.

5. Congress and the president should rebuild the government's internal oversight systems, including but not limited to the acquisitions and inspector-general offices. They should also include discussions of the government-industrial complex in the federal budget, strengthen personnel data systems, and reframe the discussion of government employment to cover both sides of the complex. They should also help their appointees, members, and citizenry understand that the federal workforce is composed of three sets of employees, not one. The term "government employee" must be redefined to include the whole.

These recommendations would raise the visibility of the government-industrial complex at little cost. If Congress wishes to create what an inspector general once described as the "visible odium of deterrence" against fraud, waste, and abuse, oversight is the answer. Given the scoring and research required under new legislative rules, Congress and the president would finally have the incentives to close the data deficit discussed in this book and start talking about the government-industrial complex in all its forms.

3. Strengthen the Motivation to Serve

The government-industrial complex cannot convert bold endeavors into achievements without highly motivated employees. Talent and energy are not enough for sustained impact; neither are extrinsic rewards such as salary, security, encouragement, benefits, promotions, and even vacation days. Every employee who works within the government-industrial complex must also have the public service motivation to make a difference for the country.[25] If federal, contract, and grant employees do not come to work each day with a commitment to the public benefit, they should not come to work at all.

The federal government has long promised to bring just these kinds of highly motivated public servants into government through a simple, fast, and fair recruiting system. "Unfortunately, this is not the system we have today," the Partnership for Public Service's president, Stier, told the Senate in April 2016. "While there have been positive steps forward, for the most part the federal hiring system, now nearly 70 years old, reflects a time when federal jobs did not require the highly-specialized knowledge and skills they do today. As currently constructed, the system poorly serves both federal employees and the American people, and is now more of a barrier than an aid to highly skilled and educated employees joining the federal government, particularly younger employees."[26]

Even if the federal government can rebuild its sluggish hiring process in time to meet the retirement bubble discussed below, it has yet to imagine a more thoughtful approach to recruiting and managing its contract and grant employees. Even though it acknowledges the "vital expertise" these employees provide, too many departments and agencies still view their contract and grant employees as commodities to be purchased and deployed with minimal, if any, oversight.[27] It wants more data on how many contract and grant employees help deliver its missions, yet it is only starting to ask just what these employees do. It wants its own employees to focus on mission but generally assumes that contract and grant employees are motivated almost entirely by extrinsic rewards. After all, they would be in government if they had public service motivation.

This theory must be amended. Recent research suggests that public service motivation does not lead only to careers in government. It is not enough for the federal government to celebrate the differences that its employees can make in helping their country; it also must confront the possibility that it competes against other sectors that offer similar opportunities to express compassion, benevolence, and commitment.[28]

Assuming life-changing events, volunteering, and religious activity are the proven antecedents of public service motivation, millions upon millions of Americans already have either the express or latent public service motivation to fill every position within the government-industrial complex. Similarly, assuming that all human beings are "soft-wired" for empathy, as evolutionary scientists suggest, perhaps they also are soft-wired for public service.[29] If so, the key to government performance is not a degree in public administration or policy, but the underlying public service motivation that might lead a student to seek a degree in creating public benefit wherever it might be found.

Shared motivation is critical for success in the best of times, but it is especially important as the baby boomers move on and the millennials finally enter the government-industrial complex in full. Assuming the government-industrial complex will exist far into future, it is time to ask how to build a commitment to public service on both sides of the divide. It would be naïve to assume that contract and grant employees will suddenly renounce their interest in pay and benefits, but it would be equally naïve to assume that public service motivation will be enough to draw the millennials to government. Hard as it may be to achieve, government and industry must create a shared commitment to the public benefit even as they provide the rewards and opportunities that millennials expect in a career.

The federal government, contract firms, and grant agencies appear to have a simple choice in dealing with their respective challenges in recruiting millennials and instilling public service motivation among their employees. They can either reform their organizations and craft new messages to appeal to their potential segments or come together to focus on the great potential of public service working for the government-industrial complex.

Can the government-industrial complex can find common purpose based on public service motivation? It warrants a try. On the one hand, public service motivation seems to be key for employees who work with nonprofit and health organizations that have long been associated with making a difference in society. On the other hand, public service motivation is often seen as tightly linked only to government careers and does not appear central to the choice of a contract firm or grant agency.

Public administration scholar Philip Crewson has even argued that profit seeking undermines public service motivation in private firms:

> Profit-seeking firms are likely to be dominated by economic-oriented employees while public-service organizations, both public and nonprofits, are likely to dominated by service-oriented employees. Although these differences in reward motivation do not appear to bias attitudes toward the role of government, evidence shows that service motivated federal employees will be more productive than economic-oriented employees.[30]

Crewson relies on well-seasoned data collected in the 1970s and early 1990s but presents one of the few rigorous comparisons of the public service motivation of public and private employees. His data are also supported by more recent work on levels of public service motivation within Denmark. According to a 2006 survey of almost 30,000 Danish public and private employees, individuals with higher levels of public service motivation were more likely to be drawn to the civil service than individuals with lower levels.[31]

Even with such a large sample, it is difficult to determine from a single sample whether the public service motivation came before, during, or after the civil servants took their posts. It is entirely possible, for example, that government puts more emphasis on intrinsic motivations such as community attachment than private firms, thereby teaching its employees to focus more on the public benefit.[32]

However, public administration scholar James Perry and his colleagues find that award-winning volunteers who had little or no history of public service administration showed high levels of public service motivation, too. The level of motivation depends in large measure on the underlying antecedents, most notably the history of volunteering, religious activity, and family socialization. These antecedents are strong predictors of public service motivation and appear to be strongly related to community involvement.[33]

Perry and his coauthors also argue that public service motivation is higher among "morally committed individuals" who had a religious or spiritual reason for their commitment to service. According to interviews with nationally recognized community volunteers, public service motivation is also tied to a need for "personal integrity or wholeness in one's life."[34] Contrary to the traditional notion that public service motivation pushes individuals inexorably toward government, Perry and his coauthors argue that the journey is not linear. Rather, public service appears to reside in a readiness to engage.

This research is particularly important for managing and motivating the federal government's multi-sector workforce. As Perry and his colleagues ask, when it is no longer clear that public service motivation (PSM) only calls government employees, "If PSM does indeed relate to more engaged, public-spirited service, the question becomes, how do we develop and maintain that in workers? Are PSM workers initially attracted to public service? Is PSM developed through their education experience? Is it developed or diminished by public job experiences?"

If research shows that common experiences such as volunteering trigger public service motivation in most participants, it seems perfectly reasonable to suggest that it might already exist among contract employees, especially among the service contract employees who sit side by side with federal employees. It also seems reasonable to ask whether public service motivation can be brought to the surface and strengthened as contract and grant employees enter the government-industrial complex.

Few would suggest that contract employees should be screened for public service motivation on Perry's well-validated indicators, or that contract employees and their managers, senior officers, and even boards be pushed toward public service motivation training of some kind. Nevertheless, the call for ethics codes and greater transparency does raise serious questions about basic commitments to the public benefit as a requirement for anyone who works in the government-industrial complex. At the very least, it is time to ask for a comparison of public service motivation within the multi-sector workforce.

Assuming Congress and the president can agree on a proper blending of the government-industrial complex, a focus on public service motivation will inevitably produce basic changes in what the complex does, where the inherently governmental functions reside, and how commercially available functions must be managed. However, the need for public service motivation throughout the complex will not change. If the complex is to deliver on the promises government makes, the nation needs a commitment to the common good on both sides of the divide.

4. Recruit the "Next Gen" Public Service

Aging may be the most significant of the fifteen pressures on the divide discussed in chapter 3. GAO predicts that almost 800,000 employees will be eligible for retirement by 2020. They will not leave at once, but their departures will widen the federal skill gaps nonetheless.[35]

The question is not whether the 800,000 will leave—age, insults, buyouts, cap, cuts, and freezes will work their will eventually. Rather, the question is how many of the resulting vacancies will be filled. Will Congress and the president cut federal employment a one-for-two, one-for-three, or even a zero-for-one replacement ratio, or will they increase employment using a one-for-one, two-for-one, or even three-for-one replacement ratio? If done through a one-for-two or three, the industry side of the government-industrial complex will grow at greater taxpayer cost.

If done through a reverse ratio, taxpayers could reap significant benefits. The reason is simple: high-level federal employees cost much more than entry-level employees. If the federal government can take its hierarchy back to where it was in the 1990s or even 1970s, a two-for-one replacement ratio could add a generation of millennials to its ranks. Instead of pulling middle-age employees up to even higher grades, a two-for-one or even three-for-one replacement ratio would invite millennials in.

The transition could bring new energy and skills to government, while giving retirees confidence in their decision. Despite their reputations as slackers, clickavists, and self-absorbed members of what *Time* called the "Me, Me, Me Generation," enough millennials already have the public service motivation to invigorate federal performance.[36]

The Pew Research Center correctly warns that generations are notoriously difficult to compare over time, if only because they are at different points in the life cycle and history when most comparisons take place.[37] So forewarned, at least for now the millennials are bringing very different attitudes into the political and economic system, including a general separation from the traditional anchors of political ideology, party identification, religion, marriage, and social institutions that their parents have used to guide their political and economic decisions.

The Case Foundation's recent "Millennial Impact" reports support the argument. According to the foundation's 2014 survey, the millennials clearly want to "do good" on the job:

> We've studied Millennials as individuals who participate in social causes. Now, we have a clearer picture of how their desire to "do good" is reflected in their employment—from the companies they consider in an initial job search to the effect an employer's work affects overall job satisfaction. The idea isn't to be recognized for doing good; rather, the point is to be able to do good and make a tangible difference through the workplace. As time progresses and Millennials move from being a small, unique segment of the overall workforce to the predominant source of employees, understanding this picture will be crucial to a company's ability to recruit and retain the best people.[38]

Government faces aggressive competition for the millennials, not the least of which comes from contract firms and grant agencies.[39] Yet, government still has a chance to recruit its fair share. Convinced that they should not spend more than five to ten years in any job, the millennials are likely to be available more than once in their careers.[40]

The millennials would be a mixed blessing on either side of the government-industrial complex.

First, the millennials would bring much greater diversity to government. According to Pew, 57 percent of the Millennials are white, compared to 72 percent of the baby boomers born between 1946 and 1964; 85 percent of millennial women are in the workforce, compared to 53 percent of baby-boomers.

Second, the millennials have very different goals than do the baby boomers. Whereas baby boomers once put their greatest emphasis on having a meaningful philosophy of life, the class of 2019 gave much more weight to financial success. First-year college students bring many objectives to school, but the 138,000 students interviewed by the University of California, Los Angeles in the fall of 2016 put financial success at the top of their objectives. Although getting a better job (85 percent) and learning more about the things that interested them (84 percent) were basically tied as the most important reasons for going to college, 82 percent said that being very well off financially was an essential or very important objective in their lives, followed by helping others at 78 percent, helping others who are in difficulty at 78 percent, raising a family at 72 percent, improving their understanding of other countries and cultures at 59 percent, becoming an authority in their fields at 59 percent, developing a meaningful philosophy of life at 47 percent, becoming a community leader at 43 percent, and influencing the political structure at 27 percent.[41]

Third, the millennials are increasingly divided between haves and have-nots, the debt-free and the debt-laden.[42] The growing income inequality is particularly visible among first-year college students. Although many students told UCLA they were concerned about financing their education, the greatest concern was exactly where one would predict, among students from lower-income families.[43]

Fourth, the millennials are less tightly anchored to tradition than the baby boomers. Although the anchors may yet emerge, the millennials surveyed were far less likely than older generations to express any religious affiliation, embrace a political party, or call themselves liberals or conservative. Few will be surprised that the millennials are far ahead of older generations in embracing the peer-to-peer economy, crowdfunding, and online giving. And they are the most likely by far to say that Twitter and Facebook are their prime sources for news.[44]

Finally, and perhaps most important, the millennials do not identify as millennials. According to Pew, only 40 percent of millennials are comfortable calling themselves by that name, compared to 79 percent of baby boomers who are quite comfortable with their generational label.[45] Asked how they would describe their generation, just 15 percent of the millennials said they are "willing to sacrifice," 17 percent said they are "moral," and 29 percent said they are "compassionate," while 59 percent said the generation is "self-absorbed," 43 percent said they are "greedy," 35 percent said they are "entrepreneurial," 36 percent said they are "hard-working," and 40 percent said they are "environmentally conscious."[46]

Even if millennials put social change and community impact at the top of their concerns, they still view the federal government as a destination of last resort in large measure because the federal government has yet to find an effective call for millennial talent. The federal government earned this reputation by mostly standing still as study after study showed threats to the future:

- A 2004 study suggested that the federal government has branded itself as a destination for "i-robots" trapped in bureaucracy.[47]
- A 2007 study argued that red tape can reduce public service motivation, while increasing employee frustration and turnover.[48]
- A second 2007 study found that government downsizing severs the employee sense of duty to the public interest.[49]
- A 2008 study demonstrated that interest in a specific job depends in part on the outspoken "publicness" of the employer.[50]
- A 2013 study of upper-division undergraduates showed that the desire for a good salary pushes students toward government, while altruism moves students toward nonprofits.[51]

- A 2014 study argued that the businesslike practices associated with reinventing government and other forms of the "New Public Management" in the 1990s and 2000s may have reduced the "stock" of public service motivation and organizational performance.[52]
- A 2015 analysis showed that graduate students lose interest in government careers as they move from their first to second year of study, even though it was related to more interaction with government.[53]
- A 2018 study showed that the effect of public service motivation is highest when employees feel a strong sense of social impact potential—in short, public service motivation appears to have less effect in the kinds of organizations that do not provide the opportunity to make a difference.[54]

The federal government is not the only destination of frustration within the government-industrial complex. Contract firms and grant agencies also face substantial challenges in recruiting the millennials. The challenges may be quite different across the three destinations, but the government-industrial complex is currently destined to fail in calling the millennials to serve.

Even if the complex succeeds in linking rewards to performance, the millennials may not stay long before moving on. Current research suggests that they do not come to work so much for the work as for the experience, which leaves plenty of room to inject public service motivation into the equation. However, the experience must involve more than pushing paper—it must also involve more than the chance to make a difference; it must involve the chance to make a difference for the country and reasonable rewards for doing so.

The federal government cannot succeed in making its case based on promises of long-term job security, especially during periods of hiring caps, cuts, and freezes. It must also address the constant pressure created by the anti-government rhetoric that framed the Trump administration's support for deconstructing the administrative state. The Whitten Amendment did not create every pressure listed in chapter 3, but it did create great stress for federal employees caught in the crosshairs. If government wants its share of scarce talent for its mission-critical occupations such as cybersecurity, engineering, information technology, and math, it must embrace immediate reform.

The survey data strongly suggest that the federal government, contract firms, and grant agencies cannot answer these challenges with their current messaging. Nor will they attract millennials through a faster hiring process that only shortens the time when millennials realize there is no chance to advance, no link between rewards and performance, and no discipline for poor performers.

Faster hiring cannot change demographics if it is merely an introduction to sluggish administrative systems, funding shortages, and fear of government breakdowns and anti-government attacks. The key to recruiting and holding the millennials may well be found in public service motivation. Despite the perfectly reasonable debate about what federal, contract, and grant employees can, should, and must do, the government-industrial complex needs to consider the possibility that its employees are all part of one public service with three destinations.

Each destination will have its own character and reputation, and some will earn tough reviews from raters, but all will have a genuine commitment to public service. Once made, this commitment can be converted into a simple set of expectations, disclosures, and even choices about who can, should, and must do what. Imagine a competition not just on cost and performance, but also on the commitment to public service motivation. It would be a competition well worth having.

Beyond Whitten

The government-industrial complex will still demand oversight even with a surge in millennial hiring and a burst of deep public service motivation. Whether motivated by public service, invited into service by the opportunity to make a difference, or drawn by security and benefits, the millennials cannot assure a proper meshing without an alert and knowledgeable citizenry by their side.

Eisenhower did have easy answers to this challenge. As noted earlier in this book, he was a realist who understood that the nation needed the military-industrial complex to fight a hostile, atheistic, ruthless, and insidious enemy. He knew the nation needed mighty arms always ready for instant action to deter aggression, yet he believed citizens could somehow find the wisdom to prevent misplaced power. And he clearly understood the risks of war, as Engle writes:

> Quite literally, for Dwight Eisenhower in 1953, it was conceivably better to be dead than red, which is not to say that atomic warfare carried much appeal. By the summer of 1956, the crushing moral weight of atomic deterrence left him hardly able to consider use nuclear bombs. These weapons, he argued, were pushing us "past the point of human endurance." By 1959, he had lost all hope of survival, warning Americans that their only option in war would be to shoot themselves.[55]

Viewed in the context of contemporary politics, Eisenhower's message is more unsettling than reassuring, if only because citizens can be easily moved by fake news, false promises, and alternative facts. More to the message in this book, Eisenhower's warning did not come with an expiration date. As he told the nation, the global conflict threatening the world would be of "indefinite duration," and he urged the nation to hold steady in meeting the threat:

To meet it successfully, there is called for, not so much the emotional and transitory sacrifices of crisis, but rather those which enable us to carry forward steadily, surely, and without complaint the burdens of a prolonged and complex struggle—with liberty the stake. Only thus shall we remain, despite every provocation, on our charted course toward permanent peace and human betterment.[56]

It is counsel well taken in protecting against unwarranted influence. Protecting liberty may reside less in a sharply divided citizenry besieged by alternative facts and fake news and much more in the public service motivation that must be cultivated on both sides of the government-industrial complex, as well as the deeper oversight of the movement across the divide. It is time to pursue both goals.

Doing so cannot begin until Congress, the president, and the American public finally move beyond Whitten. The two million cap has outlived its relevance to a government workforce composed of seven to nine million employees. If Congress and presidents want a limit, they should set it to include every federal employee, whether paid directly through the federal treasury or indirectly through contracts or grants. Americans can handle the truth if Congress and the president are ready to tell it.

NOTES

Preface

1. For pre-Iraq and Afghanistan War estimates, see Carey Luse, Christopher Madeline, Landon Smith, and Stephen Starr, *An Evaluation of Contingency Contracting: Past, President, and Future*, MBA Professional Report, Naval Postgraduate School, December 2005. The Iraq and Afghanistan estimates can be found at US Library of Congress, Congressional Research Service, *Department of Defense Contractor and Troop Levels in Iraq and Afghanistan: 2007–2017*, by Heidi M. Peters, Moshe Schwartz, and Lawrence Kapp, R44116 (2017). For a discussion of private military contractors as an emerging profession, see Scott L. Efflandt, "Military Professionalism & Private Military Contractors," *Parameters* 44, no. 2 (2014).

2. Steven L. Schooner, "Why Contractor Fatalities Matter," *Parameters* 38, no. 3 (2008): 89. For additional information on contractor casualties in Iraq and Afghanistan, see Suzanne Merkelson, "Contractor Deaths Outnumber Military Casualties in Iraq and Afghanistan," *Foreign Policy*, September 24, 2010, http://foreignpolicy.com/2010/09/24/contractor-deaths-outnumber-military-casualties-in-iraq-and-afghanistan/. See also ProPublica's "Disposable Army Project" for further details on contractor deployments during the Iraq and Afghanistan wars, https://www.propublica.org/series/disposable-army.

3. Alexander Hamilton, *Federalist*, no. 72, in *The Federalist Papers*, ed. Benjamin Fletcher Wright (Cambridge, MA: Harvard University Press, 1961), 464.

4. Sarah E. Light "The Military-Environmental Complex," *Boston College Law Review* 55, no. 3 (2014). I am unrelated to Professor Light.

5. See Eric Prince, "Contractors, Not Troops, Will Save Afghanistan," *New York Times*, August 30, 2017, for the case for using contract security personnel.

6. For a recent history of military industry, see Ronald W. Cox, "The Military-Industrial Complex and US Military Spending after 9/11," *Class, Race and Corporate Power* 2, no. 2 (2014).

7. Readers can find the list of cabinet and independent agencies included in my counts at US Office of the Federal Register, *United States Government Manual* (Washington, DC: Government Printing Office); and U.S. Executive Office of the President, Office of Management and Budget, *Historical Tables, Budget of the US Government* (Washington, DC: Government Printing Office). I do not have estimates of the number of employees who work for quasi-governmental corporations such as Amtrak.

8. Daniel Guttman, "Government by Contract: Considering a Public Service Ethics to Match the Reality of the 'Blended' Public Workforce," *Emory Corporate Governance and Accountability Review* 2 (2015): 6. For a further analysis of what Guttman calls the "shadow government," see Daniel Guttman and Barry Willner, *The Shadow Government: The Government's Multi-Billion-Dollar Giveaway of Its Decision-Making Powers to Private Management Consultants, "Experts," and Think Tanks* (New York, Pantheon Books: 1976).

9. Daniel Guttman, "Public Purpose and Private Service: The Twentieth Century Culture of Contracting Out and the Evolving Law of Diffused Sovereignty," *Administrative Law Review* 53, no. 3 (2000).

10. Dwight D. Eisenhower, "Farewell Radio and Television Address to the American People," January 17, 1961, made available online by Gerhard Peters and John T. Woolley, *The American Presidency Project*, http://www.presidency.ucsb.edu/ws/?pid=12086.

11. This draft of the speech was titled "commencement," but is undated. However, clues about its data can be found in National Archives and Records Administration files related to the speech between an October 31, 1960, memo outlining potential themes for Eisenhower's farewell address and a January 7, 1961, draft edited by the president's brother, Milton Eisenhower. As such, the draft appears to be near final. All documents related to the speech can be found at https://www.eisenhower.archives.gov/research/online_documents/farewell_address.html.

12. Eisenhower, "Farewell Radio and Television Address to the American People."

13. See Scott A. Amey, "Public Comments on the Use of Cost Comparisons: Letter to the Office of Federal Procurement Policy," Project on Government Oversight, April 2014, for the rationale underpinning these questions about the service contract workforce.

14. Guttman, "Government by Contract."

15. Paul C. Light, *The True Size of Government* (Washington, DC: Brookings Institution Press, 1999).

16. I prefer to use the term "contract firms" instead of "contractors" and the term "grant agencies" instead of "grant recipients" to identify the broad classes of employers who employ contract and grant employees.

17. Dwight D. Eisenhower, "Farewell Radio and Television Address to the American People."

18. Ibid.

19. Scholars continue to disagree about the origins of the term "military-industrial complex." Former Eisenhower aide Stephen Hess argues that the term was merely a term to tie together the words "military" and "industrial" at the end of a sentence, while others see Milton Eisenhower's hand at work. See Stephen Hess, "Eisenhower Farewell Addresses: A Speechwriter Remembers," Brookings Institution, January 9, 2017. See also Sam Roberts, "In Archive, New Light on Evolution of Eisenhower Speech," *New York Times*, December 10, 2010. According to documents collected by the US National Archive and Records Administration, the term evolved from "war-based industrial complex" into "vast military-industrial complex," and finally into "military-industrial complex." The president's brother, Milton Eisenhower, edited and initialed a January 7, 1961, copy of the typewritten address, but the available evidence strongly suggests that the term is best attributed to "unknown." The primary documents related to the speech are available at https://www.eisenhower.archives.gov/research/online_documents/farewell_address.html.

20. William J. Clinton, "Address before a Joint Session of the Congress on the State of the Union," January 23, 1996, made available online by Gerhard Peters and John T. Woolley, *The American Presidency Project*, http://www.presidency.ucsb.edu/ws/?pid=53091.

21. For a critique of the consulting industry, see Guttman and Willner, *The Shadow Government: The Government's Multi-Billion-Dollar Giveaway of Its Decision-Making Powers to Private Management Consultants, Experts, and Think Tanks* (New York: Pantheon, 1976).

Chapter 1

1. Dwight D. Eisenhower, "Farewell Radio and Television Address to the American People."

2. Ibid.

3. James Ledbetter, "Ike & *The Nation*," *The Nation*, January 24, 2011, 6.

4. Eisenhower, "Farewell Radio and Television Address to the American People."

5. See Lawrence J. Korb, Laura Conley, and Alex Rothman, "A Return to Responsibility: What President Obama and Congress Can Learn about Defense Budgets from Past Presidents," Center for American Progress, July 2011, 10.

6. Dwight D. Eisenhower, "The Chance for Peace," speech delivered before the American Society of Newspaper Editors, April 16, 1953, made available online by Gerhard Peters and John T. Woolley, *The American Presidency Project*, http://www.presidency.ucsb.edu/ws/?pid=9819.

7. US Senate, Senate Committee on Armed Services, Subcommittee on the Air Force, *Airpower*, 85th Cong., 1st Sess., 1957, Committee Print 85–29, 2.

8. Ibid, 95–97.

9. Dwight D. Eisenhower, "Annual Message to the Congress on the State of the Union," January 10, 1957, made available online by Gerhard Peters and John T. Woolley, *The American Presidency Project*, http://www.presidency.ucsb.edu/ws/?pid=11029.

10. Dolores E. Janiewski, "Eisenhower's Paradoxical Relationship with the 'Military-Industrial Complex,'" *Presidential Studies Quarterly* 41, no. 4 (2011): 667.

11. John F. Kennedy, "Inaugural Address," January 20, 1961, made available online by Gerhard Peters and John T. Woolley, *The American Presidency Project*, at http://www.presidency.ucsb.edu/ws/?pid=8032.

12. Janiewski, "Eisenhower's Paradoxical Relationship with the 'Military-Industrial Complex,'" 668.

13. See Jim Newton, "Ike's Speech," *The New Yorker*, December 20 and 27, 2010, https://www.newyorker.com/magazine/2010/12/20/ikes-speech, for a brief note on papers recently found in the lake house of Eisenhower's chief speechwriter, Malcom Moos. According to the article, the treasure trove reveals clear intent: "Some historians have regarded the Farewell Address as an afterthought, hastily composed at the end of 1960 as an adjunct to the 1961 State of the Union. Others have regarded it as the soulful expression of an aging President who was determined to warn the American people of dangers ahead. But the Moos papers make clear that the address, far from being an afterthought, was among the most deliberate speeches of Eisenhower's Presidency. Regarded in his day as inarticulate and detached, Eisenhower in these papers is fully engaged, grappling with the language of the text and the radical questions that it raised."

14. Charles J. T. Griffin, "New Light on Eisenhower's Farewell Address," *Presidential Studies Quarterly* 22, no. 3 (1992).

15. Janiewski, "Eisenhower's Paradoxical Relationship with the 'Military-Industrial Complex,'" 674.

16. Dwight D. Eisenhower, "The President's News Conference," November 5, 1958, made available online by Gerhard Peters and John T. Woolley, *The American Presidency Project*, at http://www.presidency.ucsb.edu/ws/?pid=11286.

17. Political scientist Harold D. Lasswell defined a garrison state as one in which "specialists on violence are the most powerful group in society." See Harold D. Lasswell, "The Garrison State," *American Journal of Sociology* 46, no. 4 (1941): 455.

18. Quoted in James Ledbetter, *Unwarranted Influence: Dwight D. Eisenhower and the Military Industrial Complex* (New Haven, CT: Yale University Press, 2011), 109.

19. This extract comes from Eisenhower's May 25, 1959, letter to his brother, Milton Eisenhower. This letter and the many drafts of the speech that followed is accessible at BACM Paperless Archives, "President Dwight D. Eisenhower Farewell Speech Documents," http://www.paperlessarchives.com/FreeTitles/EisenhowerFarewellSpeech Documents.pdf.

20. Kerry E. Irish, "Apt Pupil: Dwight Eisenhower and the 1930 Industrial Mobilization Plan," *Journal of Military History* 70, no. 1 (January 2006).

21. See Ledbetter, "Dwight Eisenhower & 'The Nation,'" for a discussion of the *Nation* article.

22. The UPI's Merriman Smith said Eisenhower had used these terms to describe the Democrats in a November 5, 1958, news conference immediately following a Democratic landslide, and Eisenhower did not dispute the list. See Dwight D. Eisenhower, "The President's News Conference," November 5, 1958, made available online by Gerhard Peters and John T. Woolley, *The American Presidency Project*, http://www.presidency.ucsb.edu/ws/?pid=11286.

23. Ibid.

24. Dwight D. Eisenhower, "The Chance for Peace," Remarks delivered to the American Society of Newspaper Editors, April 16, 1953, made available online by Gerhard Peters and John T. Woolley, *The American Presidency Project*, http://www.presidency.ucsb.edu/ws/?pid=9819.

25. Ibid.

26. Dwight D. Eisenhower, "Farewell Radio and Television Address to the American People."

27. For a short review of the speech, see James Ledbetter, "What Caused Ike to Criticize the 'Military-Industrial Complex?'" *Reuters*, January 14, 2011, http://blogs.reuters.com/great-debate/2011/01/14/what-caused-ike-to-criticize-the-%E2%80%9Cmilitary-industrial-complex%E2%80%9D/.

28. US Congress, House, Committee on Armed Services, Subcommittee for Special Investigations, *Employment of Retired Commissioned Officers by Defense Department Contractors*, 86th Cong., 2nd Sess., 1960, Committee, H. Doc. 49296, 29.

29. US Congress, Senate, Committee on Armed Services, *Conflict of Interest of Retired Officers*, 86th Cong., 2nd Sess., 1960, S. Doc. 1405–3, 20-21.

30. House Committee on Armed Services, *Employment of Retired Commissioned Officers*, 23.

31. Ibid., 19.

32. Ibid., 10–11.

33. Dwight D. Eisenhower, "The President's News Conference," June 17, 1959, made available online by Gerhard Peters and John T. Woolley, *The American Presidency Project*, http://www.presidency.ucsb.edu/ws/?pid=11415.

34. Ibid.

35. Dwight D. Eisenhower, "The President's News Conference," June 3, 1959, made available online by Gerhard Peters and John T. Woolley, *The American Presidency Project*, http://www.presidency.ucsb.edu/ws/?pid=11405.

36. Ralph E. Williams, "State of the Union 1961," Memorandum to the File, October 31, 1960, BACM Paperless Archives, "President Dwight D. Eisenhower Farewell Speech Documents."

37. Between 1958 and 1960, Eisenhower impounded more than $600 million in defense appropriations. See Adam M. McMahon and Andrew J. Polsky, "President Eisenhower and the Unbuilding of the American National Security State," in *The Eisenhower Presidency: Lesson for the Twenty-first Century*, ed. Andrew J. Polsky (Lexington, MA: Lexington Books, 2015) for a discussion of the Eisenhower defense agenda. See also Jordan Tama, "From Private Consultation to Public Crusade: Assessing Eisenhower's Legislative Strategies on Foreign Policy," *Congress & the Presidency* 40, no. 1 (2013).

38. Dwight D. Eisenhower, "Farewell Radio and Television Address to the American People."

39. Quoted in Robert Griffith, "Dwight D. Eisenhower and the Corporate Commonwealth," *American Historical Review* 87, no. 1 (1982): 90.

40. See Andrew Morris, "Eisenhower and Social Welfare," in *A Companion to Dwight D. Eisenhower*, ed. Chester J. Pach (New York: John Wiley & Sons, 2017), 246–63.

41. Dwight D. Eisenhower, "Farewell Radio and Television Address to the American People."

42. Rudolph G. Penner, *When Budgeting Was Easier: Eisenhower and the 1960 Budget* (Washington, DC: Urban Institute, June 2014).

43. Rudolph G. Penner, *When Budgeting Was Easier*," 9–10.

44. Dwight D. Eisenhower, "Farewell Radio and Television Address to the American People."

45. Ibid.

46. Dwight D. Eisenhower, "The President's News Conference," January 18, 1961, made available online by Gerhard Peters and John T. Woolley, *The American Presidency Project*, http://www.presidency.ucsb.edu/ws/?pid=12087.

47. Janine R. Wedel, "*Federalist* No. 70: Where Does the Public Service Begin and End," *Public Administration Review* 71, no. s1 (2011), S118.

48. Ibid., S120.

49. Ibid.

50. Guttman, "Public Purpose and Private Service," 875.

51. See Association of Federal Government Employees, "House Budget Committee Ranking Member Shines Spotlight on Expensive Contracted Workforce," Press Release, December 12, 2014, https://www.afge.org/article/house-budget-committee-ranking-member-shines-spotlight-on-expensive-contracted-workforce/. The Association quotes Van Hollen's December 5 letter as follows: "I ask that when future reports include options to reduce the number of federal employees that they also consider options to achieve savings in the contracted workforce. This would allow Congress to consider tradeoffs between all aspects of government operations." I have not been able to find a copy of the letter in any public record, but CBO referenced it in the report discussed here.

52. The text of the 2011 version of the act can be found at US House of Representatives, Committee on Oversight and Government Reform, *Reducing the Size of the Federal Government through Attrition Act of 2011*, House Report, 112–334 to accompany H.R. 3029. The final report of the Obama administration's fiscal reform commission can be found at The National Commission on Fiscal Responsibility and Reform, *The Moment of Truth: Report of the National Commission on Fiscal Responsibility and Reform* (Washington, DC: Government Printing Office, 2010), also available at http://momentoftruthproject.org/sites/default/files/TheMomentofTruth12_1_2010.pdf.

53. Jonathan Weisman, "GOP Split over Congressional Budget Office Head," *New York Times*, December 1, 2014.

54. US Congress, Congressional Budget Office, *Letter to the Honorable Chris Van Hollen, Re: Federal Contracts and the Contracted Workforce* (Washington, DC, March 15, 2015), 1.

55. Jeff Neal, "How Many Contractors Does the Government Have?" ChiefHRO.com, March 13, 2015, https://chiefhro.com/?s=how+many+contractors.

56. Charles S. Clark, "Even CBO Is Stumped on the Size of the Contractor Workforce," *Government Executive*, March 12, 2015; Josh Patrick, "CBO Report on Contract Workers: 'We Have No Idea How Many Contractors Work for Us,'" *Daily Caller*, March 11, 2015; Andy Medici, "CBO: No Clue on the Number of Contractors or Their Pay," *Federal Times*, March 12, 2015; and Josh Hicks, "No One Knows the Size of the Government's Contracted Workforce," *Washington Post*, March 12, 2015.

57. See US Acquisition Advisory Panel, *Report of the Acquisition Advisory Panel to the Office of Federal Procurement Policy and the United States Congress* (Washington, DC, 2007), 476; US Government Accountability Office, *DOD Service Acquisition: Improved Use of Available Data Needed to Better Manage and Forecast Service Contract Requirements*," GAO-16-119 (Washington, DC, 2016); 2; US Library of Congress, Congressional Research Service, *Transforming Government Acquisition Systems: Overview and Selected Issues*, L. Elaine Halchin, RL 31024 (2007); and Nancy Y. Moore, Molly Dunigan, Frank Camm, Samantha Cherney, Clifford Grammich, Judith Mele, Evan Peet, and Anita Szafran, *A Review of Alternative Methods to Inventory Contracted Services in the Department of Defense* (Santa Monica, CA: RAND Corporation, 2017), xix.

    The Advisory Panel did highlight coding mistakes at the "granular," or purchase, level of the database, but endorsed the FPDS for higher-level analysis: "In general, it seems that the FPDS-NG data at the highest level provides significant insight. However, the reliability of that data, especially on this new reporting elements, begins to degrade at the more granular level due to data specificity on elements for which those reporting may have less familiarly and training." Acquisition Advisory Panel, *Report*, 441.

    RAND made a similar point regarding the use of the FPDS in a study that was designed in 2015: "While FPDS-NG data may contain some errors in data submission, it is the authoritative system for federal contract reporting, and the quality of its data has improved over time. FPDS-NG provides, for contract actions of at least $3,000, information on the amount of the contract action, identification codes indicating whether the firm providing the service is a small business, the North American Industry Classification System (NAICS) code for the firm, the Treasury Account Symbol for the transaction funding (which can be linked to budget categories), and the Product or Service Code (PSC), a more finely grained indicator than the NAICS code regarding the exact nature of the products and services purchased. Though subject to some delay in publication due to security measures and verification, these data can give many insights on the services DoD has recently bought and, in doing so, can aid in addressing the various congressional concerns underlying the ICS requirement—namely, enabling the production of spend analyses, trend analyses, and forecasting to inform budgeting and acquisition decisions." Moore, et al., *A Review of Alternative Methods to Inventory Contracted Services in the Department of Defense*, xvii.

58. US Government Accountability Office, *Contracting Data Analysis: Assessment of Government-Wide Trends*, GAO-17-244SP (2017).

59. Scott H. Amey, "POGO Asks Pentagon for Better Tracking of Service Contracts," Project on Government Oversight, December 9, 2014, http://pogobuild.pub30.convio.net/blog/2014/12/pogo-asks-pentagon-to-keep-tabs-on-service-contracts.html?referrer=https://www.google.com/.

60. US Government Accountability Office, *Improved Use of Available Data Needed to Better Manage and Forecast Service Contract Requirements*, 1; Daniel Bryan, "Letter to the Honorable Chuck Hagel," November 25, 2015, http://pogoarchives.org/m/co/pogo_ics_ltr_to_dod_%2020141125.pdf; Project on Government Oversight, "POGO Asks Pentagon for Better Tracking of Service Contracts," December 9, 2014, http://pogobuild. pub30.convio.net/blog/2014/12/pogo-asks-pentagon-to-keep-tabs-on-service-contracts. html?referrer=https://www.google.com/; Nancy Y. Moore, Molly Dunigan, Frank Camm, Samantha Cherney, Clifford Grammich, Judith Mele, Evan Peet, and Anita Szafran, *A Review of Alternative Methods to Inventory Contracted Services in the Department of Defense* (Santa Monica, CA: RAND Corporation, 2017), xix.

61. US Government Accountability Office, *Service Contracts: Agencies Should Take Steps to More Effectively Use Government Cost Estimates*, GAO-17-398 (2017).

62. The federal employment numbers in this report come from the US Executive Office of the President, Office of Management and Budget, *Budget of the US Government: Historical Tables, Fiscal Year 2019* (Washington, DC: US Government Printing Office, 2018), Table 16.1; the active-duty military personnel numbers come from the US Department of Defense, Manpower Data Center, *Active Duty Military by Rank/Grade* (Washington, DC, 2017), and the Postal Service regular employment data come from the US Postal Service, Historian's Office, "Number of Postal Employees Since 1926" (Washington, DC: US Postal Service, March 2018).

63. CBO focused in particular on the FPDS spending codes: "FPDS also makes it difficult to summarize federal spending on contracts. For example, each purchase is assigned a single "product or service code"—but there are roughly 3,000 of those codes, and FPDS offers no useful way to group them." See Congressional Budget Office, *Letter to the Honorable Chris Van Hollen*, 3.

64. US Library of Congress, Congressional Research Service, *Defense Acquisitions: How and Where DOD Spends and Reports Its Contracting Dollars*, by Moshe Schwartz, John F. Sargent Jr., Gabriel M. Nelson, and Ceir Coral, R44010 (2015), i.

65. See for example, US Government Accountability Office, *Nonprofit Sector: Significant Federal Funds Reach the Sector through Various Mechanisms, but More Complete and Reliable Funding Data Are Needed*, GAO-09-193 (2009). GAO reached the following conclusion about tracking the federal government's increasing use of nonprofits to achieve its goals.

Due to limitations and reliability concerns with tracking systems' data, the data presently collected give an incomplete, unreliable picture of the federal government's funds reaching the nonprofit sector through various mechanisms, although they suggest these funds were significant. No central source tracks federal funds passed through an initial recipient, such as a state, and the nonprofit status of recipients was not reliably identified in FPDS-NG or FAADS. Factors contributing to data limitations include the nonprofit status of recipients being self-reported and no consistent definition of nonprofit across data systems. The development of a system to report funding through sub-awards, currently underway, may enable more complete estimates of funding to the sector in the future.

66. US Government Accountability Office, *Federal Research Grants: Opportunities Remain for Agencies to Streamline Administrative Requirements*, GAO-16-572 (Washington, DC, 2016).

67. Nation Analytics was incorporated in 2016 but dates to the 1990s when it operated as Eagle Eye Publishers.

68. US Department of Commerce, Bureau of Economic Analysis, *RIMS II: An Essential Tool for Regional Developers and Planners* (Washington, DC: Government Printing Office, 2015), chapter 1, 1.

69. Ibid., chapter 5, 8.

70. Nation Analytics removed the numbers of induced contract and grant employees found in the 2005, 2010, and 2015 estimates, while I removed the induced contract and grant employees in the 1984, 1990, 1993, 1996, 1999, and 2002 estimates using a fixed percentage based on the 2005, 2010, and 2015 totals. According to the BEA output, the number of contract-induced employees accounted for 46.1 percent of all contract employees in 2005, 46.2 percent in 2010, and 46.5 percent in 2015. In turn, the number of grant-induced employees accounted for 42.7 percent of all grant employees in 2005, 43.9 percent in 2010, and 42.6 percent

in 2015. Given this tight alignment within the 2005, 2010, 2015 contract and grant estimates, I corrected the 1984–2002 contract and grant estimates by 46 percent and 43 percent, respectively, and excluded induced employment from the 2005–2017 calculation.

71. For a critique of my past estimates, see Stan Z. Soloway, "A Visible, and Needed, Workforce," *Washington Post*, July 1, 2008. Soloway's concerns about household spending effects led me to recalculate all my contract and grant estimates dating back to 1984. See also Stan Z. Soloway, "New Report on Contractor Workforce Rife with Flaws," *Washington Technology*, July 6, 2007.

72. US Congress, Congressional Budget Office, *Replacing Military Personnel in Support Positions with Civilian Employees* (Washington, DC, 2015). This quote comes from a summary of the report from CBO's compendium at https://www.cbo.gov/budget-options/2013/44765.

73. Jennifer Lamping Lewis, Edward G. Keating, Leslie Adrienne Payne, Brian J. Gordon, Julia Pollak, Andrew Madler, Hugh G. Massey, and Gillian S. Oak, *US Department of Defense Experiences with Substituting Government Employees for Military Personnel: Challenges and Opportunities* (Santa Monica, CA: RAND Corporation, 2016), xiv–xv.

74. US Office of the Director of National Intelligence, "Key Facts about Contractors" (Washington, DC: Office of the Director of National Intelligence, 2010), https://www.hsdl.org/?view&did=21396.

75. Dana Priest and William M. Arkin, "National Security, Inc.," *Washington Post*, July 20, 2010; all articles are accessible at http://projects.washingtonpost.com/top-secret-america/articles/national-security-inc/2stories. The figures come from an expanded version of the entire *Washington Post* series in Dana Priest and William M Arken, *Top Secret America: The Rise of the New American Security State* (New York: Little Brown and Company, 2011), http://avalonlibrary.net/ebooks/Dana Priest, William M. Arkin - Top Secret America.pdf.

76. ONDI, "Key Facts about Contractors," 2.

77. Dana Priest and William M. Arkin, "National Security, Inc."

78. Ibid.

79. ONDI, "Key Facts about Contractors," 2. See also US Library of Congress, Congressional Research Service, *Intelligence Community Spending: Trends and Issues*, by Anne Daugherty Miles, R44381 (2016).

80. US Government Accountability Office, *Civilian Intelligence Community: Additional Actions Needed to Improve Reporting on and Planning for the Use of Contract Personnel*, GAO-14-692T (2014).

81. US Office of the Director of National Intelligence, *The US Intelligence Community's Five-Year Strategic Human Capital Plan* (Washington, DC: Office of the Director of National Intelligence, 2006), 6, https://www.dni.gov/files/documents/CHCO/human%20capital%20plan-2006.pdf.

82. The 2015 number of top-secret clearances can be accessed at US Office of the Director of National Intelligence, National Counterintelligence and Security Center, *2015 Annual Report on Security Clearance Determinations* (Washington, DC: Office of the Director of National Intelligence, 2015), https://fas.org/sgp/othergov/intel/clear-2015.pdf; for further details on national security clearances, see US Library of Congress, Congressional Research Service, *Security Clearance Process: Answers to Frequently Asked Questions*, by Michelle D. Christensen, R43216 (2016).

83. US Library of Congress, Congressional Research Service, *The Federal Activities Inventory Reform Act and Circular A-76*, by L. Elaine Halchin, RL 31024 (2007), 4.

84. Donald Trump, "Contract with the American Voter," October 22, 2016, https://www.donaldjtrump.com/press-releases/donald-j.-trump-delivers-groundbreaking-contract-for-the-american-vote1. Trump promised to execute the freeze on first day in office, but did not sign the order until three days later.

85. Donald J. Trump, "Address before a Joint Session of the Congress on the State of the Union," January 30, 2018, made available online by Gerhard Peters and John T. Woolley, *The American Presidency Project*, http://www.presidency.ucsb.edu/ws/?pid=128921.

86. I am grateful to Danielle Brian at the Project on Government Oversight for this reminder.

87. Ibid.

88. The most thorough investigation of contract fraud was completed in 2011 by the congressionally chartered Commission on Wartime Contracting in Iraq and Afghanistan. See Commission on

Wartime Contracting in Iraq and Afghanistan, *Transforming Wartime Contracting: Controlling Costs, Reducing Risks: Final Report to Congress* (Washington, DC: Commission on Wartime Contracting in Iraq and Afghanistan, 2011), available at https://cybercemetery.unt.edu/archive/cwc/20110929213815/http://www.wartimecontracting.gov/.

89. Scott H. Amey, "Public Comments on the Use of Cost Comparisons," Project on Government Oversight, April 15, 2013.

90. This checklist is cobbled together from several POGO documents, most notably Scott H. Amey, "Deficient Contractor Accountability Leaves Agencies and Taxpayers at Risk," Project on Government Oversight, February 28, 2011.

91. US Library of Congress, Congressional Research Service, *Federal Grant Financial Reporting Requirements and Databases.*

92. US Government Accounting Office, *Letter to the Honorable John Glenn and the Honorable John Conyers, Jr.,* January 23, 1990, 5; and US Government Accountability Office, *High-Risk Series: Progress on Many High-Risk Areas, While Substantial Efforts Needed on Others,* GAO-17-317 (Washington, DC, 2017), 269. See the 2017 table of contents at 1–2 for a set of links to each of the thirty-four items on the list.

93. Marcus Weisgerber and Caroline Houck, "Trump Proposes 10% Bump for the Pentagon—Then Four Flat Years," Defense One, February 13, 2018.

94. US Government Accountability Office, *DOD Needs to Reexamine Its Extensive Reliance on Contractors and Continue to Improve Oversight,* GAO-08-572T (2008). Walker left office the next day having served ten years of his fifteen-year term.

95. US Government Accountability Office, *DOD Inventory of Contracted Services: Timely Decisions and Further Actions Needed to Address Long-Standing Issues,* GAO-17-27 (2016).

96. Ibid., 3.

97. US Senate, Senate Committee on Homeland Security and Governmental Affairs, Ad Hoc Subcommittee on Contracting Oversight, *Improving Transparency and Accessibility of Federal Contracting Databases,* 111th Cong., 1st Sess., 2009, Committee Print 111–277, 1 (statement of Sen. Claire McKaskill).

98. See Coalition to Reduce Spending et al., "Letter to the Honorable Claire McCaskill: Contractor Accountability and Transparency Act of 2017," March 16, 2017, http://www.openthegovernment.org/sites/default/files/Support%20Letter%20McCaskill%20Post%20Contracts%20Online%2003%2016%2017.pdf.

99. John J. Dilulio Jr., "10 Questions and Answers about America's 'Big Government,'" Brookings Institution, February 13, 2017, https://www.brookings.edu/blog/fixgov/2017/02/13/ten-questions-and-answers-about-americas-big-government/. "Present-day" is a synonym for "today," of course.

100. Ibid.

101. Dilulio has pressed his case relentlessly over the past decade. See John J. Dilulio, "Want a Smaller Better Government? Hire 1 Million More Federal Bureaucrats," *Washington Post,* August 29, 2014.

102. Dilulio's estimate of 7.5 million contract in employment was based on an extrapolation of the 2005 update of my 1998 *True Size of Government* trendline. As noted in this chapter, these earlier estimates included a substantial number of contract jobs created through household spending under direct and indirect contracts. See Nick Schwellenbach, "Is the Federal Civilian Workforce Really Growing? Some Important Context," Center for Effective Government, February 11, 2014, http://www.foreffectivegov.org/is-federal-civilian-workforce-really-growing-some-important-context.

103. Dilulio, "10 Questions and Answers about America's 'Big Government.'"

104. Dilulio, *Bring Back the Bureaucrats: Why More Federal Workers Will Lead to Better (and Smaller!) Government* (West Conshohocken, PA: Templeton Press, 2014).

105. Dilulio, "10 Questions and Answers about America's 'Big Government.'"

106. George F. Will, "Big Government Sneakily Gets Bigger," *Washington Post,* February 24, 2017.

Chapter 2

1. George Washington, "First Annual Address to Congress," January 8, 1790, made available online by Gerhard Peters and John T. Woolley, *The American Presidency Project*, http://www. presidency.ucsb.edu/ws/?pid=29431.
2. Kerry E. Irish, "Apt Pupil: Dwight Eisenhower and the 1930 Industrial Mobilization Plan," *Journal of Military History* 70, no. 1 (2006).
3. Dwight D. Eisenhower, "Farewell Radio and Television Address to the American People."
4. Paul Martin, "Eisenhower Speaks His Mind: An Interview with a Member of the Staff of US News & World Report," *US News & World Report*, November 11, 1966, https://www.usnews. com/news/national/articles/2008/05/16/eisenhower-speaks-his-mind.
5. Stephen E. Ambrose, *Eisenhower: The President* (New York: Simon and Schuster, 1984), 537.
6. Several of the documents used in this book were uncovered in 2010 under a pile of dirt and pine needles in a Minnesota fishing cabinet owned by Eisenhower's chief speechwriter, Malcom Moos. See "Eisenhower's Farewell Notes Found in MN Cabin," WCCO, CBS Minnesota, December 10, 2010, http://minnesota.cbslocal.com/2010/12/10/eisenhowers-farewell-notes-found-in-mn-cabin/.
7. Dwight D. Eisenhower, "Farewell Radio and Television Address to the American People."
8. Martin J. Medhurst, "Reconceptualizing Rhetorical History: Eisenhower's Farewell Address," *Quarterly Journal of Speech* 80, no. 2 (1994): 209.
9. Lauren Carroll, "Sean Spicer's Claim of a 'Dramatic Expansion in the Federal Workforce' Is Exaggerated," *PolitiFact*, January 24, 2017.
10. CBO initially estimated the stimulus would cost $787 billion, but later raised the total to $831 billion. US Congress, Congressional Budget Office, *Estimated Impact of the American Recovery and Reinvestment Act on Employment and Economic Output from October 2011 through December 2011* (Washington, DC, 2012), 1. See also US Library of Congress, Congressional Research Service, *Department of Defense Contractor and Troop Levels in Iraq and Afghanistan, 2007–2017*, R44116 (2017) for the trends in the number of contract personnel deployed in Iraq and Afghanistan.
11. The number of Postal Service employees rose when a new personnel accounting system was implemented. See Vern K. Baxter, *Labor and Politics in the US Postal Service* (New York: Plenum Press, 1994), 169–70.
12. Ronald Reagan, "Inaugural Address," January 20, 1981, made available online by Gerhard Peters and John T. Woolley, *The American Presidency Project*, http://www.presidency.ucsb. edu/ws/?pid=43130.
13. Ronald Reagan: "Remarks on Signing the Federal Employee Hiring Freeze Memorandum and the Cabinet Member Nominations," January 20, 1981, made available online by Gerhard Peters and John T. Woolley, *The American Presidency Project*, http://www.presidency.ucsb. edu/ws/?pid=43490.
14. US Executive Office of the President, Office of Management and Budget, *Budget of the US Government: Historical Tables, Fiscal Year 2019* (Washington, DC: US Government Printing Office, 2018).
15. US Government Accounting Office, *Recent Government-Wide Hiring Freezes Prove Ineffective in Managing Federal Employment*, GAO-FPCD-82.21 (1982).
16. These contract figures come from Paul C. Light, *The True Size of Government* and were recalculated to eliminated all induced, household spending employment as described earlier in this book.
17. The number of estimated grant employees comes from recalculations of the figures I presented in the *True Size of Government*.
18. Donna Martin, "Defense Procurement Information Papers," Project on Military Procurement, August 1984, http://www.pogoarchives.org/m/ns/defense-procurement-information-papers-1984.pdf.
19. Quoted in Wayne Biddle, "Audit Cites Pentagon Contractors," *New York Times*, April 29, 1985.

20. Whatever the hammer cost, former Office of Federal Procurement Policy (OFPP) administrator, Steven Kelman called the price "an accounting artifact" produced by the Defense Department's bulk purchasing of many spare parts. Once the hammer was on the list, the department assigned equal amounts of overhead to each item. "The hammer got as much overhead as an engine," Kelman told *Government Executive* almost fifteen years later, "but nobody ever said, 'What a great deal we got on the engine.'" Quoted in Sydney J. Freeberg Jr., "The Myth of the $600 Hammer," *Government Executive*, December 7, 1998.

21. This analysis comes from Lawrence J. Korb, Laura Conley, and Alex Rothman, "A Return to Responsibility," 3.

22. Ronald Reagan, "Address to the Nation on Federal Tax Reduction Legislation," July 27, 1981, made available online by Gerhard Peters and John T. Woolley, *The American Presidency Project*, http://www.presidency.ucsb.edu/ws/?pid=44120.

23. These figures come from Veronique de Rugy, "President Reagan, Champion Budget-Cutter," American Enterprise Institute, June 9, 2004.

24. US Government Accountability Office, *Analysis of Internal Control Systems to Ensure the Accuracy, Completeness, and Timeliness of Federal Procurement Data*, GAO-PLRD-82.119 (1982). The appendix of this short report rates fifty-eight departments and agencies on the accuracy, completeness, and timeliness of their 1981 FPDS submissions.

25. US Library of Congress, Congressional Research Service, *Military Base Closures: Frequently Asked Questions*, by Daniel Else, R43425 (2014). Reagan's base closing effort was chaired by his defense secretary, Frank C. Carlucci.

26. Ronald Reagan, "The President's News Conference," August 12, 1986, made available online by Gerhard Peters and John T. Woolley, *The American Presidency Project*, http://www.presidency.ucsb.edu/ws/?pid=37733.

27. George H. W. Bush, "Address Accepting the Presidential Nomination at the Republican National Convention in New Orleans," August 18, 1988, made available online by Gerhard Peters and John T. Woolley, *The American Presidency Project*, http://www.presidency.ucsb.edu/ws/?pid=25955.

28. Ibid.

29. George H. W. Bush, "Remarks to Members of the Senior Executive Service," January 26, 1989, made available online by Gerhard Peters and John T. Woolley, *The American Presidency Project*, http://www.presidency.ucsb.edu/ws/?pid=16628. These were the first public remarks that the president made after his Inaugural Address.

30. Ibid.

31. See Glenn Kessler, "Cutting the Defense Budget," *Washington Post*, January 25, 2011. Colin Powell described the cuts in an email to Kessler as follows: "Our goal was to reduce to a Base Force level with a cut of 500,000 active duty and an overall reduction of 25 percent of the budget. The new level may not have been reached while Mr. Cheney was still there or before I left, but the reductions were in train. President Clinton cut it even more."

32. George H. W. Bush, "Address before a Joint Session of the Congress on the State of the Union," January 28, 1992, made available online by Gerhard Peters and John T. Woolley, *The American Presidency Project*, http://www.presidency.ucsb.edu/ws/?pid=20544.

33. William J. Clinton, Executive Order 12839—Reduction of 100,000 Federal Positions, February 10, 1993, made available online by Gerhard Peters and John T. Woolley, *The American Presidency Project*, http://www.presidency.ucsb.edu/ws/?pid=61535.

34. William J. Clinton, "Address before a Joint Session of Congress on Administration Goals," February 17, 1993, made available online by Gerhard Peters and John T. Woolley, *The American Presidency Project*, http://www.presidency.ucsb.edu/ws/?pid=47232.

35. William J. Clinton, "Statement on Signing the Federal Workforce Restructuring Act of 1994," March 30, 1994, made available online by Gerhard Peters and John T. Woolley, *The American Presidency Project*, http://www.presidency.ucsb.edu/ws/?pid=49886.

36. Clinton said the "era of big government is over" in his 1996 State of the Union Address. See William J. Clinton, "Address before a Joint Session of the Congress on the State of the Union," January 23, 1996, made available online by Gerhard Peters and John T. Woolley, *The American Presidency Project*, http://www.presidency.ucsb.edu/ws/?pid=53091.

37. This conclusion is confirmed in Office of Management and Budget, *Budget of the US Government: Historical Tables, Fiscal Year 2017*.

38. Reinventing government was the more common referent for the National Performance Review launched in a Rose Garden ceremony on March 3, 1993. William J. Clinton, "Remarks Announcing the National Performance Review," March 3, 1993, made available online by Gerhard Peters and John T. Woolley, *The American Presidency Project*, http://www.presidency.ucsb.edu/ws/?pid=46291. The term "reinventing government" refers to David Osborne and Ted Gaebler's best-selling government reform book, *Reinventing Government: How the Entrepreneurial Spirit Is Transforming the Public Sector* (New York: Plume 1993). Although the book had a significant impact in shaping the so-called New Public Management, reinventing government turned out to be very difficult to sustain from administration to administration. My analysis of the Minnesota case studies used in the book showed that one-third were dead by the time the paperback edition published in 1995.

39. US Government Accounting Office, *Federal Downsizing: The Status of Agencies' Workforce Restructuring Efforts*, GAO/T-GGD-96-124 (1996).

40. Paul C. Light, *A Government Ill Executed: The Decline of the Federal Service and How to Reverse It* (Cambridge, MA: Harvard University Press, 2008), 75.

41. US House, Committee on Government Oversight and Government Reform, *Lessons for the Future of Government Reform*, 113th Cong., 1st Sess., 2013, 1 (statement of Elaine Kamarck).

42. US Senate, Committee on Governmental Affairs, Subcommittee on Oversight of Government Management, *Has Government Been Reinvented?* 107th Cong., 2nd Sess. (2000), 6–8 (statement of J. Christopher Mihm).

43. Ibid., 1 (statement of Sen. Fred Thompson).

44. Most of this discussion is from Paul C. Light, "Pressure to Grow," *Government Executive*, October 1, 2000.

45. George W. Bush, "Address before a Joint Session of the Congress on Administration Goals," February 27, 2001, made available online by Gerhard Peters and John T. Woolley, *The American Presidency Project*, http://www.presidency.ucsb.edu/ws/?pid=29643.

46. Ibid.

47. Ibid.

48. For the impact of Bush and Obama's first-year legislation on subsequent budget problems, see US Library of Congress, Congressional Research Service, *The Impact of Major Legislation on Budget Deficits: 2001 to 2009*, R41135 (2010).

49. Martha Minow, "Outsourcing Power: How Privatizing Military Efforts Challenges Accountability, Professionalism, and Democracy," *Boston College Law Review* 45, no. 5 (2005): 1003.

50. Lizette Alvarez, "Senate Votes to Federalize Job of Airport Screening," *New York Times*, October 12, 2001.

51. The TSA hired its first two employees—the administrator and his deputy—in January 2002 and hired another 60,000 airport screeners by September. The federal employees replaced the contract employees who ran the screener systems in most of the nation's airports, including the two who screened the hijackers who flew the aircraft into the World Trade Center towers and the Pentagon on 9/11.

    Unfortunately, TSA had no one to monitor its $800 million contract with an untested recruiting firm and failed to flag questionable expenses such as valet parking and room service at the high-end hotels and resorts that the firm used for its assessment and hiring centers. The problems no doubt fueled at least some interest in giving airport authorities more freedom to hire contract employees again once the story hit the *Washington Post* in 2006. "The people in the agency didn't care where the money was spent," Sen. Byron Dorgan (D-ND) told the *Post* reporter. "It's an unbelievable waste of money." See also Robert O'Harrow Jr., "Report Faults TSA Security Contracting," *Washington Post*, January 5, 2006.

52. Barack Obama, "Address before a Joint Session of the Congress," February 24, 2009, made available online by Gerhard Peters and John T. Woolley, *The American Presidency Project*, http://www.presidency.ucsb.edu/ws/?pid=85753.

53. Ibid.

54. Barack Obama, "Commencement Address at the University of Michigan in Ann Arbor, Michigan," May 1, 2010, made available online by Gerhard Peters and John T. Woolley, *The American Presidency Project*, http://www.presidency.ucsb.edu/ws/?pid=87839.

55. Barack Obama, "Remarks on Fiscal Responsibility," November 29, 2010, made available online by Gerhard Peters and John T. Woolley, *The American Presidency Project*, http://www.presidency.ucsb.edu/ws/?pid=88755.

56. Ibid.

57. Barack Obama, "The President's News Conference," March 1, 2013, made available online by Gerhard Peters and John T. Woolley, *The American Presidency Project*, http://www.presidency.ucsb.edu/ws/?pid=103322.

58. Lauren Carroll, "Rand Paul Rightly Says the Government Shutdown Was More Expensive than Keeping It Open," PolitiFact, August 7, 2014, http://www.politifact.com/truth-o-meter/statements/2014/aug/07/rand-paul/rand-paul-rightly-says-government-shutdown-was-mor/. For deeper analyses see also US Government Accountability Office, *2014 Sequestration: Agencies Reduced Some Services and Investments, While Taking Certain Actions to Mitigate Effects*, GAO-14-244 (2014); see also US Library of Congress, Congressional Research Service, Government Accountability Office, *The FY 2014 Government Shutdown: Economic Effects*, by Mark Labonte, R43292 (2015); and Steve Bell, Blaise Misztal, Maj. Gen. Arnold Punaro, Shai Akabas, Brian Collins, and Ashton Kunkle, "From Merely Stupid to Dangerous: The Sequester's Effects on National and Economic Security," Bipartisan Policy Center, October 2013.

59. For a history of post–World War II defense dividends, see Lawrence J. Korb, Laura Conley, and Alex Rothman, "A Return to Responsibility."

60. US Library of Congress, Congressional Research Service, *Defense: FY2017 Budget Request, Authorization, and Appropriations*, by Pat Towell, and Lynn M. Williams, R44454 (2017), 6.

61. US Government Accountability Office, *High-Risk Series*, 280

62. Ibid, 269.

63. Barack Obama, "Address before a Joint Session of the Congress on the State of the Union," January 25, 2011, made available online by Gerhard Peters and John T. Woolley, *The American Presidency Project*, http://www.presidency.ucsb.edu/ws/?pid=88928.

64. See Steven T. Dennis, "Obama Zings Congress on Reorganization Authority," *Roll Call*, September 8, 2013, for background on Obama's ire.

65. Carrie Dann, "Obama on Exec Action: 'I've got a pen, and I've got a phone,'" NBC News, January 14, 2014.

66. For lists of the executive orders, see Joe Davidson, "Obama's Orders Protecting Federal Contract Workers Face Reversal by Trump," *Washington Post*, January 18, 2017; see also Mark Hoover, "14 White House Executive Orders Targeting Contractors," *Washington Technology*, August 12, 2015.

67. Barack Obama, "Remarks on Signing an Executive Order Establishing a Minimum Wage for Contractors," February 12, 2014, made available online by Gerhard Peters and John T. Woolley, *The American Presidency Project*, http://www.presidency.ucsb.edu/ws/?pid=104734.

68. Russell Berman, "Why Trump Wants to Ground the Next Air Force One," *Atlantic*, December 6, 2016. Trump did not criticize the profit motive, however, but later called Boeing's share "ridiculous." "I think Boeing is doing a little bit of a number. We want Boeing to make a lot of money, but not that much money."

69. Tae Kim, "Lockheed Martin Shares Fall after Trump Targets F-35 Again during New Conference," January 11, 2017.

70. Newt Gingrich, "Trump's Historic Contract with the American Voter," Fox News Opinion, October 28, 2016. Gingrich became Speaker of the House in 1995 after Republicans recaptured the majority with a similar inventory of promises titled "Contract with America."

71. "Republican Candidates Debate in Houston, Texas," February 25, 2016, made available online by Gerhard Peters and John T. Woolley, *The American Presidency Project*, http://www.presidency.ucsb.edu/ws/?pid=111634.

72. "Republican Candidates Debate in Detroit, Michigan," March 3, 2016, made available online by Gerhard Peters and John T. Woolley, *The American Presidency Project*, http://www.presidency.ucsb.edu/ws/?pid=111711.

73. Donald J. Trump, "Memorandum on the Federal Civilian Employee Hiring Freeze," January 23, 2017, made available online by Gerhard Peters and John T. Woolley, *The American Presidency Project*, http://www.presidency.ucsb.edu/ws/?pid=122514.

74. Congressional Quarterly, "White House Regular News Briefing," January 23, 2017. For a discussion of the legality of the president's freeze in lieu of statutory action, see US Library of Congress, Congressional Research Service, "President Trump Freezes Federal Civil Service Hiring," Legal Sidebar, January 26, 2017, https://fas.org/sgp/crs/misc/freeze.pdf.

75. See Lisa Rein and Andrew Ba Tran, "How the Trump Era is Changing the Federal Bureaucracy," *Washington Post*, December 30, 2017. See also Gardiner Harris, "Diplomats Sound the Alarm as They Are Pushed Out in Droves," *New York Times*, November 24, 2017, available at https://www.nytimes.com/2017/11/24/us/politics/state-department-tillerson.html, See also Michael Wald, "Turnover Up as More Workers Quit the Federal Government, *FedSmth*, March 22, 2018.

76. Michael D. Shear and Eric Lichtblau, "'A Sense of Dread' for Civil Servants Shaken by Trump Transition," *New York Times*, February 11, 2017.

77. Donald J. Trump, "Executive Order 13781: Comprehensive Plan for Reorganizing the Executive Branch," March 13, 2017, made available online by Gerhard Peters and John T. Woolley, *The American Presidency Project*, http://www.presidency.ucsb.edu/ws/?pid=123522.

78. Executive Office of the President, Office of Management and Budget, *America First: A Budget Blueprint to Make America Great Again* (Government Printing Office, March 16, 2017), https://www.whitehouse.gov/wp-content/uploads/2017/11/2018_blueprint.pdf, 2. For an analysis of the budget, see Committee for a Responsible Federal Budget, "President Trump's FY 2018 'Skinny Budget,'" March 16, 2017.

79. Annalyn Kurtz, "Trump's Budget Could Cut 200,000 Federal Jobs," *Fortune*, March 16, 2017. Review quoted in Eric Katz, "Trump's Budget Cuts Could Lead to Federal Employee Layoffs, Furloughs," *Government Executive*, February 28, 2017. For further discussion of employee morale, see Lisa Rein, "Federal Workers Grow Increasingly Nervous about Trump's Proposed Budget Cuts," *Washington Post*, March 1, 2017.

80. US Executive Office of the President, *America First: A Budget Blueprint to Make America Great Again*, 3; for a preliminary analysis of the budget, see Committee for a Responsible Federal Budget, "President Trump's FY 2018 'Skinny Budget,'" Committee for a Responsible Federal Budget, March 16, 2017.

81. Donald J. Trump, "Press Briefing by OMB Director Mick Mulvaney on a Comprehensive Plan for Reforming the Federal Government and Reducing the Federal Civilian Workforce," April 11, 2017, made available online by Gerhard Peters and John T. Woolley, *The American Presidency Project*, http://www.presidency.ucsb.edu/ws/?pid=123855.

82. Ibid.

83. Donald J. Trump: "Memorandum on the Federal Civilian Employee Hiring Freeze," January 23, 2017, made available online by Gerhard Peters and John T. Woolley, *The American Presidency Project*, http://www.presidency.ucsb.edu/ws/?pid=122514; for the text on the "skinny budget" see https://www.whitehouse.gov/sites/whitehouse.gov/files/omb/budget/fy2018/2018_blueprint.pdf. For an analysis of the budget, see Committee for a Responsible Federal Budget, "President Trump's FY 2018 'Skinny Budget,'" Committee for a Responsible Federal Budget, March 16, 2017.

84. Donald J. Trump, "Brief Remarks," March 13, 2017, made available online by Gerhard Peters and John T. Woolley, *The American Presidency Project*, http://www.presidency.ucsb.edu/report.php?pid=158.

85. John T. Bennett, "Is Trump Review Just Al Gore Reinventing Government 2.0?" *Roll Call*, March 15, 2017.

86. USGovernmentSpending.com, "Government Spending Details," http://www.usgovernmentspending.com/year_spending_2018USbn_18bs2n_3031_051#usgs302.

87. Max Fisher, "Stephen K. Bannon's CPAC Comments, Annotated and Explained," *New York Times*, February 24, 2017.

88. Donald J. Trump, "Press Briefing by OMB Director Mick Mulvaney on a Comprehensive Plan for Reforming the Federal Government and Reducing the Federal Civilian Workforce."

89. Mick Mulvaney, "Memorandum for heads of Executive Departments and Agencies: Comprehensive Plan for Reforming the Federal Government and Reducing the Federal Civilian Workforce," April 12, 2018, https://www.whitehouse.gov/sites/whitehouse.gov/files/omb/memoranda/2017/M-17-22.pdf, 1.

90. See Emmarie Huetteman, "How Republicans Will Try to Roll Back Obama Regulations," *New York Times*, January 30, 2017, for a discussion of the bill and other rollback techniques.

91. The order did not prohibit contracts with these bidders but did create a process for investigating whether the violations were willful, serious, and repetitive, and listing the findings on a government-wide database.

92. Donald J. Trump, "Remarks on Signing Legislation under the Congressional Review Act," made available online by Gerhard Peters and John T. Woolley, The American Presidency Project, http://www.presidency.ucsb.edu/ws/?pid=123645.

93. Sen. Elizabeth Warren, *Breach of Contract: How Federal Contractors Fail American Workers on the Taxpayer's Dime*, Office of Sen. Elizabeth Warren, March 17, 2017. The report was prepared by Warren's office staff and did not bear the imprimatur of any US Senate committee or subcommittee.

94. Donald J. Trump, "Remarks on Signing House Joint Resolutions 37, 44, 57, and 58 under the Congressional Review Act," March 27, 2017, made available online by Gerhard Peters and John T. Woolley, *The American Presidency Project*, http://www.presidency.ucsb.edu/ws/?pid=123645.

95. US Executive Office of the President, Office of Management and Budget, "Modernizing Government: 2019 Budget Fact Sheet," February 12, 2018, https://www.whitehouse.gov/wp-content/uploads/2018/02/FY19-Budget-Fact-Sheet_Modernizing-Government.pdf. See Eric Katz, "Transferring Responsibilities and Consolidating Offices Highlight Trump Reorganization Plan," *Government Executive*, February 12, 2018.

96. Joe Davidson, "Is Trump Joking about 'Strengthening the Federal Workforce,'" *Washington Post*, February 13, 2018.

97. US Executive Office of the President, Office of Management and Budget, *Budget of the US Government: Analytical Perspectives* (Washington, DC: US Government Printing Office, 2019), 73, https://www.gpo.gov/fdsys/pkg/BUDGET-2019-PER/pdf/BUDGET-2019-PER.pdf.

98. Eric Wagner, "OPM Director: Expect 'Full Court Press' for Civil Service Changes," *Government Executive*, April 30, 2018.

99. Joe Davidson, "Trump Thanks Federal Employees with $143.5 Billion in Retirement Cuts," *Washington Post*, May 8, 2018.

100. The Federal Funding Accountability and Transparency Act of 2006 requires detailed federal reporting on all contracts, grants, cooperative agreements, and loans. According to GAO, all but a handful of federal agencies had complied with the contract reporting by 2014, but many have failed to provide consistent or verifiable information on grant reporting. See US Government Accounting Office, *Data Transparency: Oversight Needed to Address Underreporting and Inconsistencies on Federal Award Website*, GAO-14-476 (2014).

101. US Government Accountability Analysis, *Contracting Data Analysis: Assessment of Government-wide Trends*, GAO-17-244SP (2017)

102. This summary is based on my reading of Frank Landefeld, Jamie Yachera, and Hudson Hollister, *The DATA Act: Vision & Value*, The DATA Foundation, July 2016.

103. See Ibid., Appendix III for specific definitions of the fifty-seven data elements. See also the Office of Management and Budget "Federal Spending Transparency Data Standards" list at https://max.gov/maxportal/assets/public/offm/DataStandardsFinal.htm.

104. See the DATA Foundation and Deloitte Development LLC, *DATA Act 2022: Changing Technology, Changing Culture*, Data Foundation, Deloitte Development, May 2017, for an inventory of concerns.

105. In February 2017, for example, the Treasury Department decided to use its power as DATA broker to reject all spending records with missing or inaccurate nine-digit ZIP+4 postal codes. It backed down only when it discovered that the Postal Service does not assign nine-digit numbers in many rural areas of the country. See US Government Accountability Office, *DATA ACT: As Reporting Deadline Nears, Challenges Remain That Will Affect Data Quality*, GAO-16-496 (2017), 18–19.

106. US Government Accountability Office, "The DATA Reporting Deadline Is Here: Will Agencies Show You the Money?" *WatchBlog*, May 8, 2017, https://blog.gao.gov/2017/05/08/the-data-act-reporting-deadline-is-here-will-agencies-show-you-the-money/.

107. For a summary, see Sean Moulton, "Government Earns Poor Grades for Spending Data Accuracy," Project on Government Oversight, December 1, 2017, http://www.pogo.org/our-work/articles/2017/government-earns-poor-grades-for-spending-data-accuracy.html?utm_source=weekly-reader&utm_medium=email&utm_campaign=wr-171202&utm_content=header.

108. Fred I. Greenstein, "The Hidden-Hand Presidency: Eisenhower as Leader," *Presidential Studies Quarterly* 4, no. 2 (1994).

109. Dwight D. Eisenhower, "The President's News Conference," June 3, 1959.

110. I judged the effect of each ceiling, cap, and freeze through the histories, reporting, *Congressional Quarterly Almanac*, and congressional hearings but have much more confidence in my ratings of major effects than more–nuanced, minimal, or nonexistent effects. The records in many cases are too thin for confidence and should give readers caution about any further analysis of this list. I am almost certain that I missed ceilings, caps, and freezes along the way as well, which makes the inventory potentially incomplete.

111. Steven L. Schooner, "Competitive Sourcing: More Sail Than Rudder," *Public Contract Law Journal* 33, no. 2 (2004), 277–78.

112. Guttman, "Public Purpose and Private Service," 876.

113. Congress attached Whitten's amendment to the first Korean War spending bill of 1950 and signed into law on September 27 as part of P.L. 82-843. Whitten gave this explanation on January 29, 1951; see *Congressional Record* (January 29, 1951), 82nd Cong., 1st Sess. (1951), H763.

114. US Congress, House, Committee on Post Office and Civil Service, *Federal Salaries and Classifications: Hearings before the Committee on Post Office and Civil Service*, 83rd Cong., 2nd Sess., 1954, 1129.

115. Ibid., 1147.

116. David Binder, "Jamie Whitten, Who Served 53 Years in the House, Dies at 85," *New York Times*, September 10, 1995.

117. Committee on Post Office and Civil Service, *Temporary Employees—Career Status*, H. Rpt. 90–372, Washington, DC: US Government Printing Office, June 20, 1967, 4.

118. Paul C. Light, *The True Size of Government* (Washington, DC: Brookings Institution Press, 1999), 117–23.

119. "Congress Approves Civil Service Reforms," *CQ Almanac 1978* (Washington, DC: Congressional Quarterly 1979), 818, available at http://library.cqpress.com/cqalmanac/cqal78-1237364.

120. 124 Cong. Rec. H9405; the numbers today are 142,000 federal employees, and approximately 500,000 contract and grant employees.

121. Daniel Guttman, "Contracting United States Government Work: Organizational and Constitutional Models," *Public Organization Review: A Global Journal* (September 2003): 286–87.

122. Federal employee unions supported the 1994 Federal Workforce Restructuring Act in part because its leadership was convinced that the reduction would fall heaviest on middle managers. The unions also believed that they could minimize the cuts in return for support. "We told them up front that we want to change the way we businesses; we want to be part of the solution, not part of the problem," the president of the American Federal of Government Employees later remarked, "but we certainly are not going to change the way you do business if it means the people that we represent are going to be out on the streets." See John N. Sturdivant, "Employee Benefits," Testimony before House Subcommittee on Compensation and Employee Benefits of the Committee on Post Office and Civil Service, October 13, 1993, 82–83; see also Mike Mills, "Clinton and Gore Hit the Road to Build a Better Bureaucracy," *CQ Weekly Report*, September 11, 1993. George W. Bush abolished the partnership within days of his 2001 inauguration. See Kellie Lunney, "Bush Dissolves Labor-Management Partnership Council," *Government Executive*, February 19, 2001.

123. Donald F. Kettl, *Escaping Jurassic Government: How to Recover America's Lost Commitment to Competence* (Washington, DC: Brookings Institution Press, 2016), 16.

124. John J. Dilulio, "Want a Better, Smaller Government? Hire Another Million Federal Bureaucrats," *Washington Post*, August 29, 2014. See also Dilulio, *Bring Back the Bureaucrats: Why More Federal Workers Will Lead to Better (and Smaller!) Government*, and John J. Dilulio and Paul R. Verkuil, "Want a Leaner Federal Government? Hire More Federal Workers," *Washington Post*, April 21, 2016. Verkuil was the chairman of the Administrative Conference of the United States from 2009 to 2015 and was singularly successful in rebuilding the office fifteen years after it was abolished by House Republicans in a pennywise attack on big government in 1995.

125. Kettl, *Escaping Jurassic Government*, 160.

126. Ibid., 101.

127. US General Accounting Office, *Recent Government-Wide Hiring Freezes Prove Ineffective in Managing Federal Employment*, FPCD-82.21 (1982), 5.

128. US General Accounting Office, *Personnel Ceilings—A Barrier to Effective Manpower Management*, FPCD 86–88 (1977). The description of GAO's 1982 report as "seminal" came from Rep. Stephen F. Lynch et al., "Letter to President-Elect Trump," January 9, 2017, https://lynch.house.gov/sites/lynch.house.gov/files/FINAL%20SIGNED%201-09-17%20Lynch%20Letter%20to%20President-elect%20Trump%20on%20Proposed%20Federal%20Hiring%20Freeze.pdf, 1.

129. Ibid., ii.

130. Ibid., 24.

131. US Library of Congress, Congressional Research Service, *The Relationship between Federal Personnel Ceilings and Contracting Out: Policy Background and Current Issues*, by Alice Mosher, RL 80138 (1980), 23.

132. Ibid., 2.

133. Ibid., 23.

134. Ibid., 26–27.

135. The report was footnoted in April 4, 2017, letter from Sen. Gary C. Peters and Sen. Heidi Heitkamp to US Comptroller General Gene L. Dodaro calling for a Government Accountability Office review of the Trump administration's hiring freeze.

136. US Government Accountability Office, *High-Risk Series*, 61.

137. US Committee on Governmental Affairs, Subcommittee on Civil Services and General Services, *Federal Government's Use of Consultant Services*, 96th Congress, 1st Sess. (1979), 77–78.

Chapter 3

1. David Isenberg, "The Founding Contractors," *Middle East Times*, July 7, 2008, https://www.cato.org/publications/commentary/founding-contractors. For a deep history of federal procurement, see James F. Nagle, *A History of Government Contracting*, 2nd ed. (Washington, DC: George Washington University, 2005).

2. US Senate, Committee on Governmental Affairs, *Who's Doing Work for the Government: Monitoring, Accountability and Competition in the Federal and Service Contract Workforce*, 107 Cong., 2nd Sess. (2002), 6 (statement of Stan Z. Soloway).

3. Dwight D. Eisenhower, "Farewell Radio and Television Address to the American People," January 17, 1961, made available online by Gerhard Peters and John T. Woolley, *The American Presidency Project*, http://www.presidency.ucsb.edu/ws/?pid=12086.

4. For an analysis of clever cost comparisons, see Scott H. Amey, "Public Comments on the Use of Cost Comparisons," Project on Government Oversight, April 15, 2013, which analyzes the Budget Circular A-76 process for determining the most cost-effective source for not inherently governmental, but commercially available products and services.

5. Dwight D. Eisenhower, "Farewell Radio and Television Address to the American People," January 17, 1961, made available online by Gerhard Peters and John T. Woolley, *The American Presidency Project*, http://www.presidency.ucsb.edu/ws/?pid=12086.

6. Robert M. Emmerichs, Cheryl Y. Marcum, and Albert A. Robbert, *An Executive Perspective on Workforce Planning* (Santa Monica, CA: RAND Corporation, 2004).

7. US House of Representatives, Subcommittee on the Federal Workforce, US Postal Service and Labor Policy, *Rightsizing the Federal Workforce*, 112th Cong., 1st Sess. (2011) (statement of Rep. Danny K. Davis), 63–64.

8. See Light, *The True Size of Government*, chapter 3, for a discussion of the politics of outsourcing.

9. Ibid., chapter 4, "The Tools for Sorting Out," for a discussion of the definitional problems in determining which workforce should do what jobs.

10. See Steven L. Schooner, "Competitive Sourcing Policy: More Sail Than Rudder," *Public Contract Law Journal* 33, no. 2 (2004), for a discussion of the definitions of inherently governmental and commercially available functions.

11. Office of Management and Budget, *Budget of the US Government: Analytical Perspectives*, 67.

12. Ibid., 65.

13. Davidson, "Is Trump Joking about 'Strengthening the Federal Workforce,'" *Washington Post*, February 13, 2018. I have also found Jeff Neal's perspective on the civil service system particularly helpful for framing the conversation about reform. See Jeff Neal, "(Not) the Merit System Principles," *FedSmith*, June 5, 2018.

14. Office of Management and Budget, *Budget of the US Government: Analytical Perspectives*, 65.

15. US Merit Systems Protection Board, "The Impact of Recruitment Strategy on Fair and Open Competition for Federal Jobs: A Report to the President and the Congress of the United States by the US Merit Systems Protection Board," January 2015, https://www.mspb.gov/netsearch/viewdocs.aspx?docnumber=1118751&version=1123213.

16. See Jack Moore, "OPM's Focus in Hiring Reform Shifting from Speed to Quality," *Federal News Radio*, March 26, 2014, for the background on OPM's decision to stop tracking time-to-hire statistics.

17. Andrew Chamberlain, "How Long Does It Take to Hire? Interview Duration in 25 Countries," Glassdoor, August 9, 2017, https://www.glassdoor.com/research/time-to-hire-in-25-countries/. See also Kellie Ell, "It's Taking Longer Than Ever to Get Hired, Glassdoor Survey Shows," *USA Today*, August 9, 2017.

18. United States Senate, Committee on Homeland Security and Governmental Affairs, *Federal Hiring Process Improvement Act of 2010*, 111th Cong., 2nd Sess., 115th Cong., 1st Sess., 2011, S. Rep. 111–184, 2.

19. Joe Davidson, "President Obama's Hiring Reforms Draw Applause at Personnel Agency," *Washington Post*, May 12, 2010. The reforms were codified in Barack Obama, "Memorandum on Improving the Federal Recruitment and Hiring Process," May 11, 2010, made available online by Gerhard Peters and John T. Woolley, *The American Presidency Project*. http://www.presidency.ucsb.edu/ws/?pid=87864.

20. Partnership for Public Service and LinkedIn created the new motto in *Post and Pursue: Improving Federal Hiring Using Data and Targeted Recruitment*, April 2017, https://ourpublicservice.org/publications/download.php?id=1750.

21. US Executive Office of the President, Office of Management and Budget and Office of Personnel Management, "Memorandum for the Heads of Executive Departments and Agencies: Institutionalizing Hiring Excellence to Achieve Mission Outcomes," November 1, 2016, https://www.chcoc.gov/sites/default/files/M-17-03%20%20Institutionalizing%20Hiring%20Excellence%20to%20Achieve%20Mission%20Outcomes_1.pdf.

22. Linda E. Rix, "The Irrational Escalation of Commitment to USAJOBS . . . And Other Reasons Why the Federal Hiring Process is a Deeply Broken Mess," prepared for the United States Senate, Committee on Homeland Security, and Government al Affairs Subcommittee on Regulatory Affairs, *Improving the USAJOBS Website*, April 12, 2016, CQ-Roll Call transcript, https://congressional-proquest-com.proxy.library.nyu.edu/congressional/docview/t39.d40.04122503.d60?accountid=12768, 4–5.

23. Max Stier, "Written Statement of Max Stier," prepared for the United States Senate, Committee on Homeland Security and Governmental Affairs Subcommittee on Regulatory Affairs, *Improving the USAJOBS Website*, April 12, 2016, 4.

24. As Martha Minow writes of wartime contracting, the immediate benefits in using indefinite quantity contracts to purchase labor are clear: "A private company can handpick the team for a given project, and reassemble or disassemble the team when the job is done or changes.... By depending on private companies, the military can obtain the newest technology and the staffs trained to maintain it—and even avoid the costs of retraining simply by shifting to a new team." See Martha Minow, "Outsourcing Power: How Privatizing Military Efforts Challenges Accountability, Professionalism, and Democracy," *Boston College Law Review* 46, no. 5 (2005): 1004.

25. Bernard D. Rostker, *A Call to Revitalize the Engines of Government* (Santa Monica, CA: RAND Corporation, 2008), 5.

26. These figures are based on quarterly updates to US Office of Personnel Management *Federal Employment Reports: Full-Time Permanent Age Distributions* (2016), https://www.opm.gov/policy-data-oversight/data-analysis-documentation/federal-employment-reports/reports-publications/full-time-permanent-age-distributions/#2016.

27. Jeff Neal, "What Happened to All of the Young Federal Employees?" ChiefHRO.com, July 10, 2014, https://chiefhro.com/2014/07/10/what-happened-to-all-of-the-young-federal-employees. Neal produced a second report on the problem titled "The Ticking Time Bomb in the Federal Workforce" March 2, 2016, https://chiefhro.com/2016/03/02/the-ticking-time-bomb-in-the-federal-workforce/.bid.

28. See Dan Guttman, "Government by Contract." Guttman argues that contract and grant employees get their intellectual capital working for government, but sell it to industry in the form of higher wages and dependency.

29. See US Government Accountability Office, *Federal Workforce: Additional Analysis and Sharing of Promising Practices Could Improve Employee and Engagement and Performance*, GAO-15-585 (2015); see also US Government Accountability Office, *Lessons Learned for Engaging Millennials and Other Age Groups*, GAO-16-880T (2016).

30. Nevbahar Ertas, "Turnover Intentions and Work Motivations of Millennial Employees in Federal Service," *Public Personnel Management* 44, no. 3 (2015): 401–23.

31. Seong Soo Oh, "Performance Ratings and Career Advancement in the US Federal Service," *Public Management Review* 15, no. 5 (2013): 757.

32. Henry Romero, "Grade Inflation: Does It Matter?" *Government Executive*, September 14, 2014.

33. Paul C. Light, *Thickening Government: Federal Hierarchy and the Diffusion of Accountability* (Washington, DC: Brookings Institution Press-Governance Institute, 1995).

34. US Government Accountability Office, *Distribution of Performance Ratings across the Federal Government, 2013*, GAO-16-520R (2016).

35. These figures come from US Office of Personnel Management, Office of Workforce Information, Personnel Systems and Oversight Group, *The Fact Book: Federal Civilian Workforce Statistics, 1996 Edition*, available at www.hathitrust.org, and US Government Accountability Office, *Distribution of Performance Ratings across the Federal Government, 2013*, GAO-16-520R (2016). OPM has not released federal employee performance data since 1997 nor does it provide access to its earlier data on any publicly accessible website. The steady rise in annual ratings and their relationship to promotions and pay increases is precisely documented in Seong Soo Oh, "The Impact of Performance Ratings on Federal Personnel Decisions," PhD diss., Georgia State University, 2010, http://scholarworks.gsu.edu/pmap_diss/41; see Table A.1 for the precise progression of ratings in Soo's sample of federal personnel records.

36. Government Accountability Office, *Distribution of Performance Ratings across the Federal Government*, 4.

37. US Office of Personnel Management, *Federal Employee Viewpoint Survey: Empowering Employees. Influencing Change* (Washington, DC: 2017), https://www.fedview.opm.gov/.

38. See U.S. Department of Labor, Bureau of Labor Statistics, "Economic News Release: Job Openings and Labor Turnover Survey News Release," March 6, 2018, https://www.bls.gov/news.release/archives/jolts_03162018.htm.

39. US Government Accountability Office, *Federal Workforce: Improved Supervision and Better Use of Probationary Periods Are Needed to Address Substandard Employee Performance*, GAO-15-191 (2015).

40. See Jeff Neal, "What's Really in those New Executive Orders," *FedSmith*, May 30, 2018.

41. See Nicole Ogrysko, "Interior Senior Executives Left in the Dark Amid Reorg, Reassignments," *Federal News Radio*, August 17, 2017; Sarah Kaplan, "Government Scientists Blocked from the Biggest Meeting in Their Field," *Washington Post*, December 22, 2017; Andrew Restuccia, Emily Goldberg, and Rebecca Morin, "How the Federal Government Hides Sexual Harassment Payouts," *Politico*, January 3, 2018; Joe Davidson, "Federal Agency Reports Show 'Continuum of Harm' from Workplace Sexual Misconduct," *Washington Post*, December 20, 2017; US Government Accountability Office, *Sexual Harassment: Actions Needed to Improve DOD's Efforts to Address the Continuum of Unwanted Sexual Behaviors*, GAO-18-33 (2018); and US Merit Systems Protection Board, "Update on Sexual Harassment in the Federal Workplace," March 2018.

42. Partnership for Public Service, *Embracing Change: CHCOs Rising to the Challenge of an Altered Landscape*, Partnership for Public Service and Grant Thornton, May 2014, 15.

43. Leo Shane III, "VA Firings Spiked after Trump Signed the New Accountability Law Last Year," *Military Times*, January 3, 2018. Despite the headline, the story provides year-to-year totals that mirror recent history. As the president is fond of saying, only time will tell whether firing will pick up in the future.

44. Eric Katz, "Pentagon Begins Enrolling Civilians in New Personnel System," *Government Executive*, April 1, 2016. Details on the new system can be found at www.cpms.osd.mil/Subpage/NewBeginnings/NBHome.

45. Alexander Bolton, Charles M. Cameron, John M. de Figueiredo, and David E. Lewis, "Grade Inflation in the United States Government," early draft, January 13, 2015, 28.

46. US Congress, US Congressional Budget Office, *Changes in Federal Civilian Employment* (Washington, DC: 1996), 13.

47. Dilulio, "10 Questions and Answers about America's 'Big Government.'"

48. Donald F. Kettl, *Escaping Jurassic Government: How to Recover America's Lost Commitment to Competence* (Washington, DC: Brookings Institution Press, 2016), 51.

49. National Academy of Public Administration, *No Time to Wait: Building a Public Service for the Twenty-first Century* (Washington, DC: National Academy of Public Administration, 2017), 3.

50. Ray C. Oman, Ronald L. Gabriel, Jacqueline J. Garrett, and Kenneth B. Malmberg," Actions by Political Officials Have Weakened the Federal Government Workplace: Downsizing Has Cut Lower Level Workers the Most and Replacing Federal Employees with Private Corporations Costs Much More, Creating the Need for Immediate Reform," *International Journal of Public Administration* 26, no. 10–11 (2003): 1274–75.

51. William P. Butz, Terrence K. Kelly, David M. Adamson, Gabrielle A. Bloom, Donna Fossum, and Mihal E. Gross, *Will the Scientific and Technology Workforce Meet the Requirements of the Federal Government?* (Santa Monica, CA: RAND Corporation, 2004).

52. See Ellen Nakashima, and Aaron Gregg, "NSA's Top Talent Is Leaving because of Low Pay, Slumping Morale, and Unpopular Reorganization," *Washington Post*, January 2, 2018.

53. The US Government Accountability Office draws this distinction between what it calls the "staffing" and "competency" gaps in *Federal Workforce: OPM and Agencies Need to Strengthen Efforts to Identify and Close Mission-Critical Skills Gaps*, GAO-15-223 (2015).

54. US Government Accountability Office, *High-Risk Series: An Update*, GAO-01-263 61 (2001), 8.

55. Ibid.

56. National Commission on the Public Service, *Leadership for America: Rebuilding the Public Service* (National Commission on the Public Service, 1988), 1.

57. The National Commission on the Public Service, *Urgent Business for America: Revitalizing the Federal Government for the Twenty-first Century* (National Commission on the Public Service, 2003).

58. According to the 2017 high-risk update report, skill gaps contributed to fifteen of the thirty-four programs in the 2017 report: (1) Management of Federal Oil and Gas Resources; (2) Managing Federal Real Property; (3) Improving the Management of IT Acquisitions and Operations; (4) Department of Defense (DOD) Business Systems Modernization; (5) DOD Financial Management; (6) Strengthening Department of Homeland Security (DHS) Management Functions; (7) Ensuring the Security of Federal Information Systems and Cyber-Critical Information and Protecting the Privacy of Personally Identifiable Information; (8) Protecting Public Health through Enhanced Oversight of Medical Products; (9) Transforming the Environmental Protection Agency's (EPA) Processes for Assessing and Controlling Toxic Chemicals; (10) DOD Contract Management; (11) Department of Energy (DOE)'s Contract Management for the National Nuclear Security Administration and Office of Environmental Management; (12) National Aeronautics and Space Administration (NASA) Acquisition Management; (13) Enforcement of Tax Laws; (14) Managing Risks and Improving Department of Veterans Affairs (VA) Health Care; and (15) Improving Federal Management of Indian Programs. See US Government Accountability Office, *High-Risk Series: An Update*, GAO-17-317 (2017), 81.

59. US Government Accountability Office, *OPM and Agencies Need to Strengthen Efforts to Identify and Close Mission-Critical Skills Gaps.*

60. Martin C. Libicki, David Senty, and Julia Pollak, *H4CKER5 WANTED: An Examination of the Cybersecurity Labor Market* (Santa Monica, CA: RAND, 2014), xii.

61. Libicki, et al., *H4CKER5 WANTED*, 9.

62. US Office of the Director of National Intelligence, *Key Facts about Contractors.*

63. Eric Katz, "VA Begins Using Expedited Hiring Authority to Fill Array of Critical Positions," *Government Executive*, January 18, 2018.

64. Libicki, et al., *H4CKER5 WANTED*, 9.

65. See Jason Richwine, " Government Employees Work Less than Private-Sector Employees," Heritage Foundation, September 11, 2012. Richwine uses the American Time Use Survey to argue that federal employees worked three fewer hours per week and roughly one less month per year than private-sector workers in hours from 2003 to 2010. The report is available at http://report.heritage.org/bg2724.

66. See Robert Lavigna, "Why Government Workers Are Harder to Motivate," *Harvard Business Review*, November 28, 2014, available at https://hbr.org/2014/11/why-government-workers-are-harder-to-motivate.

67. The US House of Representatives, Committee on Oversight and Management Reform, Subcommittee on Government Operations described the Department of Homeland Security and several smaller agencies as exemplars of these frustrations in a 2015 hearing titled *The Worst Places to Work in the Federal Government*, 113th Cong. 1st Sess. (2015), Committee Print 114–35, but expressed bipartisan agreement that the federal government fit the description.

68. US Office of Personnel Management, Federal Employee Viewpoint Survey: Empowering Employees, Influencing Change. The 2017 self-administered, web-based survey had a 45.5 percent response rate. See also National Academy of Public Administration, Strengthening Organizational Health and Performance in Government, January 2018. For a history and introduction to the Federal Employee Viewpoint Survey, see Doris Hausser, *Understanding the Federal Employee Viewpoint Survey*, National Academy of Public Administration, Working Paper #2, January 2018.

69. Lisa Rein, "Good News: Federal Worker Morale Has Finally Bottomed Out. Bad News: It's Still Terrible," *Washington Post*, December 8, 2015.

70. Vanderbilt University Center for the Study of Democratic Institutions, "Survey on the Future of Government Service: Executive Summary," July 16, 2015. The survey was funded in part by the Volcker Alliance.

71. Donald Fisk and Darlene Forte, "The Federal Productivity Measurement Program," *Monthly Labor Review*, May 1997. Historical data from 1967–1994 can be found at https://www.bls.gov/lpc/iprpfftp.htm.

72. Gregory B. Lewis and David Pitts, "Deciding to Retire from the Federal Service," *Review of Public Personnel Administration*, published online April 5, 2016, 18.

73. Partnership for Public Service, *The Best Places to Work in the Federal Government: Overall Findings and Private Sector Comparison*, 2017, http://bestplacestowork.org/BPTW/analysis/ . The partnership's private-sector comparisons came from surveys conducted by Sirota, a private research firm that is now part of Mercer Consulting. According to the partnership, the findings came from multiple random-sample surveys totaling 4.7 million employees from 120 organizations.

74. Paul Chassy and Scott H. Amey, *Bad Business: Billions of Taxpayer Dollars Wasted on Hiring Contractors*, Project on Government Oversight, September 2011.

75. Ibid., 13-14.

76. Ibid., 18.

77. Professional Services Council, "POGO Report ('Bad Business') Weak on Analysis, Practice Value," September 15, 2011, accessible through http://www.pscouncil.org/News2/NewsReleases/2011/PSC_POGO_Bad_Busines.aspx?WebsiteKey=fae489a9-a93a-4c2d-9230-615ba5cc8e5e.

78. Chris Edwards, "Reforming Federal Worker Pay and Benefits," Downsizing the Federal Government Project, Cato Institute, September 20, 2017, https://www.downsizinggovernment.org/federal-worker-pay.

79. US Congress, US Congressional Budget Office, *Comparing the Compensation of Federal and Private-Sector Employees, 2011-2015* (Washington, DC: 2017), 11.

80. See US Library of Congress, Congressional Research Service, *Circular A-76 and the Moratorium on DOD Competitions*, by Valerie Ann Bailey Grasso, R40854 (2013).

81. No one is quite sure where the test came from, but it is often linked to the Clinton administration's reinventing government campaign or the George W. Bush administration's privatization effort. See David Van Slyke and Alasdair Roberts, "Good Intentions, Bad Idea," *Government Executive*, August 15, 2007.

82. Keith Snavely and Uday Desai, "Competitive Sourcing in the Federal Civil Service," *The American Review of Public Administration* 40, no. 1 (2010): 83–89. See also Charles Clark, "Will Trump Bring Back Outsourcing and A-76?" *Government Executive*, December 22, 2019.

83. George Wallace, "Inspectors General Are in Demand During the Trump Era," CNN, November 15, 2017.

84. Al Gore, *From Red Tape to Results: Creating a Government that Works Better & Costs Less. Report of the National Performance Review* (Washington, DC: Government Printing Office, 1993), iii–iv.

85. The first quote comes from Bob Stone, the project's self-styled "energizer in chief" and senior project director, and comes from Charles S. Clark, "Reinventing Government— Two Decades Later," *Government Executive*, April 26, 2013. The second quote comes from Steven Kelman, Harvard University professor and former administration of the US Office of Federal Procurement Policy under Clinton, and comes from his 2007 opinion article titled "Washington's Fear Industry," published in *Federal Computer Week*, September 16, 2007.

86. Paul C. Light, *Monitoring Government: Inspectors General and the Diffusion of Accountability* (Washington, DC: Brookings Institution Press, 1993), 224.

87. Al Gore, *From Red Tape to Results*, 12.

88. Nadia Hilliard, *The Accountability State: US Federal Inspectors General and the Pursuit of Democratic Integrity* (Lawrence: University Press of Kansas, 2017).

89. Steven L. Schooner and Daniel S. Greenspahn, "Too Dependent on Contractors? Minimum Standards for Responsible Governance," *Journal of Contract Management* 9, no. 25 (2008): 10.

90. Association of Government Accountants with Kearney & Company, *Annual IG Survey: Steering through the Transition*, September 2016, available at http://www.kearneyco.com/wp-content/uploads/2017/02/2016_IG_Survey_AGA_KEARNEY.pdf.

91. Anne Joseph O'Connell, "Staffing Federal Agencies: Lessons from 1981–2016," Brookings Institution Center on Regulation and Markets, Series on Regulatory Process and Perspective, April 17, 2017, 3.

92. Gillian E. Metzger, "Appointments, Innovation, and the Judicial-Political Divide," *Duke Law Journal* 64, no. 8 (May 2015): 1624.

93. O'Connell, "Staffing Federal Agencies," 11.

94. G. Calvin Mackenzie, "Nasty & Brutish without Being Short," *Brookings Review*, March 1, 2001, https://www.brookings.edu/articles/nasty-brutish-without-being-short-the-state-of-the-presidential-appointment-process/.

95. Anne Joseph O'Connell, "Shortening Agency and Judicial Vacancies through Filibuster Reform? An Examination of Confirmation Rates and Delays from 1981 to 2014," *Duke Law Journal* 64, no. 8 (2015): 1672; and Anne Joseph O'Connell, "After One Year in Office, Trump's Behind on Staffing but Making Steady Progress," Brookings Institution Center on Regulation and Markets, January 23, 2018.

96. Jackie Calmes, "For a Washington Job, Be Prepared to Tell All," *New York Times*, November 12, 2008.

97. Terry Sullivan, "Fabulous Formless Darkness: Presidential Nominees and the Morass of Inquiry," *Brookings Review*, March 2001, https://www.brookings.edu/articles/fixing-the-appointment-process-what-the-reform-commissions-saw/.

98. These counts are based on coding of the *Federal Yellow Book* phonebooks published quarterly by Leadership Directories, Inc. Further information is available at https://www.leadershipdirectories.com/Products/LeadershipinPrint/Government/FederalYellowBook. The tables presented in this section come from the leadership directories published in the election year preceding each president's inauguration. The 2016 totals are based on the March 2016 directory.

   I have more confidence in the leadership directories as a guide to title creep than the oft-cited *Plum Book* of presidential positions and supporting positions. The House or Senate publishes the *Plum Book* in alternating cycles before every presidential election. Whereas the House and Senate stitch the *Plum Book* together from lists supplied by every department and agency, Leadership Directories, Inc., builds and validates the *Yellow Book* by unit, name, title, and phone number. *Yellow Book* sales depend on accuracy, while *Plum Book* downloads depend on urgency. The 2016 *Plum Book* is available at US Congress, US Senate Committee on Homeland Security and Governmental Affairs, *United States Government Policy and Supporting Positions* (Washington, DC: Government Printing Office, 2016), https://www.gpo.gov/fdsys/pkg/GPO-PLUMBOOK-2016/pdf/GPO-PLUMBOOK-2016.pdf.

99. US Senate, Committee on Homeland Security and Governmental Affairs, *Presidential Appointment Efficiency and Streamlining Act: Report to Accompany S. 679*, 112th Cong., 1st Sess., 2011, S. Rep. 112-24, 2. These numbers do not include the US Marshals, US Attorneys, and ambassadors who remained subject to Senate confirmation. See US Library of Congress, Congressional Research Service, *Presidential Appointee Positions Requiring Senate Confirmation and Committee Handling Nominations*, by Christopher M. Davis and Michael Greene, RL30959 (2017) for a brief history of the statute and list of appointee positions subject to confirmation as of May 2017.

100. Leadership Directories, Inc., publishes the *Federal Yellow Book* in soft cover and online. Further information about the publication can be accessed at https://www.leadershipdirectories.com/Products/LeadershipinPrint/Government/FederalYellowBook.

101. For the classic statement on the role of isomorphism in organizational structure, see Paul J. DiMaggio and Walter W. Powell, "The Iron Cage Revisited: Institutional Isomorphism and Collective Rationality in Organizational Fields," *American Sociological Review* 48, no. 2 (1983).

102. See Paul C. Light, *Thickening Government*.

103. See ibid., 82–85 for counts of the distance between the top and bottom of the chains of command from the top of departments such as Veterans Affairs all the way down to the front-line nurses.

104. The chain of command becomes even more complicated when it involves policy or budget decisions, which are generally passed down layer by layer to the front line. Suddenly, the

chain of command for Veterans hospital nurses jumps to 41 layers for policy decisions and 63 for budget reviews, while the chain of command for air traffic controllers jumps to 87 for policy and 84 for budget.

105. For the transcript of the interview, see Chris Cillizza, "Donald Trump's A+/C+ Presidency," *Washington Post,* February 28, 2017.

106. Jesse Byrnes, "Trump on Lack of Nominees: 'I am the Only One That Matters,'" *The Hill,* November 2, 2017.

107. I used this phrase in an NPR interview with Bryan Naylor on March 6, 2017; see Bryan Naylor, "Trump Has Many Jobs Unfilled; Is He 'Deconstructing the Administrative State'?" NPR, March 6, 2017.

108. Partnership for Public Service, Political Appointee Tracker, https://ourpublicservice.org/issues/presidential-transition/political-appointee-tracker.php, accessed March 1, 2018.

109. Al Shaw, Justin Elliott, and Derek Kravitz, "Trump Town," *ProPublica,* March 8, 2017, updated March 17, 2018, https://projects.propublica.org/trump-town/.

110. Kathryn Dunn Tenpas, "Why Is Trump's Staff Turnover Higher than the 5 Most Recent Presidents?" Brookings Institution, January 19, 2018, updated March 7, 2018, https://www.brookings.edu/research/why-is-trumps-staff-turnover-higher-than-the-5-most-recent-presidents/.

111. Compare Paul C. Light, *Government's Greatest Achievements: From Civil Rights to Homeland Security* (Washington, DC: Brookings Institution Press, 2000) with Paul C. Light, "Vision + Action = Faithful Execution: Why Government Daydreams and How to Stop the Cascade of Breakdowns That Now Haunts It," 2015 John Gauss Award Lecture, *PS,* 2016.

112. The was the term used to describe the mindset of US intelligence agencies in the weeks and months preceding the 9/11 terrorist attacks. See National Commission on Terrorist Attacks on the United States, *The 9/11 Commission Report: Final Report of the National Commission on Terrorist Attacks upon the United States* (Washington, DC: Government Printing Office, 2004), 336, http://govinfo.library.unt.edu/911/report/911Report.pdf.

113. Pew Research Center, "Government Gets Lower Ratings for Handling Health Care, Environment, Disaster Response," December 14, 2017, http://www.people-press.org/2017/12/14/government-gets-lower-ratings-for-handling-health-care-environment-disaster-response/.

114. Ibid.

115. Ibid.

116. Ibid. For a July, 2018 update, see Pew Research Center, "Majorities Express Favorable Opinions of Several Federal Agencies, Including the FBI," February 14, 2018, http://www.people-press.org/2018/07/24/growing-partisan-differences-in-views-of-the-fbi-stark-divide-over-ice.

The update shows continued public support for many federal agencies, most notably the National Park Service, but increasing division toward the Justice Department, Environmental Protection Agency, and Immigration and Customs Enforcement (ICE). ICE came under fire for its role in the zero-tolerance immigration policy that led to the June and July family separations at the US border. Forty-seven percent of Pew's respondents were unfavorable toward ICE, including majorities of women, Democrats, and 18- to 39-year-olds the most unfavorable. Pew had never asked the public about ICE before the zero-tolerance breakdown, and therefore had no comparable data.

117. Vanessa S. Williamson, *Read My Lips: Why Americans Are Proud to Pay Taxes* (Princeton, NJ: Princeton University Press, 2017), vi. See also Vanessa S. Williamson, "Tax Me. Please." *New York Times,* October 8, 2016.

118. Light, "What Americans Want from Reform." The questions used in this brief analysis varied somewhat over time follows:

The following two questions were used to create the 1997, 2001, and 2010 data points in Figure 3.1:

1. "Imagine a scale from one to six where one represents someone who generally believes that federal government programs should be cut back greatly to reduce the power of government, and six represents someone who feels that federal government programs

should be maintained to deal with important problems. Where on the scale of one to six would you place yourself?"

2. "Which of these statements comes closest to your view? The federal government needs very major reform, or the federal government is basically sound and needs only some reform, or the federal government doesn't need much change at all."

The following two questions were used to create the 2015 data points in Figure 3.1:

1. "Which of these statements comes closest to your view: Government should do more to solve programs or government is doing too many things better left to business and individuals?"

2. "Which of these statements comes closest to your view? The federal government needs very major reform, or the federal government is basically sound and needs only some reform, or the federal government doesn't need much change at all."

The following two questions were used to create the 2016 and 2018 data points in Figure 3.1:

1. "If you had to choose, would you rather have a smaller government delivering fewer services or a bigger government delivering more services?"

2. "Which of these statements comes closest to your view? The federal government needs very major reform, or the federal government is basically sound and needs only some reform, or the federal government doesn't need much change at all."

Respondents who said programs should be cut back (positions 1–3 on the scale, government is doing too much, or government should be smaller and deliver fewer services) and government needs very major reform are defined as dismantlers; respondents who said programs should be maintained or be bigger (positions 4–6 on the scale, government should do more to solve programs, or government should be bigger and deliver more services) were defined as rebuilders; respondents who said government programs should be cut back and government is basically sound and doesn't need much change were defined as streamliners; and respondents who said government programs should be maintained or be bigger and government is basically sound and doesn't need much change were defined as expanders. Readers should note that I referred to the rebuilders in past work as the priority-setters and the expanders in past work as the reinventors. I have changed both names here to provider a tighter description of what the two groups now favor.

The Pew Research Center collected the 1998, 2010, and 2015 data presented in this figure, Princeton Survey Research Associates collected the 2001 and 2016 data, and SSRS collected the 2018 data. The Pew Research Center data are publicly available. The Brookings Institution's Presidential Appointee Initiative provided the funding needed to collect the 2001 data, while the Volcker Alliance provided the funding needed to collect the 2016 and 2018 data. I conducted all the analysis presented here.

119. Pew Research Center, "Beyond Distrust: How Americans View Their Government," November 23, 2015, http://w.people- press.org/ 2015/ 11/ 23/ beyond- distrust-howamericans-view- their- government/. Author's analysis.

120. Paul C. Light, "What Americans Want from Reform: An Update," July 2018.

121. Hannah Fingerhut, "In Politics, Most Americans Feel They're on the Losing Side," Pew Research Center, November 25, 2015, http://www.pewresearch.org/fact-tank/2015/11/25/winners-and-losers-in-politics/. See also, Pew Research Center, "Partisan Shifts in Views of the Nation, but Overall Opinions Remain Negative," August 4, 2017. http://www.people-press.org/2017/08/04/partisan-shifts-in-views-of-the-nation-but-overall-opinions-remain-negative/.

122. See Charles E. Lindblom, "The Science of 'Muddling Through," *Public Administration Review* 19, no. 2 (1959), for the classic statement on making decisions by muddling through.

123. Thomas E. Mann and Norman J. Ornstein, *It's Even Worse than It Looks: How the American Constitutional System Collided with the New Politics of Extremism* (New York: Basic Books, 2012), 4. See also Thomas E. Mann and Norman J. Ornstein, "Finding the Common Good in an Era of Dysfunctional Governance," *Daedalus* 142, no. 1 (2013).

124. Partnership for Public Service, *Government Disservice: Overcoming Washington Dysfunction to Improve Congressional Stewardship of the Executive Branch* (Washington, DC: Partnership for Public Service, September 2015), 37.

125. US Senate, Committee on Homeland Security and Governmental Affairs, *The Costs and Impacts of Crisis Budgeting*, 113 Cong., 1st Sess. (2013), 6 (Statement of Philip Joyce).

126. US Government Accountability Office, *Budget Issues: Continuing Resolutions and Other Budget Uncertainties Present Management Challenges*, GAO-18-368T (2018). Further analysis of shutdowns and budget uncertainty can be found at Philip G. Joyce, *The Costs of Budget Uncertainty: Analyzing the Impact of Late Appropriations*, IBM Center for the Business of Government, September 2013, http://www.businessofgovernment.org/report/costs-budget-uncertainty-analyzing-impact-late-appropriations; US Government Accountability Office, *Budget Issues: Effects of Budget Uncertainty from Continuing Resolutions on Agency Operations*, GAO-13-464T (2013).

127. Kathryn Dunn Tenpas, "Shutdowns Break Government . . . and Its Workers," Brookings Institution, September 28, 2015; https://www.brookings.edu/blog/fixgov/2015/09/28/shutdowns-break-government-and-its-workers/.

128. A. R. "Trey" Hodgins, "Let's Give Americans an Early Holiday Gift by Returning to Regular Order," *Tech Wonk Blog*, Information Technology Industry Council, December 7, 2017.

129. Paul C. Light, *The Tides of Reform: Making Government Work, 1945–1995* (New Haven, CT: Yale University Press, 1997); see also Paul C. Light, "The Tides of Reform Revisited: Patterns in Making Government Work, 1945–2002," *Public Administration Review* 66, no. 1 (2006).

130. Alexander Hamilton, *Federalist*, no. 68, in *The Federalist Papers*, ed. Benjamin Fletcher Wright, 441 (Cambridge, MA: Harvard University Press, 1961).

131. Pew Research Center, "Beyond Distrust: How Americans View Their Government," 194.

132. Daniel I. Weiner, Lawrence Norden, and Brent Ferguson, "Requiring Government Contractors to Disclose Political Spending," Brennan Center for Justice at New York University School of Law, March 27, 2015, 2.

133. Barack Obama, "Address before a Joint Session of the Congress on the State of the Union," January 12, 2016, made available online by Gerhard Peters and John T. Woolley, *The American Presidency Project,* http://www.presidency.ucsb.edu/ws/?pid=111174.

134. See OpenSecrets.org for the latest inventory of dark-money expenditures https://www.opensecrets.org/outsidespending/nonprof_summ.php.

135. Zeke J. Miller, "Obama Completes His Slow About-Face on Super PACS," *Time*, February 28, 2014.

136. Sandy Keeney, "The Foundations of Government Contracting," *Journal of Contract Management* 43, no. 3 (2007): 8.

137. Quoted in Miguel Forbes, "Paul Volcker Launches Volcker Alliance," *Forbes,* May 12, 2015.

138. I cannot find an original source for this quote, but have encountered it many times over the years; the most recent use appears in Peter J. Dombrowski and Andrew L. Ross, *Transforming the Navy: Punching a Feather Bed*, Naval War College, November 21, 2012.

Chapter 4

1. See James C. Brown, *Printed Hearings of the House of Representatives in the National Archives of the United States 1824–1958* (Washington, DC: National Archives and Records Service, 1974).

2. These numbers come from a July 2018 search of the ProQuest Congressional database of published House and Senate hearings. The search used the following search string to cull hearing titles: "contract" AND ("fraud" OR "waste" OR "abuse"). For an introduction to the ProQuest database, see http://www.proquest.com/libraries/academic/databases/proquest-congressional.html. Given the vagaries of history and indexing, readers should use the figures presented here as approximations.

3. The search used the following search string: "active duty military" OR "armed forces" OR "civil service employees" OR "contractors" OR "contract employees" OR "consultants" OR "federal employees" OR "government employees" OR "postal workers" OR "mail carriers" OR "military personnel." The search results presented here should be taken with caution given the indexing errors that accumulate over time and the natural errors associated with long search strings, but my reading of the hearing titles and abstracts strong suggest that the historical patterns summarized in this chapter are fair.

4. The search used the following search string: "A-76" OR "commercially-available sourcing" OR "competition in contracting" OR "contracting out" OR "downsizing" OR "inherently

governmental" OR "insourcing" OR "outsourcing." See the following hearings as examples of the ongoing battles over the sixty-year battle over contracting out: US House of Representatives, Committee on Post Office and Civil Service, Subcommittee on Manpower Utilization, *Contracting Out Government Responsibility for Administrative and Management Services*, 86th Cong., 1st session (1959); US House of Representatives, Committee on Post Office and Civil Service Operations, Subcommittee on Human Resources, *Contracting Out and Its Impact on Federal Personnel and Operations*, 101st Cong., 1st and 2nd sessions (1989–1990); US House of Representatives, Committee on Government Reform and Oversight, *Contracting Out—Successes and Failures*, 105th Cong., 1st Sess. (1997); US Senate, Committee on Governmental Affairs, Subcommittee on Oversight of Government Management, the Federal Workforce and the District of Columbia, *Then and Now: An Update on the Bush Administration's Competition Sourcing* Initiative, 108th Congress, 1st Sess. (2001); US Senate, Committee on Banking, Housing, and Urban Affairs, Subcommittee on Financial Institutions and Consumer Protection, *Outsourcing Accountability? Examining the Role of Independent Consultants*, 113th Congress, 1st Sess. (2013).

5. Sixteen of these hearings were held before 1975, 274 were held between 1975 and 2001, and 65 were held between 2001 and July 2018.

6. The search used the following search string: "blended workforce" OR "human capital" OR "multi-sector workforce" OR "right-size" OR "rightsizing" or "strategic workforce planning" OR "strategic human capital." For examples, see US House of Representatives, Committee on Government Reform, Subcommittee on Technology and Procurement Policy, *The Best Services at the Lowest Price: Moving beyond a Black and White Discussion of Outsourcing*, 107th Cong., 1st Sess. (2001); US Senate, Committee on Governmental Affairs, *Who's Doing Work for the Government: Monitoring, Accountability and Competition in the Federal and Service Contract Workforce*, 107th Cong., 2nd Sess. (2002); US Senate, Committee on Governmental Affairs, Subcommittee on Civil Service and Agency Organization, and US House of Representatives, Committee on Government Reform, Subcommittee on Civil Service and Agency Organization, *The Human Capital Crisis-Offering Solutions and Delivering Results*, 108th Cong., 1st Sess. (2003); US Senate, Committee on Homeland Security and Governmental Affairs, Subcommittee on Oversight of Government Management, the Federal Workforce, and the District of Columbia, *Balancing Act: Efforts to Right-Size the Federal Employer-to-Contractor Mix*, 111th Cong., 2nd Sess. (2010); US House of Representatives, Subcommittee on the Federal Workforce, US Postal Service and Labor Policy, *Rightsizing the Federal Workforce*, 112th Cong., 1st Sess. (2011); and US House of Representatives, Committee on Small Business, Subcommittee on Contracting and Workforce, *Insourcing Gone Awry: Outsourcing Small Business Jobs*, 112th Cong., 1st Sess. (2011).

7. "Rightsizing" is a pliable term that generally references other terms such as "reinventing," "reorganizing," "reshaping," and "retrenching." It also implies precise answers to difficult questions such as, "What is the right size for a city?" "What is the right size for a small railway system?" and "What is the right-size plant?" For a discussion of the term and its use in public management, see Richard C. Box, "Running Government Like a Business: Implications for Public Administration Theory and Practice," *American Review of Public Administration* 29, no. 1 (March, 1999): 19–43; and Janet Anderson, "Rightsizing Government: The Literature and the Detroit Experience," *State and Local Government Review* 43, no. 3 (2011): 224–33.

8. US Senate, Committee on Governmental Affairs, Subcommittee on Oversight of Government Management, Restructuring and the District of Columbia, *High Risk: Human Capital in the Federal Government*, 107th Cong., 1st Sess., 2001, 8 (Statement of Comptroller General of the United States, David M. Walker).

9. For an early example of the department/agency focus, see US House of Representatives, Committee on Government Reform, Subcommittee on National Security, Emerging Threats and International Relations, *Strategic Workforce Planning at USAID*, 108th Cong., 1st Sess. (2003). For an early example of the growing emphasis on the human-capital crisis, see US Senate, Committee on Governmental Affairs, Subcommittee on the Government Management, the Federal Workforce, and the District of Columbia, *Building the Twenty-First Century Federal Workforce: Assessing Progress in Human Capital* Management, 108th Cong., 2nd Sess. (2004).

10. House of Representatives, Committee on Government Reform, Subcommittee on Technology and Procurement Policy, *The Best Services at the Lowest Price: Moving beyond a Black and White Discussion of Outsourcing*, 107th Cong., 1st Sess. (2001); US Senate, Committee on Homeland Security and Governmental Affairs, Subcommittee on Oversight of Government Management, the Federal Workforce, and the District of Columbia, *Balancing Act: Efforts to Right-Size the Federal Employer-to-Contractor Mix*, 111th Cong., 2nd Sess. (2010).

11. US House of Representatives, *Rightsizing the Federal Workforce*, 6.

12. US House of Representatives, *Reducing the Size of the Federal Government Through Attrition Act of 2011*, 112th Congress, H.R. 3029, September 22, 2011.

13. Ibid, 8.

14. Mulvaney's quote can be found at FEDmanager, "Legislation Introduced to Cut Federal Workforce through Attrition," September 27, 2011, https://www.fedmanager.com/columns/from-the-hill/178-legislation-introduced-to-cut-federal-workforce-through-attrition.

15. For a history of the BRAC process, see US Library of Congress, Congressional Research Service, *Military Base Closures: A Historical Review from 1998 to 1995*, by David E. Lockwood, Order Code 97-305 F (2004); see US Library of Congress, Congressional Research Service, *Military Base Closures: Frequently Asked Questions*, by Daniel H. Else, R43425 (2014).

16. These party convention quotes can be accessed at Gerhard Peters and John T. Woolley, *The American Presidency Project*, http://www.presidency.ucsb.edu/ws/?pid=25953 (Carter), http://www.presidency.ucsb.edu/ws/?pid=25970 (Reagan), http://www.presidency.ucsb.edu/ws/?pid=25955 (George H.W. Bush), http://www.presidency.ucsb.edu/ws/?pid=25958 (Clinton), http://www.presidency.ucsb.edu/ws/?pid=25954 (George W. Bush), http://www.presidency.ucsb.edu/ws/?pid=78284 (Obama), and http://www.presidency.ucsb.edu/ws/index.php?pid=117935 (Trump). In turn, the government reform summaries are based on Paul C. Light, *The Tides of Reform: Making Government Work, 1945–1995* (New Haven, CT: Yale University Press, 1997); see also Paul C. Light, "The Tides of Reform Revisited: Patterns in Making Government Work, 1945–2002," *Public Administration Review* 66, no. 1 (2006) and more recent analyses such as US Library of Congress, Congressional Research Service, *The President's Management Agenda: A Brief Introduction*, by Virginia A. McMurtry, RS2146 (2009).

17. Charles T. Goodsell read all reports and documents in this "Mount Everest" of paperwork, "The Grace Commission: Seeking Efficiency for the Whole People?" *Public Administration Review* 44, no. 3 (May/June 1984). James P. Pfiffner followed Goodsell's precedent in reviewing the documents assembled by Gore's National Performance Review in "The National Performance Review in Perspective," *International Journal of Public Administration* 20, no. 1 (1997), where he offers an early assessment of how reinventing government fit into the history of government reform.

18. US Library of Congress, Congressional Research Service, *The President's Management Agenda: A Brief Introduction*, by Virginia A. McMurtry, RS2146 (2009).

19. Christopher Lee, "Bush Plan to Contract Federal Jobs Falls Short," *Washington Post*, April 25, 2008.

20. Stephen Barr, "The Candidates Sound Off on Government Jobs," *Washington Post*, May 30, 2007, http://www.washingtonpost.com/wp-dyn/content/article/2007/05/29/AR2007052902060.html.

21. Joe Davidson, "If I Were the Boss . . .," *Washington Post*, August 20, 2008.

22. Barack Obama and Joseph Biden, *The Change We Need in Washington*, September 22, 2008, http://obama.3cdn.net/0080cc578614b42284_2a0mvyxpz.pdf, author's files, 9.

23. Barack Obama, "Remarks in Green Bay, Wisconsin," September 22, 2008, made available online by Gerhard Peters and John T. Woolley, *The American Presidency Project*, http://www.presidency.ucsb.edu/ws/?pid=84331.

24. Barack Obama and Joseph Biden, *The Change We Need in Washington*, 6.

25. Barack Obama, "Remarks in Green Bay, Wisconsin."

26. This summary is based on Barack Obama, "Address before a Joint Session of the Congress," February 24, 2009, made available online by Gerhard Peters and John T. Woolley, *The American Presidency Project*, http://www.presidency.ucsb.edu/ws/?pid=85753; Barack Obama, "Remarks on Federal Contracting," March 4, 2009, *Public Papers of the Presidents*

of the United States: Barack Obama, Book 1, (Washington, DC: U.S. Government Publishing Office, 2009), 180–182. and Barack Obama, "The President's News Conference," March 24, 2009, made available online by Gerhard Peters and John T. Woolley, *The American Presidency Project*, http://www.presidency.ucsb.edu/ws/?pid=85909.

27. Barack Obama, "Address before a Joint Session of the Congress on the State of the Union," January 25, 2011.

28. Barack Obama, "Press Release—President Obama Announces Proposal to Reform, Reorganize, and Consolidate Government," January 13, 2012, made available online by Gerhard Peters and John T. Woolley, *The American Presidency Project*, http://www.presidency.ucsb.edu/ws/?pid=121767. I cannot overstate Zients' tireless commitment in Obama's broad reorganization effort. He held steady year after year despite the frustrations and lack of congressional support.

29. Seven T. Dennis, "Obama Zings Congress on Reorganization Authority," *Roll Call*, July 8, 2013.

30. Thomas J. Laubacher, "Simplifying Inherently Government Functions: Creating a Principled Approach from Its Ad Hoc Beginnings," *Public Contract Law Journal* 46, no. 4 (2017): 793; Jonathan D. Breul, "Practitioner's Perspective: Improving Sourcing Decisions," *Public Administration Review* 70, no. S1 (2010): S199.

31. The bill was authored by John "Jimmy" Duncan (R-TN) and introduced as the Freedom from Government Competition Act of 1997, H.R. 716, 105th Cong. (1997).

32. For further details of the ongoing debate about words and meanings, see US Library of Congress, Congressional Research Service, *Definitions of "Inherently Governmental Function" in Federal Procurement Law and Guidance*, by Kate M. Manual, R41209 (2010).

33. Ibid., 3–4.

34. See US Government Accountability Office, *Competitive Contracting: The Understandability of FAIR Act Inventories Was Limited*, GAO/GGD-00-67 (2000). For a discussion of the importance of words in limiting discretion, see Mona Vakilifathi, "Constraining Bureaucrats Today Knowing You'll Be Gone Tomorrow: The Effect of Legislative Term Limits on Statutory Discretion," *Policy Studies Journal*, August 25, 2017.

35. See US Government Accountability Office, *Civilian Agencies' Development and Implementation of Insourcing Guidelines*, GAO-10-58R (2009), 3.

36. Laubacher, "Simplifying Inherently Government Functions," 823.

37. Ibid.

38. Ibid, 823–29.

39. Ibid.

40. US Government Accountability Office, *DOD Service Acquisition: Improved Use of Available Data Needed to Better Manage and Forecast Service Contract Requirements*, GAO-16-119 (2016), 31.

41. Guttman, "Government by Contract," 5-6.

42. Ibid., 6.

43. Louis D. Brandeis, "What Publicity Can Do," *Harper's Weekly*, December 20, 1913, http://3197d6d14b5f19f2f440-5e13d29c4c016cf96cbbfd197c579b45.r81.cf1.rackcdn.com/collection/papers/1910/1913_12_20_What_Publicity_Ca.pdf; my emphasis.

44. Daniel I. Weiner, Lawrence Norden, and Brent Ferguson, "Requiring Government Contractors to Disclose Political Spending," 1.

45. Center for Responsive Politics, "Dark Money Basics," https://www.opensecrets.org/dark-money/dark-money-basics.php.

46. Elliott V. Converse III, *History of Acquisition in the Department of Defense, Volume I: Rearming for the Cold War: 1945-1960* (Washington, DC: Historical Office, Office of the Secretary of Defense, 2012), 31.

47. Ibid., 655.

48. US Library of Congress, Congressional Research Service, *The Federal Acquisition Regulation (FAR): Answers to Frequently Asked Questions*, by Kate M. Manuel, L. Elaine Halchin, Erika K. Lunder, and Michelle D. Christensen, R42826 (2015).

49. The term "scandal proof" comes from G. Calvin Mackenzie and Michael Hafkin, *Scandal Proof: Do Ethics Laws Make Government Ethical?*" (Washington, DC: Brookings Institution Press, 2002).

50. Dennis F. Thompson, "Obama's Ethics Agenda: The Challenge of Coordinated Change," *The Forum: A Journal of Applied Research in Contemporary Politics* 7, no. 1 (2009): 3.

51. Social responsibility is frequently advertised as a source of business success in the literatures on doing well by doing good. See Yvon Chouinard, Jib Ellison, and Rick Ridgeway, "The Sustainable Economy," *Harvard Business Review*, 89 no. 10 (2011), while potential pitfalls are summarized in Olivier Boiral, "Sustainability Reports as Simulacra? A Counter-account of A and A 1 GRI Reports," *Accounting, Auditing, & Accountability Journal* 26, no. 7 (2013).

52. Herman Aguinis and Ante Glavas, "Embedded versus Peripheral Corporate Social Responsibility: Psychological Foundations," *Industrial and Organizational Psychology* 6, no. 3 (2013).

53. The President's Blue Ribbon Commission on Defense Management, *A Quest for Excellence: Final Report to the President* (Washington, DC: Government Printing Office, 1986), 77-78.

54. See Michael Payne, "Contractors Now Required to Prepare a Code of Business Ethics and Conduct and to Implement Internal Controls and Ethics Training," Federal Construction Contracting Blog, January 7, 2008, http://federalconstruction.phslegal.com/2008/01/articles/federal-procurement-policy/contractors-now-required-to-prepare-a-code-of-business-ethics-and-conduct-and-to-implement-internal-controls-and-ethics-training/.

55. The code can be accessed at https://www.fhwa.dot.gov/construction/cqit/ethcmodl.cfm.

56. US Government Accountability Office, *Defense Contracting Integrity: Opportunities Exist to Improve DOD's Oversight of Contractor Ethics Programs*, GAO-09-591 (2009).

57. Ibid., 18.

58. Pratap Chatterjee, "How Sunlight Can Improve Federal Contracting," Center for American Progress, March 2012.

59. Ibid., 14-15.

60. See Neil Gordon, "POGO Gets a Peek inside FAPIIS," Blog Post, Project on Government Oversight, February 27, 2015, http://www.pogo.org/blog/2015/02/pogo-gets-a-peek-inside-FAPIIS.html?referrer=https://www.google.com/.

61. See Lawrence Lessig, "Against Transparency," *New Republic*, October 9, 2009.

62. Howard Seavoy Leach, ed., *The Public Papers of Woodrow Wilson*, Vol. 1 (New York: Kraus Reprint Company, 1970), 333.

63. US Government Accountability Office, *Federal Spending Accountability: Preserving Capabilities of Recovery Operations Center Could Help Sustain Oversight of Federal Expenditures*, GAO-15-814 (2015).

64. Dennis F. Thompson, "Obama's Ethics Agenda: The Challenge of Coordinated Change," 12.

65. US Library of Congress, Congressional Research Service, *Sourcing Policy: Selected Developments and Issues*, by L. Elaine Halchin, R42341 (2012); *Inherently Governmental Functions and Department of Defense Operations: Background, Issues, and Options for Congress*, by John R. Luckey, Valerie Bailey Grasso, and Kate M. Manuel, R40641 (2009).

66. Ibid.

67. Don K. Price, *The Scientific Estate* (Cambridge, MA: Harvard University Press, 1965), 50. For the Obama administration's definition of terms such as inherently governmental, closely associated with inherently governmental, and critical to inherently government, see US Executive Office of the President, Office of Management and Budget, Office of Federal Procurement Policy, "Performance of Inherently Governmental and Critical Functions, Policy Letter 1101," *Federal Register* 76, no. 176 (September 12, 2011): 56227–42.

68. See Barack Obama, "Memorandum on Government Contracting," March 4, 2009, made available online by Gerhard Peters and John T. Woolley, *The American Presidency Project*, http://www.presidency.ucsb.edu/ws/index.php?pid=85815.

69. Barack Obama, "Remarks on Government Contracting," March 4, 2009, made available online by Gerhard Peters and John T. Woolley, *The American Presidency Project*, http://www.presidency.ucsb.edu/ws/?pid=85821.

70. According to Steven Schooner, rebuilding the acquisition workforce was the most important piece of the Obama memorandum. "Realistically, if we want the government's procurement dollars spent wisely, the government may need to hire tens of thousands of qualified, motivated, trained and responsible acquisition professionals," he told the *Washington Post*.

"That's everything." Schooner was quoted in Scott Wilson and Robert O'Harrow Jr., "President Orders Review of Federal Contracting System," *Washington Post,* March 5, 2009.

71. For the OMB directive, see Barack Obama, "Executive Order 13494—Economy in Government Contracting," January 30, 2009, made available online by Gerhard Peters and John T. Woolley, The American Presidency Project, http://www.presidency.ucsb.edu/ws/ ?pid=85715; for the genesis of the OFPP letter, see Barack Obama, "Remarks on Government Contracting."

72. For a summary of the letter, see US Library of Congress, Congressional Research Service, *Inherently Governmental Functions and Other Work Reserved for Performance by Federal Government Employees: The Obama Administration's Proposed Policy Letter,* by L. Elaine Halchin, Kate M. Manuel, Shawn Reese, and Moshe Schwartz, R41209 (2010).

73. The comments were easy to summarize, in large part because 30,100 were submitted by the same form letter. See Office of Management and Budget, Office of Federal Procurement Policy, "Performance of Inherently Governmental and Critical Functions."

74. US Library of Congress, Congressional Research Service, *Sourcing Policy: Selected Developments and Issues,* by L. Elaine Halchin, R42341 (2012), 3–5.

75. Daniel Gordon, "Feature Comment: Reflections on the Federal Procurement Landscape," *The Government Contractor* 54, no. 7 (2012): 51.

76. Office of Management and Budget, Office of Federal Procurement Policy, "Performance of Inherently Governmental and Critical Functions."

77. Matthew Weigelt, "The Rise of the 'Critical Function': A New Way to Think about Acquisition," *Federal Computer Week,* February 17, 2010.

78. Office of Management and Budget, Office of Federal Procurement Policy, "Performance of Inherently Governmental and Critical Functions."

79. Ibid.

80. Schooner, "Competitive Sourcing Policy: More Sail than Rudder," 277–78.

81. Both quotes come from Robert Brodsky, "Administration Puts Its Stamp on 'Inherently Governmental,'" *Government Executive,* March 31, 2010.

82. Office of Management and Budget, Office of Federal Procurement Policy, "Performance of Inherently Governmental and Critical Functions."

83. US Congress, Committee of Conference, *The Supplemental Appropriation Bill, 1951: Conference Report to Accompany H.R. 9526,* 82nd Cong., 1st Sess., 1951, H. Rep. 82-3096, 2–3.

84. Rep. Whitten speaking on amendments to the Defense Production Act of 1950, *Congressional Record,* 82nd Cong., 1st Sess. (1951), 8472. I made several small grammatical changes in the final sentence to give Whitten more grammatical precision.

85. US Government Accountability Office, *DOD Service Acquisition,* 1.

86. Project on Government Oversight, "POGO Asks Pentagon for Better Tracking of Service Contracts," December 9, 2014; Project on Government Oversight, "POGO Highlights DoD Effort to Kill Beneficial Service Contract Inventory System," November 25, 2014.

87. See Nancy Y. Moore, Molly Dunigan, Frank Camm, Samantha Cherney, Clifford Grammich, Judith Mele, Evan Peet, and Anita Szafran, *A Review of Alternative Methods to Inventory Contracted Services in the Department of Defense;* see also US Government Accountability Office, *DoD Inventory of Contracted Services;* and US Department of Defense, Office of the Inspector General, *Independent Auditor's Report on Agreed-Upon Procedures for DoD Compliance With Service Contract Inventory Compilation and Certification Requirements for FY 2014* (Washington, DC: 2016),

88. US Executive Office of the President, Office of Federal Procurement Policy, "Memorandum for Chief Acquisition Officers and Senior Procurement Executives: Service Contract Inventories," December 19, 2011, https://obamawhitehouse.archives.gov/sites/default/ files/omb/procurement/memo/service-contract-inventory-guidance.pdf.

89. US Government Accountability Office, *DoD Inventory of Contracted Services.*

90. US Department of Defense, Office of the Under Secretary of Defense for Acquisition, Technology, and Logistics, *Report to Congress: Fiscal Year Inventory of Contracted Services* (Washington, DC: Department of Defense, 2015), https://fas.org/man/eprint/contract-2014.pdf.

91. Ibid. The Defense Department states that its forty-one department components such as Defense Health Affairs, Defense Logistics Agency, Defense Acquisition University, and even the Defense OIG spent a total of $131,642,262,228 billion to support 641,428 contractor full-time equivalents, which averages to $203,674 per full-time equivalent.

92. The Caucus's Facebook page describes its mission as follows: "To advocate for public policies that promote the utilization of and reliance upon the private sector by government at all levels and that eliminate unfair government-sponsored competition with private, for profit enterprise, including small business." The invitation to potential members was issued by the caucus on January 14, 2014, http://governmentcompetition.org/uploads/Yellow_ Pages_Caucus_Dear_Colleague__1-15-14_.pdf.

93. Dana Priest and Anne Hull, "Soldiers Face Neglect, Frustration at Army's Top Medical Facility," *Washington Post*, Sunday, February 18, 2007.

94. US Library of Congress, Congressional Research Service, *Walter Reed Army Medical Center (WRAMC) and Office of Management and Budget (OMB) Circular A-76: Implications for the Future*, by Valerie Ann Bailey Grasso, RL34140 (2007), 20.

95. US Library of Congress, Congressional Research Service, *Circular A-76 and the Moratorium on DOD Competitions*.

96. Quoted in Mark Rockwell, "Congress Mulls Changes to 'Inherently Governmental' Activities," *FCW*, July 8, 2016, https://fcw.com/articles/2016/07/08/inherently-governmental.aspx.

97. Curtis Grimm and Xinyi Ren, "Supply Chain Management Research in Management Journals: A Review of Recent Literature (2004-2013)," *International Journal of Physical Distribution & Logistics* 44, no. 3 (2014).

98. Nancy Y. Moore, Laura H. Baldwin, Frank Camm, and Cynthia R. Cook, *Implementing Best Purchasing and Supply Management Practices* (Santa Monica, CA, RAND Corporation, 2002), iii.

99. For guidance on the Better Buying Power 3.0 initiative, see US Department of Defense, Under Secretary of Defense, *Implementation Directive for Better Buying Power 3.0— Achieving Dominant Capability through Technical Excellence and Innovation* (Washington, DC: Department of Defense, 2015).

100. US Government Accountability Office, *Strategic Sourcing: Leading Commercial Practices Can Help Federal Agencies Increase Savings When Acquiring Services*, GAO-13-417 (Washington, DC: 2013), 2.

101. See Christopher S. Tang, "Perspectives in Supply Chain Risk Management," *International Journal of Production Economics* 103, no. 2 (2006) for a summary of the business literature at the time.

102. US House of Representatives, Committee on Small Business, Subcommittee on Contracting and Workforce, *Putting the Strategy in Sourcing: Challenges and Opportunities for Small Business Contractors*, report prepared by subcommittee staff, 113th Cong., 1st Sess. (2013).

103. Executive Office of the President, Office of Management and Budget, Office of Federal Procurement Policy, "Performance of Inherently Governmental and Critical Functions."

104. Ibid., 56238.

105. For a summary of the distinctions between terms such as "inherently governmental" and "commercially available," see US Library of Congress, Congressional Research Service, *Defense Outsourcing: The OMB Circular A-76 Policy*, by Valerie Bailey Grasso. RL 30392 (2005).

106. Executive Office of the President, Office of Management and Budget, Office of Federal Procurement Policy, "Performance of Inherently Governmental and Critical Functions."

107. Ibid., 56238.

108. US Library of Congress, Congressional Research Service, *Definitions of "Inherently Governmental Function" in Federal Procurement Law and Guidance*.

109. US Government Accountability Office, *Inventory of Contracted Services Actions Needed to Help Ensure Inventory Data Are Complete and Accurate*, 22.

110. Barack Obama, "Remarks on Federal Contracting.

111. Barack Obama, "Memorandum for the Heads of Executive Departments and Agencies— Subject: Government Contracting," March 4, 2009, and Barack Obama, "Memorandum on

Government Contracting," March 4, 2009, made available online by Gerhard Peters and John T. Woolley, *The American Presidency Project*, http://www.presidency.ucsb.edu/ws/ ?pid=85815.

112. Pratap Chatterjee, "Insourcing: How Bringing Back Essential Federal Jobs Can Save Taxpayer Dollars and Improve Services," March 2012, 2.

113. Executive Office of the President, Office of Management and Budget, Director's Office, "Memorandum for the Heads of Departments and Agencies: Managing the Multi-Sector Workforce," M-09-26 (2009) 1. This is my interpretation of the awkward phrasing in the memo. The full sentence reads as follows: "In particular, overreliance on contractors can lead to the erosion of the in-house capacity that is essential to effective government performance. Such overreliance has been encouraged by one-sided management priorities that have publicly rewarded agencies for becoming experts in identifying functions to outsource and have ignored the costs stemming from loss of institutional knowledge and capability and from inadequate management of contracted activities."

114. Ibid.

115. US Department of Defense, Office of the Deputy Secretary of Defense, *Memorandum for Secretaries of the Military Departments, Chairman of the Joint Chiefs of Staff, Commanders of the Combat Commands, Director, Administration and Management, Directors for the Defense Agencies, Directors of the DOD Field Activities: In-Sourcing Contracted Services— Implementation Guidance* (Office of the Deputy Secretary of Defense: 2009), 1, http:// www.asamra.army.mil/scra/documents/DepSecDef%20Memo%2028MAY09%20In-sourcing%20Implementation%20Guidance.pdf.

116. Ibid., 5.

117. Jessie Riposo, Irv Blickstein, Stephanie Young, Geoffrey McGovern, and Brian McInnis, *A Methodology for Implementing of Department of Defense's Current In-Sourcing Policy* (Santa Monica, CA: RAND Corporation, 2011).

118. US Government Accountability Office, *Civilian Agencies' Development and Implementation of Insourcing Guidelines*, GAO-10-58R (2009), 7.

119. Executive Office of the President, Office of Management and Budget, Director's Office, "Memorandum for the Heads of Departments and Agencies: Managing the Multi-Sector Workforce," July 29, 2009; the only online copy still available is at http://www.asamra.army. mil/scra/documents/OMB%20Memo%2029%20JUL%2009%20Managing%20the%20 Multi-Sector%20Workforce.pdf.

120. The quotes in this paragraph come in order from Robert Brodsky, "Industry Group Seeks to Highlight Impact of Insourcing on Small Businesses," *Nextgov*, May 10, 2010; Robert Brodsky, "Insourcing Isn't the Only Ingredient of Workforce Rebalancing," *Government Executive*, May 20, 2010; Elizabeth Newell Jochum, "Federal Employee Union to Propose Insourcing Legislation," *Government Executive*, February 9, 2009; Loren Thompson, "Pentagon Insourcing Binge Begins to Unravel," *Forbes,* March 7, 2011; and Charles S. Clark, "Boomerang Effect," *Government Executive*, August 1, 2011.

121. Loren Thompson, "Pentagon Insourcing Binge Begins to Unravel," *Forbes*, March 7, 2011.

122. Emelie Rutherford, "Insourcing Critics Seize on Gates' Halting of Most Job Conversions," *Defense Daily*, August 10, 2010.

123. Marjorie Censer, "Now Too Much Federal 'Insourcing'?" *Washington Post*, December 13, 2010.

124. John D. Donahue, "The Wrong Question about Business and Government," *Governing*, April 28, 2010.

125. The federal employee hiring estimate comes from the OPM's online "Hiring Process Analysis Tool," https://www.opm.gov/policy-data-oversight/human-capital-management/hiring-reform/hiring-process-analysis-tool/; the firing estimate comes from the US Government Accountability Office, *Federal Workforce: Improved Supervision and Better Use of Probationary Periods Are Needed to Address Substandard Employee Performance*, GAO-15-191 (2015).

126. US Library of Congress, Congressional Research Service, *"Fast Track" Legislative Procedures Governing Congressional Consideration of a Defense Base Closure and Realignment (BRAC) Commission Report*, by Christopher M. Davis, R43102 (2015).

127. See David S. Sorenson, *Shutting Down the Cold War: The Politics of Military Base Closure* (New York: St. Martin's Press, 1998).

128. Kenneth R. Mayer, "The Base Realignment and Closure Process: Is It Possible to Make Rational Policy?" New York University John H. Brademas Center on Congress, December 2007, 15.

129. See Paul C. Light, *Still Artful Work: The Continuing Politics of Social Security Reform* (New York: McGraw Hill, 1995).

Chapter 5

1. Jeffrey A. Engel, "Not Yet a Garrison State: Reconsidering Eisenhower's Military-Industrial Complex," *Enterprise & Society* 12, no. 12 (2011): 177–78.

2. "Commencement Speech," undated draft, available at the BACM Paperless Archives, "President Dwight D. Eisenhower Farewell Speech Documents," http://www.paperlessarchives.com/FreeTitles/EisenhowerFarewellSpeechDocuments.pdf.

3. Dwight D. Eisenhower, "The President's News Conference," January 18, 1961.

4. Stephen Ambrose, *Eisenhower: Soldier and President (The Renowned One-Volume Life)* (New York: Simon & Schuster, 1991), 321. The "trick" in the 141 figure was the change to counting bombers in wings instead of groups.

5. Donald Alan Carter, "Eisenhower versus the Generals," *Journal of Military History* 71, no. 4 (2007): 1170.

6. David A. Stockman, "Yes We Can: How Eisenhower Wrestled Down the US Warfare State," *The Globalist*, April 29, 2014.

7. Dwight D. Eisenhower, "The President's News Conference," March 19, 1953, made available online by Gerhard Peters and John T. Woolley, *The American Presidency Project*, http://www.presidency.ucsb.edu/ws/?pid=9798.

8. The Eisenhower letter is referenced by Robert Maranto, "Praising Civil Service but Not Bureaucracy," *Review of Public Personnel Administration* 22, no. 2 (2002): 177.

9. Herman Miles Somers, "The Federal Bureaucracy and the Change of Administration," *American Political Science Review* 48, no. 1 (1954): 131.

10. Allison Stanger, *One Nation under Contract: The Outsourcing of American Power and the Future of Foreign Policy* (New Haven, CT: Yale University Press, 2009), 14.

11. For a history of the policy, see US Library of Congress, Congressional Research Service, *Insourcing Functions Performed by Federal Contractors, Legal Issues*, by Kate M. Manuel, and Jack Maskell, R41810 (2013). Eisenhower's bulletin was revised in 1957 and 1959, and survives to this day in the form of Budget Circular A-76. See also Beryl A. Radin, *Federal Management Reform in a World of Contradictions* (Washington, DC: Georgetown University Press, 2012), for further details on this history.
    The current version of the policy can be found at US Executive Office of the President, Office of Management and Budget, *CIRCULAR NO. A-76 (REVISED)*, May 29, 2003, https://www.whitehouse.gov/sites/whitehouse.gov/files/omb/circulars/A76/a76_incl_tech_correction.pdf.

12. Dwight D. Eisenhower, "Telegram to Fred Herman, Chairman, Small Businessmen for Ike," October 22, 1956, made available online by Gerhard Peters and John T. Woolley, *The American Presidency Project*, http://www.presidency.ucsb.edu/ws/?pid=10664.

13. Aaron L. Friedberg, *In the Shadow of the Garrison State* (Princeton, NJ: Princeton University Press, 2000), 249.

14. Aaron L. Friedberg, "Why Didn't the United States Become a Garrison State?" *International Security* 16, no. 4 (1992): 141–42.

15. Kenny, "The Foundations of Government Contracting," 8.

16. Alexander Hamilton, *Federalist*, no. 70, in *The Federalist Papers*, ed. Benjamin Fletcher Wright, 451 (Cambridge, MA: Harvard University Press, 1961).

17. Ibid., 455.

18. Ron Chernow, *Alexander Hamilton* (New York: Penguin Books, 2005), 340.

19. Janine R. Wedel, "*Federalist* No. 70: Where Does the Public Service Begin and End," S124. Publius is the pseudonym that Alexander Hamilton, John Jay, and James Madison used as the authors of the eighty-five papers they wrote to promote ratification of the Constitution.
20. Carroll, "Sean Spicer's Claim of a 'Dramatic Expansion in the Federal Workforce' Is Exaggerated."
21. US Department of Defense, Deputy Secretary of Defense, *In-Sourcing Contracted Services—Implementation Guidance*, 5-6.
22. See Paul C. Light, *Government's Greatest Achievements: From Civil Rights to Homeland Security* (Washington, DC: Brookings Institution Press, 2000). I updated my list of post-World War II endeavors in 2012 to include new statutes such as the Bipartisan Campaign Reform Act of 2002, the Patient Protection and Affordable Care Act of 2010, and the USA PATRIOT Act of 2001.
23. Alexander Hamilton, *Federalist*, no. 72, *The Federalist Papers*, ed. Benjamin Fletcher Wright, 451 (Cambridge, MA: Harvard University Press, 1961).
24. Ibid., 462.
25. See Partnership for Public Service and the National Association of Colleges and Employers, "College Students Are Attracted to Federal Service, but Agencies Need to Capitalize on Their Interest," Issue Brief, March 2014, 4.
26. US Senate Committee on Homeland Security and Government Affairs, Subcommittee on Regulatory Affairs and Federal Management, *Improving the USAJobs Website*, 3 (Statement by Max Stier)
27. Peter Orszag used this term to describe contractors in US Executive Office of the President Office of Management and Budget, Director's Office, "Memorandum for the Heads of Departments and Agencies: Managing the Multi-Sector Workforce," 1.
28. These destinations are suggested in the discussion of antecedents to public service motivation in James L. Perry, Jeffrey L. Brudney, David Coursey, and Laura Littlepage, "What Drives Morally Committed Citizens? A Study of the Antecedents of Public Service Motivation," *Public Administration Review* 68, no. 3 (2008): 445-58.
29. Francis B. M. de Waal makes the soft-wired argument in "The Antiquity of Empathy," *Science* 296, no. 5573 (2012).
30. Philip E. Crewson, "Public-Service Motivation: Building Empirical Evidence of Incidence and Effect," *Journal of Public Administration Research and Theory* 7, no. 4 (1997), 515.
31. Bram Steijn, "Person-Environment Fit and Public Service Motivation," *International Public Management Journal* 11, no. 1 (2014). See also Marc Buelens and Herman Ven den Broeck, "An Analysis of Differences in Work Motivation between Public and Private Sector Organizations," *Public Administration Review* 67, no 1 (2007).
32. Adrian Ritz, Gene A. Brewer, and Oliver Neumann, "Public Service Motivation: A Systematic Literature Review," *Public Administration Review* 76, no. 3 (2016).
33. James L. Perry, Jeffry L. Brudney, David Coursey, and Laura Littlepage, "What Drives Morally Committed Citizens? A Study of the Antecedents of Public Service Motivation," *Public Administration Review* 68, no. 3 (2008).
34. Ibid. The study is based on a 2004 survey of 525 community award winners.
35. US Government Accountability Office, *OPM and Agencies Need to Strengthen Efforts to Identify and Close Mission-Critical Skills Gaps*, 6.
36. Joel Stein, "Millennials: The Me, Me, Me Generation," *Time*, May 20, 2013.
37. Pew Research Center, "The Whys and Hows of Generational Research," Pew Research Center, September 3, 2015, http://www.people-press.org/2015/09/03/the-whys-and-hows-of-generations-research/.
38. Achieve, "Inspiring the Next Generation Workforce: The 2014 Millennial Impact Report," Case Foundation, Millennial Impact Project, 2014, 23.
39. For a recent update on the rise of the millennials, see Richard Fry, "Millennials Projected to Overtake Baby Boomers as America's Largest Generation," Pew Research Center, March 1, 2018, http://ww.pewresearch.org/fact-tank/2018/03/01/millennials-overtake-baby-boomers/.
40. Paul C. Light, "In Search of Public Service," Policy Brief, Brookings Institution and New York University, 2003, http://www.brookings.edu/~/media/research/files/reports/2003/6/governance-light/search.pdf, 17.

41. Kevin Eagan, Ellen Bara Stolzenberg, Hilary B. Zimmerman, Melissa C. Aragon, Hannah Whang Sayson, and Cecilia Rios-Aguilar, *The American Freshman: National Norms Fall 2016*, University of California, Los Angeles, Higher Education Research Institute, Cooperative Institutional Research Program (University of California, Los Angeles: 2017), 46.

42. See Edward N. Wolff, *Top Heavy: The Increasing Inequality of Wealth in America and What Can Be Done about It* (New York: New Press, 2002).

43. Kevin Eagan et al., *The American Freshman: National Norms Fall 2015*, 10-16.

44. Aaron Smith, "Shared, Collaborative, and On Demand: The New Digital Economy," Pew Research Center, May 19, 2016, http://www.pewinternet.org/2016/05/19/the-new-digital-economy/.

45. Pew Research Center, "Most Millennials Resist the 'Millennial' Label," Pew Research Center, September 3, 2015 http://www.people-press.org/2015/09/03/most-millennials-resist-the-millennial-label/.

46. Ibid., 12-13.

47. See Partnership for Public Service, *A New Call to Service for an Age of Savvy Altruism: Public attitudes About Government and Government Workers* (Washington, DC: Partnership for Public Service, November 2004), 1; see also Jack K. Ito, "Career Mobility and Branding in the Civil Service: An Empirical Study," *Public Personnel Management* 27, no. 2 (2003).

48. Donald P. Moynihan and Sanjay K. Pandey, "The Role of Organizations in Fostering Public Service Motivation," *Public Administration Review* 67, no. 1 (2007).

49. Mary Ann Feldman, "Public Sector Downsizing and Employee Trust," *International Journal of Public Administration* 30, no. 3 (2007).

50. Wouter Vandenabeele, "Government Calling: Public Service Motivation as an Element in Selecting Government as an Employer of Choice," *Public Administration* 86, no. 4 (2008).

51. Roger P. Rose, "Preferences for Careers in Public Work: Examining the Government-Nonprofit Divide among Undergraduates through Public Service Motivation," *American Review of Public Administration* 43, no. 4 (2013).

52. Nicola Bellé and Edoardo Ongaro, "NPM, Administrative Reforms, and Public Service Motivation: Improving the Dialogue between Research Agendas," *International Review of Administrative Services* 80, no. 2 (2014).

53. Leonard Bright and Cole Blease Graham Jr., "Why Does Interest in Government Careers Decline among Public Affairs Graduate Students?" *Journal of Public Affairs Education* 21, no. 4 (2015).

54. Nina van Loon, Anne Mette Kjeldsen, Lotte Andersen, Wouter Vandenbelle, and Peter Leisink, "Only When the Societal Impact Potential Is High? A Panel Study of the Relationship Between Public Service Motivation and Perceived Performance," *Review of Public Personnel Administration* 38, no. 2 (2018).

55. Engle, "Not Yet a Garrison State," 190.

56. Dwight D. Eisenhower, "Farewell Radio and Television Address to the American People."

INDEX

Tables and figures are indicated by an italic *t* and *f* following the page/paragraph number.